DATE DUE

NEGOTIATING
PEACE
War Termination as
a Bargaining Process

NEGOTIATING
PEACE

War Termination as
a Bargaining Process

Paul R. Pillar

PRINCETON UNIVERSITY PRESS

Library of Congress Cataloging-in-Publication Data
Pillar, Paul R., 1947–
Negotiating peace.

Bibliography: p.
Includes index.
1. Peace.   2. Armistices.   3. War.   4. Negotiation.
5. International relations.   I. Title.
JX5166.P54   1983   327.1′72   83-42572
ISBN 0-691-07656-1

Publication of this book has been aided by the
Louis A. Robb fund of Princeton University Press

This book has been composed in Linotron Times Roman
with Helvetica display.

Princeton University Press books are printed on acid-free paper and
meet the guidelines for permanence and durability of the Committee on
Production Guidelines for Book Longevity of the Council on Library Resources

Printed in the United States of America by
Princeton Academic Press

3   5   7   9   10   8   6   4   2

To my father

CONTENTS

TABLES AND FIGURES

ACKNOWLEDGMENTS

The largest debt I have accumulated in writing this book is to Klaus Knorr, whom I have been privileged to know as both an academic mentor and a professional colleague. He supervised the dissertation research on which the book is based, and has continued to be a valued source of advice and encouragement. Jeffrey Hart also served as an adviser while the original version of this work was being prepared. Harrison Wagner and I. William Zartman have read the manuscript and provided many useful comments.

Bonnie Lee deserves special credit not only for typing the final version of the manuscript with admirable speed and accuracy but also for her other help in upholding the author's morale. Robin Wolfgang skillfully prepared the graphics. Elizabeth Gretz of Princeton University Press has been consistently helpful while shepherding this work into print.

I am solely responsible for any remaining errors. The views in this book are my own and not necessarily those of my current employer, the Central Intelligence Agency, or of the United States Government.

P.R.P.

NEGOTIATING
PEACE
War Termination as
a Bargaining Process

INTRODUCTION

How do wars end? Given the misery and destruction caused by warfare through the centuries, and the impact it has had on human history, the importance of this question seems self-evident. Yet, unlike attempts to explain how wars begin, the effort devoted to understanding how they end has been scant. This book is intended to increase that understanding.

The book's subject is in one sense broad, in another sense narrow.

It is broad insofar as it explores many sides of the fundamental question of how wars end. It is not confined to identifying and describing a moment that marks a transition from war to peace (*"When* do wars end?"). It is instead intended to illuminate entire patterns of diplomatic and military behavior which belligerents display when they attempt to bring a war to a satisfactory conclusion. How do governments determine what terms of settlement to demand? How do they use military force to support those demands? How does combat affect diplomacy, and vice versa? Simple questions are not posed, and simple answers will not be offered, because to do so would not befit the complexity of the subject. Indeed, to demonstrate this complexity is one purpose of the study.

The subject is narrow insofar as it explores this array of questions from one particular perspective: it views warfare as a process of *bargaining* between two belligerents, and the making of peace as the striking of a bargain. This is a restriction, in two different but related senses, on the subject of war termination. The first sense is that the study is chiefly concerned with wars that end in a particular way— viz., with a negotiated settlement, and more specifically with a settlement that is completely negotiated while combat continues. It does not focus attention on wars that end through means other than negotiation, nor does it concern negotiations that have taken place at post-war "peace conferences" such as those at Vienna and Versailles. Instead, it addresses the making of armistices—i.e., agreements that end combat. ("Cease-fire" and "truce" will be used interchangeably with "armistice.") But in another sense, the perspective of warfare-as-bargaining is a restriction not so much on the kind of wars to be studied as on the method used to examine the endings of wars in general. This is, for two reasons, a valid way to view the scope of this book even though most of the empirical material in it is drawn from a few wars ending with negotiated settlements that combined an armistice with other peace terms. One reason will be the argument of Chapter 1: that this form of war ending, though infrequent in the past, will be more common in the future. The other reason, also discussed in Chapter 1, is that even many of the wars which do not conclude with this kind of negotiated settlement (e.g., ones that end when one side capitulates) contain elements of a bargaining process.

The overall purpose of the study is to spell out the implications of being part of a bargaining relationship in which violence is used— what the determinants of diplomatic and military decisions are, what problems are encountered in reaching those decisions, and how these problems tend to be resolved. It should be borne in mind that this is still only one side of the subject of war termination. Not every war can be described chiefly as a bargaining process, and the ones which can have other aspects as well. Discussion of these other aspects will be confined mainly to pointing out how they limit or qualify the principal conclusions about bargaining in warfare. But the underlying premise is that to view the ending of wars as a bargaining problem is a fruitful way, and probably the most fruitful way, to study the subject. The argument is that much of the military and diplomatic behavior in a war, particularly in its final stages, is comprehensible when we interpret it as the reaching of a bargain, even if it is incomprehensible when viewed in some other way (such as a contest which culminates in a "win" for one side and a "loss" for the other).

The intention is more to describe and explain than to prescribe. The wartime decision-maker faces many constraints, and we will see how some events are virtually predetermined by the forces which bear upon him. Nevertheless, he still has considerable latitude for acting wisely or unwisely, for committing mistakes or avoiding them. The occasions for doing so will be pointed out along the way, and some additional advice to the statesman will be offered in the final chapter and in Appendix A.

There have been some fine accounts of the negotiated settlement of individual wars (several of which are relied upon in the present study), but general works on war termination are strikingly scarce. This deficiency has begun to be remedied only during the past decade, when the national anguish in the United States over the Vietnam War inspired new work on the subject.[1] This neglect has stemmed partly from prevailing attitudes in the community of peace researchers, who have viewed war more as a disease to be eradicated than as a beast to be controlled.[2] Such an outlook admits studies of the prevention of war, and hence of its outbreak and causation, but not of what to do with it once it is underway. The neglect has also been rooted in a more widespread tendency, particularly prevalent in the United States, to view war and peace as two distinct states, intrinsically different from one another, which must be managed and analyzed in different ways.[3] This discourages the examination of war termination, a process which bridges the two domains. Although these few efforts have provided some valuable insights, they still constitute only a scratch on the surface of the subject.

The most systematic of these works have employed quantitative techniques to search for recurring relationships among such measures as casualties, force ratios, and the duration of wars.[4] This work has been directed more to the question of *when* wars end than to how they end, but even within this limited frame of reference the

---

[1] Book-length studies of the subject are: H. A. Calahan, *What Makes a War End?* Paul Kecskemeti, *Strategic Surrender;* Clark C. Abt, *The Termination of General War;* Fred C. Iklé, *Every War Must End;* Robert F. Randle, *The Origins of Peace;* and Stuart Albert and Edward C. Luck (eds.), *On the Endings of Wars.* [The bibliography contains complete citations of all works mentioned in the footnotes.] See also two collections of articles, one edited by Berenice A. Carroll in the *Journal of Peace Research,* 6 (1969, No. 4), and the other edited by William T. R. Fox in the *Annals of the American Academy of Political and Social Science,* 392 (November 1970).

[2] For a development of this and other explanations, see William T. R. Fox, "The Causes of Peace and Conditions of War," *Annals of the American Academy of Political and Social Science,* 392 (November 1970), 1–13 at pp. 3–6.

[3] Robert E. Osgood, *Limited War, passim;* and Morton H. Halperin, *Limited War in the Nuclear Age,* p. 19.

[4] One of the earliest such studies was sponsored during World War II by the United States government, which sought to determine if past wars revealed any patterns that would indicate when Japan would surrender. (Significantly, the United States was not seeking a negotiated peace.) The principal investigator, Frank L. Klingberg, published the results in "Predicting the Termination of War: Battle Casualties and Population Losses." A more recent example of work in the same genre is much of the material in Melvin Small and J. David Singer, *Resort to Arms.*

results have not been particularly conclusive. They point to some trends, such as changes in casualty ratios or the size of armies, that may be associated with the end of a war, but the relationships among these military measures are not clear and there is little or no evidence of any threshold, such as of total casualties, associated with the end of combat.[5]

The effectiveness of this approach is limited not so much by the quantitative methodology as by its focus on military events to the exclusion of political and diplomatic events. The view of war and diplomacy that underlies this approach also underlay Lewis F. Richardson's pioneering work on arms races and war moods. A war, in Richardson's view, must be studied the way one would study the weather—the subject of his own work as a meteorologist—which follows its own dynamic regardless of the interests, decisions, or intentions of the people who are rained or shined upon. This conception implies that if one wants to understand the course of wars, including how and when they end, examining diplomatic evidence is a waste of time. The only connection that Richardson himself made between war and diplomcy was the negative one that each inhibits the other. "To attempt both at the same time," he wrote, "feels as unnatural as to swing the arms in phase with the legs in marching, instead of in the usual antiphase."[6] But as statesmen themselves realize, politics and diplomacy *are* relevant to wars, and certainly to war endings. Although some wars have at times resembled Richardson's conception of a mindless physical struggle, in most wars political purpose is not completely lost in the confusion, and diplomacy does not fall into disuse. The political and diplomatic sides of an armed struggle may be less susceptible than combat statistics to rigorous analytical techniques, but they cannot simply be ignored if one seeks to understand how wars end.

There is a much larger literature which does relate military force to diplomacy, although without any special attention to the ending of wars. Most of this work has centered on international crises—con-

---

[5] Klingberg, pp. 167–168; and Small and Singer, Chap. 11. Donald Wittman in "How a War Ends: A Rational Actor Model," p.753, showed a negative correlation between the length of wars and battle deaths per capita per month, but without suggesting how the termination of combat might be associated with any particular level or pattern of casualties.

[6] Lewis F. Richardson, "War Moods: I," p. 155. Richardson's conception and methods have inspired many investigations of topics in international relations other than war termination. For a compendium of recent efforts, see Dina A. Zinnes and John V. Gillespie (eds.), *Mathematical Models in International Relations*, Part 3.

frontations in which the deployment of armed forces and the possibility of their use are important, but in which the protagonists are not already at war.[7] Some of the same principles governing military and diplomatic behavior in crises apply as well to wars, and so the crisis literature is a source of insights for the present study. In fact, a subsidiary purpose of this book is to offer additional insights which apply not just to the termination of wars but also to other armed confrontations, including crises. The richness of military and diplomatic behavior during the terminal stage of a war makes it a fertile field for generating such ideas. But this very richness is the basis for important differences between crises and wars, thus limiting the usefulness of the crisis literature in attempting to understand war termination. For one thing, the diplomatic process leading to an armistice agreement is usually far more complex than the diplomacy involved in resolving most crises. A government's objective in a crisis may not even be an explicit agreement but rather the adversary's taking (or refraining from) some unilateral act.[8] The crisis literature therefore does not delve as deeply as this study does into the complex interplay of concessions, counterconcessions, package proposals, and changes in patterns of diplomacy during the course of a negotiation. It tends instead to pose the simpler question of which side will back down in a confrontation, and searches for reasons why one side is more likely to do so than the other.[9] Furthermore, with a war in progress, military behavior is also more complex than it is in a crisis. In Chapter 4 we will see just how complex it can become even when the discussion is limited to uses of armed force that are intended to influence the terms or timing of a peace agreement. The ingredients of military decision-making described there go well beyond what is covered in studies of armed confrontations in which violence is only threatened and not actually employed.

Finally, none of these previous works—either on war termination or on such related topics as crises—develops very far the implications of treating its subject as a bargaining process. The term "bar-

---

[7] Among the most important studies of this subject are: Oran R. Young, *The Politics of Force;* Ole R. Holsti, *Crisis Escalation War;* Alexander L. George, David K. Hall, and William E. Simons. *The Limits of Coercive Diplomacy;* Glenn H. Snyder and Paul Diesing, *Conflict Among Nations;* and Richard N. Lebow, *Between Peace and War.*

[8] As will be demonstrated in Chapter 1, most wars *do* end with an explicit agreement.

[9] This is particularly true of the George, Hall, and Simons book.

gaining'' crops up frequently, but often without spelling out exactly what it means, and seldom attempting to make extensive use of the insights of those who have analyzed other kinds of bargaining problems or the bargaining process in general. This book aims to do both.

Most of the analysis in the pages that follow tacitly employs a "rational actor" conception of foreign policy and interstate behavior. That is, each belligerent is viewed as a unitary actor having a consistent set of objectives and behaving in the way calculated to bring it closest to those objectives.[10] The choice of this perspective does not imply that alternative conceptions would be useless in shedding light on the subject. To the contrary, a sensitivity to the irrational elements in international politics and to divisions within a warring state or alliance can enhance our understanding of many details of diplomatic and military behavior. This book will occasionally depart from the rational actor perspective to take note of each. But, given the present state of knowledge of war termination, an analysis of the *logic* of negotiating peace—of the strategic structure of the kind of conflict under study—seems most useful.

Within this general conception, and the more specific perspective of warfare and its termination as a bargaining process, this book uses a diversity of analytical methods and sources of insight. The most important source is the historical record of actual wars and peace negotiations. The selection of empirical material is based on the presentation in Chapter 1 concerning the form of past and future war endings; further comment on how this material was chosen and how it is to be used will be made at the end of that chapter. Apart from the wars themselves, the propositions in this study have several other sources.

Among these are abstract models of bargaining, which will be utilized particularly in Chapters 3 and 4. Although most of these were created by economists who had bilateral monopoly—especially labor-management negotiations—in mind, the model-builders have usually claimed that their work is applicable to bargaining problems in general. There are several reasons to refer to such abstract models in the present study. First, the models are a genuine source of some nonobvious ideas and propositions; at the very least, the source needs to be acknowledged. Second, even when a point is more obvious, reference to one of the models may be the quickest and clearest way to make it. And, third, drawing upon this work and

[10] Cf. Graham T. Allison, *Essence of Decision*, Chap. 1.

putting the claims of general applicability to the test may advance our understanding of bargaining in general—another subsidiary purpose of this study—and of the ways in which peace negotiations resemble or differ from other bargaining problems. A related point is that this kind of exercise provides feedback to the model-builders, indicating which of their psychological assumptions or decision rules are realistic and which are not.[11] Because they are greatly simplified versions of an inherently complex process, no one of these models can provide any more than a partial truth, although in certain circumstances the truth provided may be the most important one. Identifying which assumptions or rules tend to be operable in which circumstances will be a major part of the task ahead.

Another source of insights is experimental research on bargaining, which has generated an immense literature over the past two decades. Because this approach to the subject has occupied the time and talents of so many researchers—in this case, social psychologists—it would be shortsighted to ignore this work. Besides, laboratory experiments have advantages of control and observation which make them useful in confirming tendencies suspected to exist in interactions outside the laboratory. A statesman may be unavailable for comment after making a diplomatic or military decision, but a questionnaire administered to an experimental subject who has just made an analogous decision may provide an insight regarding the statesman's likely motivations.[12]

Yet another source is research on real-life bargaining situations other than peace negotiations, particularly contract negotiations between labor unions and corporations. Using this research does not presuppose that peace negotiations are always similar to labor negotiations. In fact, some important differences, as well as similarities,

---

[11] On the role of such assumptions or decision rules in economic models, see J. Pen, "A General Theory of Bargaining," p. 27; and Alan Coddington, *Theories of the Bargaining Process*, p. 63.

[12] Furthermore, the point about supplying feedback to the model-builders applies as well to experimental research.

On the general relevance of experimental research to the study of conflict, bargaining, and international relations, see Herbert C. Kelman, "Social-Psychological Approaches to the Study of International Relations," in Kelman (ed.), *International Behavior*, pp. 598–600; Charles Lockhart, *Bargaining in International Conflicts*, pp. 28–32; Dean G. Pruitt, *Negotiation Behavior*, pp. 11–12; and Barry R. Schlenker and Thomas V. Bonoma, "Fun and Games: The Validity of Games for the Study of Conflict."

will be pointed out. But, like the abstract models and the experimental findings, this research does suggest some useful propositions.

The opening chapter will present an inventory of past war endings to determine to what extent a concentration of attention on bargaining, and on pre-armistice peace negotiations, is justified in studying war termination. It will also identify the principal sources of empirical material to be used in the remainder of the book. Chapter 2 discusses the opening of peace negotiations and the problems commonly encountered in getting talks underway. Chapter 3 analyzes diplomatic movement in a peace conference, describing the various meanings of concessions and using them to search for patterns as the belligerents converge toward an agreement. Chapter 4 discusses the variety of ways in which military force is used to induce an enemy to concede. Chapter 5 analyzes diplomatic responses to armed force, explaining why a military action often elicits an unexpected or unwanted reaction from the enemy. Chapter 6 addresses the problems and opportunities associated with negotiating several issues simultaneously. Chapter 7 concludes the study by noting the principal lessons for the scholar and for the statesman.

CHAPTER ONE

Patterns of
War Termination

An inquiry into the process of negotiating peace must begin by identifying the part that negotiation plays in war termination generally. The present chapter presents a brief but systematic tabulation of past war endings, revealing patterns that suggest how future wars will be likely to end. The tabulation also reveals which past wars can yield the most insights about how peace agreements are likely to be negotiated in the future.

Following some preliminary remarks about the basis of the tabulation, the first section presents a typology of war endings. The next section uses this typology to summarize how past wars have ended. The results reveal changes in patterns of war termination which suggest that most future international wars will end with negotiated settlements. This argument is then extended, showing why most of these settlements will be negotiated prior to an armistice. Based on these findings, war termination is then described as a bargaining problem. The final section notes the implications of the results for the study of peace negotiations and identifies the sources of material to be used in subsequent chapters.

The tabulation below includes wars that ended between 1800 and 1980. It thus roughly covers the period of the modern mass army, which was born in the wars of the French Revolution. The period is also sufficiently long to reveal trends.

Several lists of wars have been published, though none were compiled to study how wars have ended and none include any data on that subject.[1] The list in this chapter is based principally on the most

---

[1] The author of one of the compilations, however, addressed the subject elsewhere: Quincy Wright, "How Hostilities Have Ended: Peace Treaties and Alternatives," *Annals of the American Academy of Political and Social Science*, 392 (November 1970), 51–61.

recent compilation of wars of the nineteenth and twentieth centuries, found in Melvin Small and J. David Singer's *Resort to Arms*. Their criteria for inclusion as an international war involve the number of casualties and the status of the entities that fought. They include a conflict in their list if it involved at least one member of the interstate system[2] and caused at least 1,000 battle deaths among all the members of the interstate system that were belligerents. Further, if a war involving only one member of the interstate system lasts longer than one year, that member's battle deaths must reach an annual average of 1,000.[3] The list in this chapter includes all 111 international wars ending between 1816 and 1980 identified by Small and Singer. The list is extended back to 1800 by drawing on Quincy Wright's earlier compilation, which adds 10 interstate wars.[4]

The peace negotiations discussed in this book have mainly occurred in international wars. We should also take note of how civil wars have ended, however, not only because of their intrinsic importance but also because this will permit some later comparisons that will clarify the conditions in which negotiated settlements are most likely. Small and Singer present a list of civil wars in *Resort to Arms,* but their definition is a broad one which includes instances of mass violence that some others would describe as riots rather than civil wars. For our present purpose we will thus use Wright's more restrictive list, taking from it all conflicts that Small and Singer, in an earlier version of their work on international wars, state that they exclude solely because they are civil wars.[5] This adds 11 wars through 1965 (when Wright's list ends), and applying what appears to be Wright's standard for civil wars to the portion of Small and Singer's list for 1966 to 1980 adds 10 more. The final list includes 142 wars that concluded between 1800 and 1980, from the French Revolutionary Wars ending in 1801 to the civil war in Zimbabwe ending in 1979.

Two minor problems with the list should be mentioned. The first is that the list includes several multilateral wars which were really clusters of struggles grouped together under a single name, not all of

---

[2] Prior to 1919, membership is defined as having a population of at least 500,000 and exercising a fair degree of sovereignty and independence. After 1919, it requires either meeting the population minimum and receiving recognition by at least two major powers, or membership in either the League of Nations or United Nations.

[3] Small and Singer, *Resort to Arms,* pp. 36–57.

[4] Quincy Wright, *A Study of War,* Appendices XX and C.

[5] J. David Singer and Melvin Small, *Wages of War,* pp. 82–128.

which ended together. These are the French Revolutionary and Napoleonic wars, the Latin American wars for independence, the two world wars of the twentieth century, the Bolshevik regime's struggle against several opponents during its first years, and the various Arab-Israeli wars. Rather than attempting to break these conglomerate wars into individual components, which would in effect mean constructing a new list, the end of each will be taken to be the end of fighting on the last front to fall quiet. Given the small number of these conglomerate wars in comparison with the overall total of 142, this procedure is unlikely to distort any patterns. Besides, most of the conflicts in each conglomerate war tended to have similar endings anyway.

The other minor difficulty results from the way Small and Singer use their casualty criteria to determine the duration of a war. Some colonial and imperial wars were stop-and-go affairs or dragged out over several years at a low level of violence. The purpose of the 1,000-deaths-per-year standard is to include only the violent phases of such conflicts. This is acceptable if the concern is to measure the duration of violence (one of Small and Singer's concerns), but less desirable in examining how violence has ended, because in a couple of cases the Small-Singer cutoff point was only a temporary interruption of a war that concluded definitively sometime later. To adjust their dates, however, would mean losing the precision of the casualty criterion and substituting something else that might entail begging the very questions which the exercise is designed to answer. Therefore, the casualty criterion will be retained to identify when a war ended as well as whether it belongs on the list in the first place, and the cases in which this raises difficulties will be noted individually.

How Wars Can End

This chapter is concerned with the structure or form of war endings, and not with the substance or legal status of peace settlements. The distinctions we are exploring involve whether and how the conclusion of a war is related to political decisions, who takes such decisions, and when they are taken. Figure 1 depicts a typology of war endings that makes these distinctions. The initial basis for classification is whether fighting ends when the war does. The question is genuine because some of the wars that appear on a list such as

FIGURE 1. **Types of war endings.**

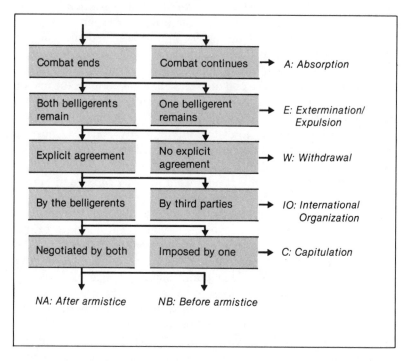

Small and Singer's never reached their own conclusion. Instead, they became part of a larger war (which they may have helped to trigger), with additional participants, its own place on the list and its own settlement. In such cases, the concluding date of the smaller war only marks the start of the larger one. The smaller war may be said to have ended by *absorption* (A). (One might prefer to think of this not as the end of a war but only as a quirk of this kind of list. At least it serves as a reminder that the level of violence can go up as well as down.) If the fighting does cease, we may next ask whether it did because both belligerents decided that it should cease. If one side stops fighting without having taken a decision to stop, it means that its opponent has rendered it incapable of continuing the fight, either through *extermination* (of an organized force, not necessarily of individuals) or *expulsion* (E) from the country or theater in which the war is fought. When a war ends instead through decisions taken by both parties, it may be without any explicit agreement—i.e., through a simple *withdrawal* (W) from combat—or through acceptance of a written accord. The parties could have drafted such an accord themselves or accepted one written by a third party. Virtually the only kind of third party that has served this function is an *international organization* (IO). If the agreement was not the work of a third party, it might have been imposed, without discussion or modification, by one side upon the other. This would be *capitulation* (C). Capitulations may include "unconditional" surrenders as well as agreements that are much less one-sided; all that matters is how the agreement was reached. The alternative to imposition by one side is *negotiation* by both sides. Finally, negotiated peace agreements differ according to the sequence of negotiation and cease-fire. In some cases, the principal peace agreement is negotiated *after* (NA) the establishment of an armistice. In others, the only peace agreement reached is the one which establishes the cease-fire; the negotiation which led to it took place *before* (NB) the armistice. This distinction depends solely on whether or not there was a post-armistice agreement that was part of the process of war termination, not on the substance or legal form of an agreement.

Not every war fits neatly into one of the boxes. For example, when an insurrection gradually loses strength and finally ends without any explicit agreement, it may be unclear whether the end came because the remaining leadership of the insurrection decided to give up the struggle (withdrawal) or because they lost all of their troops (extermination/expulsion). When there is an explicit agreement, the line between capitulation and negotiation can be fuzzy. In common parlance the two terms are usually distinguishable; negotiation suggests at least the possibility of give-and-take, whereas capitulation is a matter of one side signing on the dotted line. The ambiguity that does occur reflects the lack of a generally accepted definition of negotiation. This in turn is at least partly the result of a confusion— often deliberate—of the concept of negotiation itself, with the concept of negotiating behavior that is "reasonable" or "in good faith." An easy way to criticize one's opponent is to accuse him of not negotiating at all. However, to define negotiation so that it requires not just that reciprocity be possible but that it actually occur would mean that in many encounters commonly described as negotiations, true negotiation is not taking place most of the time. Furthermore, such a definition would confuse or prevent some comparisons between individual negotiations that are useful in studying questions of successful versus unsuccessful negotiating strategies, easy versus difficult negotiations, etc. Accordingly, a peace settlement is considered to have been negotiated if it emerged from a face-to-face session which at least one of the parties entered with the apparent intention not of capitulating, but of jointly writing an agreement.[6]

How Wars Did End

Table I lists the 142 wars which ended between 1800 and 1980, in order of their ending dates. The table provides two pieces of information about each war, in addition to the dates. One is a classification of the wars themselves into three types, which is taken from Small and Singer: (1) interstate wars, in which a member of the state system fought on each side; (2) extra-systemic wars, which were colonial or imperial conflicts involving a member of the state system on only one side; and (3) civil wars. These distinctions will be referred to again in a moment. The other is the classification of war endings, following the typology in Figure 1. The sources consulted are listed in the bibliography and keyed to the numbers in this table. The most questionable cases are asterisked and explained further in notes. In addition to the seven basic categories, an additional coding scheme in parentheses indicates wars which, though not falling within the NB category, share some of its attributes. The notation (I) indicates that some political issues were settled through indirect negotiations (conducted through intermediaries, broadcasts, or written messages) prior to the armistice. (P) means that the armistice agreement itself incorporated substantial political provisions, usually as a "preliminary peace treaty." (U) indicates that face-to-face negotiations were conducted on the terms of settlement prior to an armistice but did not succeed in producing an agreement.

The Prevalence of Explicit Agreements

The totals at the bottom of the table show that a substantial majority of the wars ended with an explicit agreement between the two sides. In most of the ones that did not, one of the parties was exterminated or expelled. As long as both belligerents remain, in

[6] There is actually only one case, the Russo-Finnish War of 1939–1940, that is classified as a negotiation under this rule but that looks very much like a capitulation. The Finns came to Moscow with the intention of negotiating, even though they wound up signing a document which the Soviets had drafted and refused to change by so much as a comma.

other words, it is rare for combat to end without a written agreement. It is perhaps even more rare than the total of seven withdrawals indicates, because five of these seven are questionable or special cases. An agreement to end the Spanish-Santo Dominican War was negotiated and signed in 1865, but it was effectively discarded when the Dominican leaders repudiated their own negotiators and word arrived that Madrid had decided to evacuate its forces from the island. Spain and Chile also signed an armistice agreement and peace treaty after their war in 1865–1866, but these came so long after the actual end of hostilities that the case is classified as a withdrawal. The French adventure in Mexico during the same decade ended when Napoleon decided to withdraw his troops, but the imperial forces within Mexico put up some further resistance before capitulating. The fighting between Britain and the followers of the Mahdi in the Sudan in the 1880's ended with a British withdrawal back to Egypt. However, this omits (because British deaths did not meet the casualty criterion) the further fighting in the 1890's, when the British under Kitchener returned to crush the dervishes at the battle of Omdurman and exterminate their rebellion. Finally, the civil strife in Colombia which ran from the 1940's through the early 1960's is one of those instances of an insurrection gradually petering out, and which could be considered either a withdrawal or an extermination. There are only two wars on the list which unambiguously ended through withdrawal: China's border clashes with India in 1962 and with Vietnam in 1979.

Withdrawals probably would not be quite so scarce if the casualty criteria for inclusion in the list were relaxed. At low levels, military force is sometimes used demonstratively, to assert a claim or to issue a warning. The Chinese Communists' periodic shelling of the offshore islands in the Taiwan Strait is an example, as perhaps were their larger actions against India and Vietnam. When force is used only to demonstrate, and not to eliminate an adversary or to change his will, the advantages of explicitness in an agreement are irrelevant because no agreement is sought.

An instance of armed conflict growing out of more ambitious aims but which would also be classified as a withdrawal if it qualified for the list is the Communist insurgency in Greece between 1946 and 1949. That struggle ended when the rebels announced that they were ending military operations and withdrew what was left of their army and government to Albania. The conflict in Greece is worth mentioning because, despite its small scale, it influenced the thinking of

TABLE 1
How Wars Ended, 1800–1980

Type of war
1: Interstate
2: Extra-systemic
3: Civil

Type of ending
A: Absorption
E: Extermination/Expulsion
W: Withdrawal
IO: International Organization
C: Capitulation
NA: Negotiation after armistice
NB: Negotiation before armistice
(I): Indirect negotiations before armistice
(P): Political terms combined with armistice
(U): Unsuccessful negotiations before armistice

An asterisk indicates an explanatory note at
the end of the table.

1.	French Revolutionary (1792–1801)	1	NA(P)
2.	Haitian Revolt (1802–1803)	2	C
3.	1st British-Maharattan (1802–1804)	2	C
4.	Russo-Swedish (1808–1809)	1	NA
5.	Russo-Turkish (1806–1812)	1	NA
6.	Russo-Persian (1804–1813)	2	NA
7.	War of 1812 (1812–1815)	1	NB
8.	Nepoleonic (1803–1815)	1	NA(U)
9.	Austria-Naples (1815)	1	E
10.	2nd British-Maharattan (1817–1818)	2	C
11.	Franco-Spanish (1823)	1	C
12.	Latin American Revolt (1810–1824)	2	C
13.	1st Anglo-Burmese (1823–1826)	2	C
14.	Russo-Persian (1826–1828)	2	NA
15.	Greek (1821–1828)	2	A
16.	Russo-Turkish (1828–1829)	1	C
17.	Javanese (1825–1830)	2	C
18.	1st Polish (1831)	2	E
19.	1st Syrian (1831–1832)	2	C

20.	Texan (1835–1836)	2	C
21.	2nd Syrian (1839–1840)	2	C
22.	Peruvian-Bolivian (1841)	2	NA
23.	1st British-Afghan (1838–1842)	2	E
24.	1st British-Sikh (1845–1846)	2	C
25.	Franco-Algerian (1839–1847)	2	C
26.	Mexican-American (1846–1848)	1	NB
27.	Austro-Sardinian (1848–1849)	1	NA(I)
28.	1st Schleswig-Holstein (1848–1849)	1	NA
29.	Hungarian (1848–1849)	2	C
30.	2nd British-Sikh (1848–1849)	2	C
31.	Roman Republic (1849)	1	C
32.	La Plata (1851–1852)	1	E
33.	1st Turco-Montenegran (1852–1853)	2	NA
34.	Crimean (1853–1856)	1	NA(U,P)
35.	Anglo-Persian (1856–1857)	1	NB
36.	Sepoy (1857–1859)	2	E
37.	2nd Turco-Montenegran (1858–1859)	2	NA
38.	Italian Unification (1859)	1	NA
39.	Spanish-Moroccan (1859–1860)	1	C
40.	Italo-Roman (1860)	1	C
41.	Italo-Sicilian (1860–1861)	1	C
42.	Ecuadorian-Colombian (1863)	1	NA
43.	China (1850–1864)	3	E
44.	2nd Polish (1863–1864)	2	E
45.	2nd Schleswig-Holstein (1864)	1	NA
46.	United States (1861–1865)	3	C
47.	Spanish-Santo Dominican (1863–1865)	2	W(U)
48.	Spanish-Chilean (1865–1866)	1	W*
49.	Seven Weeks (1866)	1	NA(I)
50.	Franco-Mexican (1862–1867)	1	W*
51.	Spain (1866–1868)	3	E
52.	Lopez (1864–1870)	1	E
53.	Franco-Prussian (1870–1871)	1	NA
54.	Spain (1872–1876)	3	E
55.	Balkan (1875–1877)	2	A*
56.	Ten Years (1868–1878)	2	C
57.	Dutch-Achinese (1873–1878)	2	C*
58.	Russo-Turkish (1877–1878)	1	NA(I)
59.	Bosnian (1878)	2	E
60.	British-Zulu (1879)	2	C
61.	2nd British-Afghan (1878–1880)	2	E

62.	Pacific (1879–1883)	1	C
63.	Franco-Indochinese (1882–1884)	2	A
64.	Mahdist (1882–1885)	2	W
65.	Sino-French (1884–1885)	1	NA(U)
66.	Central American (1885)	1	NA
67.	Serbo-Bulgarian (1885)	2	NA
68.	Sino-Japanese (1894–1895)	1	NA
69.	Franco-Madagascan (1894–1895)	2	C
70.	Cuban (1895–1898)	2	A
71.	Italo-Ethiopian (1895–1896)	2	NA
72.	Greco-Turkish (1897)	1	NA
73.	1st Philippine (1896–1898)	2	A
74.	Spanish-American (1898)	1	NA(I)
75.	Boxer Rebellion (1900–1901)	1	NA(P)
76.	2nd Philippine (1899–1902)	2	E
77.	Boer (1899–1902)	2	C
78.	Ilinden (1903)	2	E
79.	Russo-Japanese (1904–1905)	1	NB
80.	Central American (1906)	1	NA
81.	Central American (1907)	1	NA
82.	Spanish-Moroccan (1909–1910)	1	C
83.	Italo-Turkish (1911–1912)	1	NB
84.	1st Balkan (1912–1913)	1	NA(I,P)
85.	2nd Balkan (1913)	1	NA
86.	World War I (1914–1918)	1	NA(I)
87.	Hungarian Allies (1919)	1	E
88.	Russo-Polish (1919–1920)	1	NA(P)
89.	Russian Nationalities (1917–1922)	2	E*
90.	Greco-Turkish (1919–1922)	1	NA
91.	Riffian (1921–1926)	2	C
92.	Druze (1925–1926)	2	E
93.	Sino-Soviet (1929)	1	NB
94.	Manchurian (1931–1933)	1	C
95.	Chaco (1932–1935)	1	NA(P,I)*
96.	Italo-Ethiopian (1935–1936)	1	E
97.	Changkufeng (1938)	1	NB
98.	Spain (1936–1939)	3	E(U)
99.	Nomohan (1939)	1	NB
100.	Franco-Thai (1940–1941)	1	NA
101.	Sino-Japanese (1937–1941)	1	A
102.	Russo-Finnish (1939–1940)	1	NB
103.	World War II (1939–1945)	1	C

104.	Paraguay (1947)	3	E
105.	Hyderabad (1948)	2	C
106.	Madagascan (1947–1948)	2	E
107.	China (1927–1949)	3	E
108.	Indonesian (1945–1946)	2	NA(U,P)*
109.	1st Kashmir (1947–1949)	2	NB*
110.	Palestine (1948–1949)	1	IO*
111.	Bolivia (1946–1952)	3	C
112.	Korean (1950–1953)	1	NB
113.	Indochina (1945–1954)	2	NB
114.	Russo-Hungarian (1956)	1	E
115.	Sinai (1956)	1	IO
116.	Tibetan (1956–1959)	2	E
117.	Algerian (1954–1962)	2	NB
118.	1st Laos (1959–1962)	3	NA*
119.	Sino-Indian (1962)	1	W
120.	Colombia (1948–1964)	3	W
121.	Cyprus (1963–1964)	3	IO(I,U)
122.	2nd Kashmir (1965)	1	IO(I)*
123.	Six Days (1967)	1	IO
124.	Football (1969)	1	IO
125.	Yemen (1962–1970)	3	NB
126.	Nigeria (1967–1970)	3	C(U)
127.	Israeli-Egyptian (1969–1970)	1	IO*
128.	Jordan (1970)	3	NB
129.	Sri Lanka (1971)	3	E
130.	Bangladesh (1971)	1	C*
131.	2nd Laos (1963–1973)	3	NB
132.	Yom Kippur (1973)	1	IO*
133.	Angola (1962–1974)	2	NA
134.	Mozambique (1964–1974)	2	NB
135.	Turco-Cypriot (1974)	1	IO
136.	Cambodia (1967–1975)	3	C
137.	Vietnam (1957–1975)	3	C*
138.	Lebanon (1975–1976)	3	NB
139.	Sino-Vietnamese (1979)	1	W
140.	Ugandan-Tanzanian (1978–1979)	1	E
141.	Nicaragua (1978–1979)	3	C
142.	Zimbabwe (1972–1979)	3	NB

Summary:

	A	E	W	IO	C	NA	NB	
1	1	7	4	8	11	28	10	69
2	5	12	2	0	20	9	4	52
3	0	7	1	1	6	1	5	21
	6	26	7	9	37	38	19	142

Notes to Table 1

[48] Spanish-Chilean (1865–1866). Combat ceased when the Spanish fleet withdrew from the Chilean coast in May 1866. A formal armistice was signed in 1871, and a final peace treaty in 1879.

[50] Franco-Mexican (1862–1867). Napoleon decided in 1866 (under pressure from the United States) to withdraw all French troops from Mexico. The last of these were gone by March 1867, though Mexican forces supporting Maximilian continued to fight until capitulating in May.

[55] Balkan (1875–1877). Serbia and Turkey signed an armistice in November 1876 and a final peace treaty in March 1877. The other anti-Turkish forces were still fighting, however, when the Russo-Turkish War broke out in April.

[57] Dutch-Achinese (1873–1878). Pacification was accomplished through the surrender of some of the rebellious chiefs and the capture of others.

[89] Russian Nationalities (1917–1922). The Bolshevik regime's fight for survival ended in different ways on different fronts. The foreign interventionary forces were withdrawn, the Baltic republics signed peace treaties with the Bolsheviks, and most of the other nationalist resistance movements were crushed. The last fighting was in Turkestan, where the rebellion was extinguished in the late summer of 1922.

[95] Chaco (1932–1935). There were numerous attempts at mediation, conciliation, and direct talks during this war. The parties finally agreed to a cease-fire in June 1935, with the understanding that their dispute would be submitted to arbitration. A final peace treaty was signed in July 1938.

[108] Indonesian (1945–1946). The 1945–1946 phase of the fighting, which is the only one that meets the Small-Singer criteria, had two different efforts to negotiate a peace. The first was unsuccessful; the second led to a cease-fire in October 1946, which was followed closely by the Linggadjati agreement in November. The vague terms of this agreement led to further controversy and two more rounds of fighting before peace was finally restored in 1949.

[109] 1st Kashmir (1947–1949). The cease-fire followed a conference between the two sides in New Delhi, although the UN Commission for India and Pakistan was also actively involved.

[110] Palestine (1948–1949). The cease-fire which took hold in January 1949 was in response to action by the UN Security Council. The so-called "armistice agreements" concluded over the following months between Israel and the Arab states did not create armistices, but rather concerned the administration of one already in effect.

[118] 1st Laos (1959–1962). The United States accepted a Geneva conference only after insisting on a preliminary cease-fire. Some fighting did continue, however, while the conference was in session.

[122] 2nd Kashmir (1965). The UN-sponsored cease-fire in September was followed by talks between the two sides in Tashkent, although the Tashkent Declaration in January 1966 contained little of substance.

[127] Israeli-Egyptian (1969–1970). The war ended when both sides accepted a U.S. proposal that included a promise to observe earlier cease-fire resolutions of the UN Security Council.

[130] Bangladesh (1971). What brought the war to an end was the unconditional surrender of all Pakistani forces in East Pakistan on 16 December. A cease-fire was declared on the western front the following day.

[132] Yom Kippur (1973). As with the 1948–1949 Middle East war, Israel and the Arab states later concluded agreements covering the administration of an armistice that had already been established under the auspices of the Security Council.

[137] Vietnam (1957–1975). The civil war ended with Saigon's surrender in April 1975. The period of American involvement had ended with the Paris agreements of January 1973.

---

decision-makers, at least in the United States, who directed later and larger wars. In Congressional testimony in May 1951 (less than two months before the start of the Korean truce talks), General Omar Bradley, the Chairman of the Joint Chiefs of Staff, acknowledged that the fighting in Korea might end in the Greek pattern rather than with a formal agreement.[7] And during the early part of the Vietnam War, American officials again were thinking in terms of a unilateral withdrawal from combat by the Communists, rather than an explicit agreement with them.[8] But the important point here is that, despite such thinking, these later wars nevertheless ended with formal agreements.

[7] *Military Situation in the Far East,* hearings, Committees on Armed Services and Foreign Relations, U.S. Senate, 82nd Congress, 1st session, Part 2, pp. 971–972.

[8] See a memorandum by Robert McNamara dated 20 July 1965 in *The Pentagon Papers,* Vol. 4, pp. 27–28; and a report on thinking among U.S. officials in Saigon in the *New York Times,* 19 January 1966, p. 2. See also Townsend Hoopes's criticism of this pattern of thought in a memorandum by himself which he quotes in *The Limits of Intervention,* p. 45.

The Huk rebellion in the Philippines and the Communist insurgency in Malaya, both of which faded out in the early 1950s without explicit agreements, also influenced the thinking of some of the Vietnam War planners. Unlike the Greek rebellion, however, there was no evidence in either of these conflicts of a decision by the rebel leaders to suspend operations when such a decision could still have made a difference. Instead, they would be classified as cases of extermination. Given that the United States never had the objective of exterminating the Hanoi regime, the Philippine and Malayan conflicts were inappropriate models.

Divisibility of the Stakes

It is easier to interpret the totals for the other categories by considering the different kinds of wars that are involved, which is why the three-fold typology of wars based on Small and Singer was included in Table 1. Eliminating the three lightly populated categories of war endings (absorption, withdrawal, and action by an international organization), collapsing the two categories of negotiation, and cross-tabulating the remaining three categories with the three types of war produces Table 2. The table suggests that what kind of war is being fought affects what kind of ending it will probably have.[9]

The likelihood that the two sides in any dispute can negotiate a settlement depends greatly on whether compromise agreements are available. If the stakes are chiefly indivisible, so that neither side can get most of what it wants without depriving the other of most of what it wants, negotiations are less apt to be successful.[10] Stakes are usually less divisible in civil wars than in other types of war; the issue is whether one side or the other shall control the country. The very fact that a civil war has broken out indicates the weakness of any mechanisms for compromise, and the war itself tends to polarize whatever moderate elements may have existed. Furthermore, each side in a civil war is a traitor in the eyes of the other and can never expect the enemy to let it live in peace. The struggle for power becomes a struggle for survival as the options narrow to the single one of a fight to the finish.[11] As a result, few civil wars end through negotiation unless they become highly internationalized. In all six of the wars in the upper right-hand cell of Table 2, the country whose future was at stake had become a pawn in a larger conflict, with outside powers becoming directly involved as belligerents or negotiators. These included the two wars in Laos (in which the Vietnam-

---

[9] The wars on the list do not constitute a true sample, but the chi-square test is applicable if they are construed as a sample of all possible wars which might have been fought during the same period.

[10] This has been demonstrated experimentally: Myron L. Joseph and Richard H. Willis, "An Experimental Analog to Two-Party Bargaining."

[11] In such conditions, not only is a successful negotiation next to impossible; even a capitulation may be ruled out. In the Spanish civil war of 1936–1939, fears of the fate that their followers would suffer in the hands of the Nationalists discouraged Republican leaders from surrendering to Franco even after their cause had become hopeless. The Republican government sought and obtained last-minute negotiations, but evidently only as a means of delay so that any of its sympathizers who wished to flee the country could do so. Hugh Thomas, *The Spanish Civil War*, pp. 551, 599–600.

TABLE 2
Types of Wars and Types of War Endings

	Interstate	Extra-systemic	Civil	
Negotiation	38 (68%)	13 (29%)	6 (32%)	57 (48%)
Capitulation	11 (20%)	20 (44%)	6 (32%)	37 (31%)
Extermination/ Expulsion	7 (13%)	12 (27%)	7 (37%)	26 (22%)
	56	45	19	120

Percentages shown are within columns.
chi-square = 18.88, $p < .001$

ese were participants), the Yemeni civil war (where Egypt became deeply involved), the fighting in Jordan in 1970 and Lebanon in 1975–1976 (both of which included Syria and the PLO), and the insurgency in Zimbabwe (in which Britain, as the responsible colonial power, arranged a settlement).[12]

Extra-systemic wars are a mixed group. They include some conflicts in which one belligerent only narrowly misses qualifying as a member of the state system, and so resemble interstate wars. They also include colonial wars in Africa and Asia, in which a European power usually had superior armed strength, was in no mood to compromise, and was fighting what it considered to be an internal rebellion that deserved only to be crushed. As the table indicates, the endings of these wars are also mixed.

Because both participants in an interstate war are full-fledged members of the state system, the continued existence of neither one as a nation-state is usually at stake, even though the existence of a government or regime may be. In this respect, such a war is the opposite of a civil war. The result, shown in the first column of the table, is that two-thirds of such wars end through negotiation, and the overwhelming majority end with some explicit coming to terms. Of the seven interstate wars which ended by extermination/expulsion, all but one resembled civil wars in that the major issue was the

[12] For further observations on the difficulty of negotiation in civil wars, see Iklé, *Every War Must End*, p. 95; George Modelski, "International Settlement of Internal War," in James N. Rosenau (ed.), *International Aspects of Civil Strife*, pp. 141–142; and Leslie H. Gelb, "Vietnam: The System Worked," pp. 150–153.

internal legitimacy of the regime that was eliminated. These were: Austria's overthrow of Napoleon's protégé Murat in Naples in 1815; Brazil's toppling of the Argentinian dictator Rosas in 1852; Brazil and Argentina's toppling of the Paraguayan dictator Lopez in 1870; the crushing of the Bela Kun regime in Hungary by Czech and Romanian forces in 1919; the crushing of the Imre Nagy regime in Hungary by Soviet forces in 1956; and the overthrow of Idi Amin in Uganda by Tanzanian forces in 1979. The only instance of a belligerent in an interstate war exterminating or expelling its enemy not to allow its replacement by a regime of the same nationality, but instead to annex its country, was the Italo-Ethiopian War of 1935–1936.

The Transition Toward Negotiation

Further conclusions follow when we examine changes over time. In doing so, we need first to return to the categories omitted from Table 2. One of these (withdrawal) was already discussed, and another (absorption) is an artifact of constructing the list. The remaining category—action by an international organization—must be included in any discussion of the termination of interstate wars because eight of the nine wars in it were of this type (the exception being Cyprus 1963–1964, a civil war). This form of termination has become important in recent years: all nine cases occurred within the last thirty years, and nearly one-fourth of the conflicts since World War II have ended this way. One reflection of this is that, compared to war termination in general, the peacemaking activities of international organizations have been relatively well studied.[13] But the use of international organizations to stop wars has been limited to a few locales and participants. Of the nine wars which have ended this way, the body taking action in eight of them was the United Nations Security Council. Five of these were rounds in the Arab-Israeli dispute, two concerned Greek versus Turk in Cyprus, and one was between India and Pakistan. The other case was the 1969 football war between El Salvador and Honduras, in which the Organization of American States was the body taking action. In none of these instances was a major power a belligerent (which is consistent with

[13] See, e.g.: Ernst B. Haas, Robert L. Butterworth, and Joseph S. Nye, *Conflict Management by International Organization;* Alan James, *The Politics of Peacekeeping;* and J. S. Nye, *Peace in Parts.*

the vision of the Security Council's role that was held by the authors of the UN Charter in 1945), though major powers have been involved in several other wars ending in the past thirty years. All but one of these conflicts lasted less than a year, though much longer and costlier wars have been fought during the same period. In short, for a limited range of possible wars, action by an international organization is an important method of ending combat. Outside that range, there is no reason to expect it to supplant other forms of war endings.

These other forms exhibit their own changes over time. One of the most important is the decreased frequency of capitulations in international (i.e., both interstate and extra-systemic) wars. Only two noncivil wars since World War II have ended through capitulation: India's quick conquest and annexation of Hyderabad in 1948, and the Indo-Pakistani war that gave birth to Bangladesh in 1971. The classification of the latter war is questionable, because although combat ended when the Pakistani army in East Bengal surrendered unconditionally, there remained an independent Pakistani army and government in the west.

The increased scarcity of capitulations has two causes, one a change in the international system and the other a change in the way military events are interpreted.

The web of international politics has fewer seams than ever before. Diplomatic or military movement on one part of the globe tugs (or what may be just as important, appears to tug) at statesmen on another part of it more swiftly, more strongly, and more surely than it used to. A general reason for this is the improvement in capabilities for communication and transportation. A more specific reason is the emergence after World War II of ideological links which convert what would otherwise be conflicts between states or groups into contests between alternative values and ways of life. Caught in the web, statesmen feel less free to choose when and where they will compete. They are contestants whether willing or not. They do not believe they have the luxury of waiting to fight until the prospects are good or of cutting bait when the prospects are bad. This has been most true of the leaders of major powers. The Truman administration, for example, made its decisions to fight in Korea in June 1950—and to keep fighting in January 1951 despite the possibility that the allied army might be forced off the peninsula—not so much because South Korea had intrinsic importance but because it saw the war as part of a worldwide Communist challenge.[14] These were decisions taken by men who felt they had little choice but to meet the challenge.

This change in the international political system means that states enter, and stay in, frays which in an earlier age they would have avoided as unprofitable. The prospect of stalemate is now less likely to keep a government out of a war, implying that more wars are fought which do in fact become stalemated. This effect has been accentuated by a concurrent expansion in the destructive capabilities of major states. The awesome capacity for mass destruction in the nuclear age, far from being a means for obtaining sudden military decisions, has been a heavy restraint on statesmen at war. The danger of catastrophic escalation provides a strong incentive scrupulously to observe limitations on the use of violence.[15] This combination of constraints—the inability to avoid entering a war and the inability to make full use of military capabilities once in it—means that wars which formerly would either never have been fought in the first place, or fought to a swift and decisive conclusion, are now fought in a restrained and carefully controlled way. This encourages deadlock and compromise and reduces the likelihood of capitulation.

The other reason for the decline in capitulations is a breakdown of consensus on how military outcomes should translate into political outcomes.

"War," writes Clausewitz on the first page of *On War,* "is nothing but a duel on an extensive scale."[16] Like a duel, a war is a physical procedure for reaching a decision on an issue which the two parties found unable to resolve through less violent means. And, also like a duel, the nature of that procedure, and the indices of success or failure in carrying it out, need not be directly related to the issue that led to it in the first place. The capture of a city may have no closer connection to the issues that divide two warring states than the drawing of blood with a rapier does to a quarrel between two gentlemen. Sometimes there is such a connection; if possession of the city is the political issue, the military outcome of its capture (or retention) translates naturally into a political out-

---

[14] See Truman's letter to MacArthur in January 1951, explaining his war aims, quoted in Harry S Truman, *Memoirs,* Vol. 2: *Years of Trial and Hope,* pp. 435–436.

[15] Robert E. Osgood and Robert W. Tucker, *Force, Order, and Justice,* pp. 190–191.

[16] Carl von Clausewitz, *On War,* Vol. 1, p. 1.

come. In other instances, however, the political objective is not the same as the military objective because it is less vulnerable than other possible military objectives or because it is something intangible that cannot be captured directly at all. In the past, this nonidentity of political and military objectives did not spoil warfare's value as duel-like decision mechanism because the two sides often had a common standard of success and failure in the military contest, particularly when that contest was unidimensional: a province was captured or retained, a front moved east or west. Thus, the belligerents could agree on who had done better in the military duel and was therefore entitled to a better political outcome.[17] This provided a basis for the notion of "winning" and "losing" a war; the common standard of military success and failure could serve the same function that an objective defined in the rules serves in an athletic contest. A common view of victory and defeat in turn provides a basis for capitulation, because capitulation is seen as an acknowledgment of defeat. A government does not capitulate unless it perceives itself as defeated and believes that the enemy perceives the situation the same way.

But war has now lost much of its duel-like quality.[18] Two individuals will engage in a duel only if they both see a certain symmetry of justice and motivation in their dispute. If one party believes that justice is entirely on his side, he will be less inclined to submit the dispute to a decision mechanism in which justice plays no part. Even more important, if he sees himself as having a greater interest than his opponent in the outcome, and hence as being more willing to endure costs to obtain a favorable outcome, he has no incentive to force a decision by resorting to a duel. Instead, he prefers to outwait his opponent, imposing on both of them whatever costs are associated with disagreement. One characteristic of world politics in the last three decades is the emergence of numerous governments or movements, some of which have engaged in warfare, that believe they have such an advantage of righteousness or motivation over their adversaries. This is the result of nationalist and eschatological ideologies which have so taken root among mass publics that their

[17] The idea of war as a decision mechanism is discussed in Paul Kecskemeti, "Political Rationality in Ending War," *Annals of the American Academy of Political and Social Science,* 392 (November 1970), pp. 106–107.

[18] This does not imply a criticism of Clausewitz. His comparison of war to a duel was only the starting point in a presentation that went on to argue that the outcome of a war depends not only on who subdues whom in the physical contest, but also on calculations of costs and benefits.

leaders feel it necessary, whatever their own beliefs, to stand up to foreign pressures if they intend to remain in power. This phenomenon is most apparent in the less-developed countries, which would usually be the militarily weaker parties in wars against more highly developed opponents. As a consequence, governments now often keep fighting despite military setbacks that, in an earlier age, would have induced them to capitulate.[19] The apparent loser in the military duel refuses to accept the military outcome as a basis for resolving the issues, and what might have ended with a surrender instead drags on until it concludes with a negotiated settlement.

Thus the scarcity of capitulations in interstate wars of recent times is rooted in the environment in which these wars have taken place. Another change over time that can be projected into the future is the decreasing frequency of the other type of international war—extra-systemic wars. Almost all of the more recent conflicts of this type were the death throes of European empires in Asia and Africa. The end of these empires marks the end of opportunities for wars of this kind to break out. When this observation is coupled with the decline in capitulations and the previously noted infrequency of interstate wars ending with extermination or expulsion, it follows that the left and middle columns of Table 2 will tend to collapse into the upper left-hand cell: interstate wars ending through negotiation. A future international war, if it is not of the restricted type suitable for handling by an international organization, will probably have a negotiated settlement. Anyone who seeks to understand the making of peace in future international wars must understand the negotiation of peace.

Negotiations Before and After Armistices

Table 1 indicates that, of the wars ended through negotiation, two-thirds of the final settlements were reached after combat had ceased. This understates, however, the true extent to which issues have been resolved prior to armistices. This is suggested somewhat by the parenthetical notations in Table 1 showing indirect or unsuccessful negotiations and the incorporation of political terms into armistice agreements. Beyond this, even a truce agreement that ostensibly is purely military usually affects the resolution of political issues. This

---

[19] Klaus Knorr, *The Power of Nations,* pp. 111–112.

can happen when the military arrangements incidental to a cease-fire unavoidably have direct political implications, such as the disposition of territory. At the 1954 Geneva conference that ended the war between France and the Viet Minh, all the participants agreed that some sort of consolidation or regroupment of forces would be required for a workable cease-fire. Given the absence of a clear front line, the task was to sort things out in an effort to guarantee that hostilities would not resume.[20] But any designation of zones would itself be a political arrangement. General Paul Ely, France's military and political chief in Indochina at the end of the war, acknowledged this when he later wrote that the distinction between a cease-fire with guarantees and a cease-fire after a political settlement was so slight as to be only "theoretical."[21] This war did not have a separate post-armistice peace agreement (partly because of this very problem), but it illustrates how, in ones that do, the armistice agreement can predetermine the resolution of issues. Even when military armistice arrangements do not directly impinge on substantive issues in this way, they may nevertheless influence how they are resolved in later negotiations by affecting each side's potential for resuming combat, or for credibly threatening to resume it. This is clearest when the military outcome is one-sided enough for a belligerent to be able to insist on armistice arrangements that effectively disarm its opponent. The political settlement of World War I was negotiated after combat ended, but it was the crippling armistice terms imposed on Germany in November 1918 that made it possible for the Allied statesmen to act so independently at Versailles.[22]

An even more important point emerges from looking once again for changes over time. During the first quarter of the twentieth century there was a marked transition away from post-armistice peace settlements in favor of pre-armistice peace negotiations. The demise of the post-armistice peace treaty, which has been noted elsewhere,[23] emerges clearly from Table 1. Of the 38 peace settlements

[20] See, e.g., the remarks by one of the co-chairmen, Anthony Eden, in *Documents Relating to the Discussion of Korea and Indo-China at the Geneva Conference*, pp. 122–123.

[21] Paul Ely, *Mémoires: L'Indochine dans la Tourmente*, p. 105.

[22] Abt, *The Termination of General War*, pp. 96–97; and B. H. Liddell Hart, *Thoughts on War*, pp. 43–44.

[23] Berenice A. Carroll, "How Wars End: An Analysis of Some Current Hypotheses," *Journal of Peace Research*, 6 (1969, No. 4), pp. 296–297; and Wright, "How Hostilities Have Ended: Peace Treaties and Alternatives," *Annals of the American Academy*, 392 (November 1970), pp. 59–61.

negotiated after an armistice, only five occurred during the past half century (specifically, since the Treaty of Lausanne which ended the Greco-Turkish conflict of 1919–1922). All five were complicated or special cases. Two of them, the Chaco War of 1932–1935 and the Indonesian war for independence in 1945–1946, were on-again-off-again encounters which had several partial agreements and unsuccessful cease-fires and considerable activity by third parties. Either one could easily be coded differently. The Franco-Thai conflict of 1940–1941 ended when Japan—a nonbelligerent—pressured the Vichy government into stopping its attacks on the Thais and then making territorial concessions. Similarly, the settlement of the Laotian war of 1959–1962 was largely in the hands of nonbelligerent great powers, and the cessation of combat was due to the successful coercive diplomacy of the United States rather than anything that was happening in Laos itself. The Angolan insurgency was peculiar in that, by the time it ended in 1974, the most important struggle was not the one against the Portuguese but rather the one among three rival resistance movements. Each accepted a preliminary cease-fire in order to become a legal political party and establish a headquarters in the capital, thus maintaining its position relative to the other two. The other side of the statistic regarding post-armistice negotiations is that, of the nineteen wars with a settlement negotiated prior to the armistice, all but three were fought in the twentieth century.

The chief reason for the transition from post-armistice to pre-armistice negotiations is an increase in the technical capacity to coordinate combat and diplomacy. The point may be made through two quotations, the first of which is a message from President Lincoln to General Grant written during the closing days of the Civil War, shortly after Grant had received a peace feeler from General Lee. Lincoln instructed Grant, through a telegram signed by Secretary of War Stanton, as follows:

> The President directs me to say to you that he wishes you to have no conference with General Lee unless it be for the capitulation of General Lee's Army, or on some minor and purely military matter. He instructs me to say that you are not to decide, discuss, or confer upon any political question. Such questions the President holds in his own hands, and will submit them to no military conferences or convention. Meanwhile you are to press to the utmost your military advantage.[24]

[24] Quoted in Bruce Catton, *Never Call Retreat*, p. 432.

The second quotation is from General of the Army Douglas MacArthur, in testimony at Senate hearings held after his dismissal by President Truman in April 1951. MacArthur stated:

A theater commander, in any campaign, is not merely limited to the handling of his troops; he commands that whole area politically, economically, and militarily. You have got to trust at that stage of the game when politics fails, and the military takes over, you must trust the military.[25]

The telegram to Grant expresses a concern held by political leaders throughout history who have led nations in wartime: to avoid losing control over policy to their military commanders in the field without taking away the commander's capacity for military initiative. (It also suggests how the retention of political control becomes particularly important during the closing stage of a war.) This has been difficult to accomplish because of the truth that lies behind MacArthur's dictum—viz., that a military commander's actions inevitably have political as well as military repercussions. And, conversely, political decisions depend on military results. This was a greater problem before the advent of modern electronic communications, because the military commander was out of immediate contact with his government. The coordination of diplomacy and combat over long distances was difficult or impossible. Governments in the past responded to this problem in three different ways.

One was to follow the prescriptive aspect of MacArthur's statement: to turn the general into a proconsul by giving him the political power to make peace as well as the military power to wage war. This, of course, did not keep political control in the capital. Instead, it was a recognition of the impossibility of doing so and a placing of the government's trust in one able man who would personally coordinate diplomacy and combat in the field. This is what the British did in most of their imperial wars in Asia during the nineteenth century. The method was more necessary in those wars than in most others because of the extreme remoteness of the theaters in which they were fought. It was also a suitable method because the British were aiming for the capitulation or elimination of their Asian enemies; the political objectives were simple and the proconsul was unlikely to diverge much from what London would have wanted him to do.

[25] *Military Situation in the Far East,* Part 2, p. 28.

In wars between two equal members of the state system, however, creating a proconsul was less suitable because the political objectives were more complicated. Simple capitulation or elimination was less likely to be possible or desirable, and the political leaders could not surrender the coordination of the political and military fronts to a general merely because he was in a convenient location. A solution was for the political leaders to put *themselves* in a convenient location—i.e., to travel with their armies. The main difficulty with this, the second possible response to the problem of military-diplomatic coordination, was that while this was convenient for running the war, it was terribly inconvenient for conducting any other business. Only the most momentous struggle justified a leader's absenting himself from his capital for an extended period. In fact, this method was used only during the closing months of the Napoleonic Wars in 1814, when the principal Allied statesmen— including foreign ministers, chancellors, and even an emperor— traveled in the train of their armies as they pushed the French westward. Their presence, and the fact that their opponent was an emperor-general who combined the military command and the supreme political power in his own person, made possible the political negotiations that took place at Châtillon in February and March while the fighting continued. Even in this case it was difficult to talk peace while waging war, since Napoleon could not be at the conference table and on the battlefield at the same time. As it was, he stayed on the battlefield, and his representative at Châtillon complained to him: "I am given necessity for rule, but necessity arises from events. . . . [W]hen I know nothing of what is going on, when Your Majesty sends me no news, I find myself reduced to march in obscurity and without guide."[26]

The limitations and difficulties of these two responses led statesmen to place greater reliance on the third. This was the creation of a *temporal* division between the military and diplomatic arenas, with a political settlement to be negotiated after the guns fell silent. The soldiers would first do their job, after which the diplomats could take their time and be careful about doing theirs. Neither would be hindered by the activity of the other. The post-armistice peace settlement thus became the most common method of managing the conclusion of wars.

---

[26] Caulaincourt to Napoleon, 8 February 1814, quoted in R. B. Mowat, *The Diplomacy of Napoleon,* pp. 288–289.

All three of these responses were necessitated by the inadequacies of the communications linking capital, battlefield, and conference table. But this communications gap no longer exists, and hence neither does the need for the procedures which were devised to cope with it. The statesman can now coordinate combat and diplomacy as he could not do before. This means, more specifically, that it is now more feasible for a government to negotiate a political settlement prior to an armistice than it ever was before.[27]

It is worth noting that one of the incidents that precipitated MacArthur's dismissal concerned the management of peacemaking in Korea. The general issued a communique in March 1951 in which he proclaimed his readiness "to confer in the field with the commander in chief of the enemy forces in an earnest effort to find any military means whereby the realization of the political objectives of the UN in Korea . . . might be accomplished without further bloodshed."[28] He made this declaration on his own initiative, and it torpedoed a Presidential peace statement that was being carefully drafted in Washington.[29] MacArthur's actions as a proconsul brought him into conflict with the political leadership in the capital because a proconsul was no longer needed. His expansive view of the powers of a military commander in a remote theater—no doubt nourished by his prolonged absence from the United States, his political duties during the occupation of Japan, and the relatively free hand he had been given during the first part of the Korean conflict—had already been made obsolete by communications which made it possible for combat and diplomacy to be controlled from the capital even when both the battlefield and the conference table were thousands of miles away. What goes for MacArthur's response to the problem of coordinating combat and diplomacy goes as well for the second response and, most important, for the third as well. Governments no longer postpone a peace settlement to after the armistice because they no longer *need* to postpone it. While negotiating, governments can attempt to strengthen their bargaining position through the continued use of armed force. As long as at least one of the parties believes it is advantageous to do so, fighting will continue while the peace settlement is written.

[27] Cf. Alfred Vagts, *Defense and Diplomacy,* p. 477.

[28] *New York Times,* 24 March 1951, p. 2.

[29] Truman, pp. 438–440. There were other portions of MacArthur's communique, including a scarcely veiled threat to expand the war, that also helped to produce this effect.

A subsidiary reason for the shift to pre-armistice negotiations is a breakdown of certain legal principles regarding war and peace. Because the post-armistice peace settlement was well suited to the conditions in which wars were fought for so many years, it acquired the status of a legal norm. Traditional writing on international law described it as the standard way to end a war, with pre-armistice peace negotiations viewed as aberrations.[30] The legal doctrine came to exert an influence of its own, at least among the Western nations, where traditional international law developed. But the entry into the state system of nonwestern nations, which has led to the breakdown or revision of so much else in this body of law, has also contributed to the breakdown of the norm regarding the form of peace settlements.[31]

If a single date were selected as the turning point in this change, it would be the eighth of February 1904. This marked, not the end of a war, but the beginning of one, when the Japanese attacked the Russian fleets at Port Arthur and Inchon. It was a surprise attack, preceded by no declaration of war, thus foreshadowing Pearl Harbor thirty-seven years later. To start a war in this manner was not completely unprecedented (as the Japanese were quick to point out), but it clearly departed from prevailing practice. An attack without a declaration of war and a peace negotiation without an armistice are two sides of the same coin: a rejection of the temporal—and legal— division between peace and war. And, in fact, the Russo-Japanese War ended with a pre-armistice peace negotiation, making it the first twentieth-century war to do so. The point to note is that this break from prior legal forms, which initiated the modern era of fighting-while-negotiating, was accomplished by an Oriental nation, one which had not participated in the creation of traditional international law. Conversely, the post-armistice peace settlements that were reached over the next twenty years, despite the changes already taking place in communications and in the technology of warfare, all involved western nations. These included two wars in Central America, the two Balkan wars preceding World War I, World War I itself, and the conflicts that followed it between Russia and Poland and between Greece and Turkey.

[30] See, e.g., Coleman Phillipson, *Termination of War and Treaties of Peace*, pp. 56–59.

[31] Janice Gross Stein, "War Termination and Conflict Reduction or, How Wars Should End," p. 3.

War Termination as a Bargaining Problem

A bargaining problem has three essential characteristics. The first is that the two[32] parties both realize that they could improve their lots if they made some sort of agreement—struck a bargain—with each other. This may be viewed in either of two ways: (1) disagreement is mutually costly, and so the parties seek to end it; (2) agreement is profitable, and so the parties seek to attain it. In some bargaining situations, the only costs of disagreement are opportunity costs. In most buyer-seller relationships, failure to agree on a price does not mean outright deprivation of something of value; the only thing that either party can lose is the opportunity to exchange a good or sum of money for something more useful to him. In other situations, there are costs that go beyond mere lost opportunities. When a union and management bargain during a strike or lockout, they are not just missing the improvements over the old contract that each side might expect to be in the new one; each is also paying a price in the form of lost wages or lost production.

The second characteristic is that mutual action is required to reach an agreement; there is no such thing as a unilateral bargain. Correspondingly, disagreement persists if even one of the parties wants it to persist; neither party, acting alone, can remove it. Removing disagreement should not be confused with dissolving the bargaining relationship. A buyer in a bazaar, having decided after unsuccessful haggling that a seller will not lower his price to what he—the buyer—considers to be the value of the merchandise, may simply walk away. He dissolves the bargaining relationship because he no longer sees any possibility of raising his utility through an agreement with that particular seller. But he has not removed the disagreement; the disagreement persists, even though in this instance the buyer no longer perceives it to entail any opportunity costs.

The third feature of a bargaining problem is that there exists more than one possible agreement. Specifically, there are at least two possible agreements that are: (1) each mutually preferred to continued disagreement; and (2) ordered differently on the prefer-

---

[32] This study treats each side in a war as a unit, meaning that the concern is with bilateral bargaining. Multilateral bargaining, while having special features of its own, shares the three general characteristics described here.

ence scales of each party. In most bargaining situations there is a range of many possible agreements, as when a labor union and management bargain over an hourly wage.

To what extent do warfare and the termination of wars exhibit these attributes? The first characteristic raises the issue of whether warfare—i.e., warfare itself, not objectives that might be gained through recourse to it—is costly. To some individuals or groups, it may not always be so. Elements within the military, for instance, may value combat for its glory or adventure. Nevertheless, warfare inflicts obvious and often immense costs on the military and civilians alike. These include the human costs of casualties and dislocation and the direct material costs of property damage and the expenditure of supplies. There are also opportunity costs: e.g., diversion of attention and resources from other endeavors and the curtailment of peacetime intercourse such as trade. On balance, the costly features of warfare probably outweigh the desirable ones for most individuals and, more to the point, for most national leaders. Governments wage war not because war is attractive but because it is a means of obtaining other benefits or avoiding other costs. This is especially true during the later stages of a war—those most relevant to understanding its termination—when motives such as adventure and glory have diminished and the awareness of suffering and deprivation has increased.

As for whether mutual action is required to reach a peace agreement, the answer is clearly yes; a unilateral bargain is no more of a possibility in warfare than it is elsewhere. The role of agreements in war termination varies, however. The type of war ending in which an agreement between the belligerents is most clearly essential to the cessation of combat is the one at the bottom right of Figure 1: negotiation before an armistice. With this type of ending, the disagreement costs of warfare cease only when the belligerents reach an explicit accord on the issues dividing them. Although the NB ending was found to be relatively infrequent in the past, this does not mean that few wars resemble a bargaining problem. For one thing, we have already seen why most future international wars are likely to end this way. Furthermore, other types of endings have some of the characteristics of a bargaining process, although to a diminishing degree as we move back toward the top of Figure 1. As previously noted, many of the political issues in NA wars are settled at the time of the armistice. A capitulation is not negotiation, but it may nevertheless follow considerable bargaining, perhaps indirect or tacit, between the belligerents.[33] Action by an international organization is invariably preceded by considerable bargaining in the corridors, usually involving the belligerents or their principal supporters. When a withdrawal occurs, bargaining is entirely tacit and therefore harder to discern, but it is present nonetheless. It is only when we retreat to the category of extermination and expulsion that the conclusion of a war can no longer be described as a bargain. Even here, however, bargaining could have been intended, and even attempted, earlier in the war.

For wars not ending in extermination or expulsion, the mutual act of agreement is even more important than it is in many other bargaining problems. This is because a bargaining relationship in warfare is not readily dissolved, as when the buyer walks away from the seller in the bazaar. Wars do not have a conclusion corresponding to "no sale." The buyer in the bazaar can dissolve his relationship with the seller by walking away because he carries with him the only thing we could lose through a bad bargain—his money. Stakes such as a country, a province, or a population are not so easily removed. If a warring state extricates itself from combat without incapacitating the opponent, it does so only by accepting, at least tacitly, a resolution of the issues favorable to the adversary. In such a case the two sides, whether or not they both admit it, have in effect reached an agreement. The United States, for example, could have unilaterally withdrawn its forces from the Indochina theater at any time during the Vietnam War. This would have ended American involvement in the war, because Hanoi had neither the capability nor the willingness to attack the U.S. homeland. But the United States could have done this only by accepting what Hanoi wanted: a free hand in the affairs of South Vietnam. It could have moved its own citizens out of Hanoi's reach, but it could not also have moved a non-Communist South Vietnam out of reach. The only instance of a government's attempting to dissolve a warring relationship unilaterally was Leon Trotsky's proclamation of "no war—no peace" on the German-Russian front in 1918. As we know, Trotsky's tactic failed. One week later, after recovering from their astonishment, the

---

[33] In his *Strategic Surrender*, Paul Kecskemeti has shown how much the Axis states had to bargain with near the end of World War II.

Germans resumed their offensive. One month later a peace treaty was signed.[34]

Even if both belligerents consider warfare to be costly and both seek an agreement, there remains the question of whether a multiplicity of possible agreements exists. Given the costs and issues in most wars, it would seem that if the other characteristics of a bargaining problem are present then this one probably is too. Peace terms are often subject to minute variation—with quantitative issues the number of possible variations can be infinite—and if both sides find one possible set of peace terms preferable to continued disagreement they are likely to find several others preferable to it as well. Besides, war costs often become sufficiently great to produce a bargaining range large enough to accommodate even gross differences among possible agreements. This does not imply that the limits of this range are always clear, especially in the early stages of bargaining. When one side rejects a proposed settlement, neither the opponent nor an outside observer may know for sure whether it was rejected as being worse than a continued war or rejected in an attempt to make acceptable terms even better. Nor does it imply that the limits of the bargaining range remain fixed. It is more common for them to fluctuate in the course of a war as costs increase or decrease, opportunities open or close, and hopes appear or disappear. It is only if the range vanished entirely, as it would if either side became willing and able to exterminate or expel the other, that a bargaining situation would no longer exist.

The Use of Evidence from Individual Wars

We have found that most future international wars will probably end in a way that makes them describable as bargaining processes, even though few past wars have had the type of ending (NB) that most fully embodies the characteristics of a bargaining problem. The fact that a phenomenon expected to prevail in the future has been relatively rare in the past simplifies, in a way, the task of studying it. The pile of relevant evidence is manageably small without having

[34] Probably the closest thing to an exception to the point made in this paragraph would be the flight of a nomadic tribe or a band of pirates that has used violence to extort easily transportable riches. If it has no home of its own to be destroyed, and it escapes retribution by fleeing with its booty, it has unilaterally dissolved—at least for a time—the relationship with its enemies.

been made small through an arbitrary selection process. Furthermore, the list of nineteen wars that were settled through a pre-armistice negotiation effectively shortens when one considers what insights each has to offer. Selection occurs, not arbitrarily, but as a necessary consequence of the limitations of the available evidence. The negotiations in the Sino-Soviet conflict of 1929, the Changku-feng incident of 1938, the Russo-Japanese conflict of 1939, the Yemeni civil war of 1962–1970, and the 2nd Laotian War of 1963–1973 all took place out of the view of western observers. Consequently, few details about them are on the record. The Anglo-Persian War of 1856–1857 is less obscure, though only slightly so in terms of what historians have written about it. The war for independence in Mozambique and the civil war in Zimbabwe are too recent to have received historical treatment, and journalistic accounts of them provide few details of negotiations. The periods of negotiation in the Mexican-American War of 1846–1848, the Russo-Finnish War of 1939–1940, the 1st Kashmir War of 1947–1949, the Jordanian civil war of 1970, and the Lebanese civil war of 1975–1976 were all very short, and hence are not very fertile fields from which to extract insights on the present subject. In the two earliest twentieth-century wars in which a settlement was negotiated prior to an armistice— Russia vs. Japan in 1904–1905 and Italy vs. Turkey in 1911–1912—a virtual de facto cease-fire was in effect during the peace conference. They are, therefore, not very instructive regarding the relation of military to diplomatic events while a negotiation is in progress.

That leaves four wars which are classified NB in Table 1 and are rich in material relevant to the topics considered in this study because they share three other attributes: (1) a long period of direct negotiations (at least long enough for an observer to discern diplomatic movement); (2) a continuation of intense combat during this period; and (3) a reasonably complete and accessible record of both military and diplomatic events, in the form of documents, recollections of participants, journalistic accounts, and histories. The earliest of the four is the War of 1812 (1812–1815) between Britain and the United States. Its settlement was reached in a conference at Ghent, Belgium, attended by three British and five American peace commissioners. The conference began in early August 1814 and concluded four and a half months later with the signing of a treaty on Christmas Eve (although because of communication lags the fighting continued into January 1815). The other three conflicts have all occurred since World War II. One is the Korean War (1950–1953), in which negotiations were in progress during most of the war. An armistice conference opened at Kaesong in July 1951 (thirteen months after the start of the war), later moved to Panmunjom, and after several interruptions ended with an armistice agreement in July 1953. Another is the war between France and the Viet Minh in Indochina (1945–1954), which was settled in a multilateral conference at Geneva that included client states and major allies as well as the two principals. The Geneva conference was the shortest of the peace negotiations being singled out as instructive cases, lasting from early May to late July 1954, but there was plenty of diplomatic activity during this time. The overall settlement which became known as the "Geneva accords" comprised both military armistice agreements signed by the belligerents and an unsigned Final Declaration of the conference. The other modern case is the struggle between France and the Front de la Liberation Nationale (FLN) in Algeria (1954–1962). The first formal, direct talks between the two sides took place in June 1960. Over the next twenty-one months they met in various locations, usually either informally in Switzerland or in formal sessions in the French Alps. The final agreement signed at Evian in March 1962 made it possible for the FLN to take power in an independent Algeria. To these four wars may be added a fifth, one which eventually ended with a capitulation but which had an earlier phase concluding with a negotiated settlement: the period of American involvement in the Vietnam War.[35] It had the longest negotiation period of all—more than four and a half years of public and private sessions from the first talks in May 1968 until the signing of the Paris agreements in January 1973. It is from these five wars that most, though by no means all, of the empirical material in the pages to follow is drawn. Subsequent references to the "major cases" are references to these five.

Clausewitz listed four ways in which historical examples might be used in the study of war: (1) explanation of an idea; (2) application of an idea; (3) proving the possibility of a fact or event; (4) true proof (by which he really meant corroboration) of a proposition or theory.[36] The examples in this study are used mainly for the first three of these purposes, which is to say in an illustrative manner. Occasionally they are used as well for the fourth, by noting some pattern

---

[35] In keeping with general usage, the "Indochina War" will henceforth always mean the French War ending in 1954, the "Vietnam War" the later conflict involving the United States.

[36] *On War*, Vol. 1, p. 158.

which has existed in each of the major cases and taking its recurrence as evidence of the validity of a proposition. Confining oneself to the latter procedure alone would mean forfeiting the opportunity to explore important theoretical avenues. Many of the ideas in subsequent chapters could not be applied or tested using a fixed group of cases, either because of gaps in the historical record or simply because the circumstances in any one case are such that one question or issue arises but another one does not. This is not a reason for not advancing the idea; it is a reason for being flexible in one's search for evidence to support or explain it. Accordingly, many examples are drawn from wars other than the major five.

Another reason not to confine one's purview entirely to a small, fixed set of cases is to avoid having one's conclusions influenced by the effects of circumstances which are common to most or all of these cases but nevertheless are irrelevant to the questions being studied. The major cases, especially the four modern ones, have many characteristics in common. Some of these shared attributes reflect the practical criteria used to narrow the list or are ones which, given the discussion earlier in this chapter, we would expect to be associated with wars classified NB in the first place. (E.g., the fact that a major western power—France or the United States—was involved in each war means that more information about it is accessible to the western observer, and also that it is not the type of conflict amenable to settlement through an international organization.) There are undoubtedly other common characteristics, however, which affected the course of these wars and their settlements but which are irrelevant to a general inquiry into the negotiation of peace. A little evidence from other wars (even of a rather superficial sort, performing Clausewitz's third function of merely demonstrating a possibility) can thus be useful in correcting for the effects of these characteristics. This is not to say that these other similarities cannot provide a basis for useful comparative analyses of the substance of the agreements.[37] But the present purpose is instead to use these wars as vehicles for learning about the *process* of negotiation and about the principles of bargaining between enemies committing violent acts against each other.

---

[37] Two examples of this kind of comparison, both of which considered possible settlements to the Vietnam War while it was still in progress, are Frank Baldwin, "A 'Korean Solution' For Vietnam?" and Stanley Hoffmann, "Vietnam: An Algerian Solution?"

CHAPTER TWO

The Opening
of Negotiations

A peace negotiation has several turning points. The final reaching of agreement obviously is one. There are some others that will be identified in Chapter 3. But the opening of negotiations is surely another. As such, it deserves a separate examination, which is the purpose of the present chapter. Two overall questions are discussed here.

The first is the question of *when* peace negotiations open. In none of the past wars ending with a settlement negotiated prior to an armistice did negotiations take place throughout the conflict. I.e., any prewar negotiations on disputed issues ended when hostilities broke out, and it was only after a period of fighting without talking that the parties began to talk once again. The opening of a peace conference is thus a change in the state of war. What accounts for this change? Why is it that one or both belligerents decide to talk at a given moment rather than sooner or later? The first section below outlines what enters into such decisions, and offers a general answer to the question of when negotiations usually open. Agreement on the opening of a peace conference is shown to be a bargaining problem similar to the problem of arriving at a peace settlement itself.

The other question is *how* negotiations open—the problems and procedures entailed in establishing contact and getting talks underway. The second section identifies several barriers that frequently inhibit the opening of talks. Some of these result from the necessities of combat, others from expectations concerning the future course of negotiations. The third section describes the methods that belligerents use to overcome the barriers.

The fourth section returns to the issue of the sequence of negotiation and armistice, an issue often raised in connection with the opening of negotiations.

The Decision to Talk

A government seeks a peace negotiation if it hopes to benefit from: (1) a peace agreement; and/or (2) other consequences of the negotiation—side-effects, as Fred Iklé has called them.[1] We leave side-effects for the time being to inquire under what circumstances governments seek peace agreements.

This question is more often a matter of *when* a government chooses to negotiate than of *whether* it wants the war to terminate with a negotiated settlement at all. One reason for this is the conclusion reached in the previous chapter—viz., that, for a large class of wars, we can expect the belligerents to sit down at some point and negotiate peace terms while combat continues. Another reason is that the distinction between a negotiated settlement and a capitulation—the principal alternative to negotiation in international wars— is fundamentally a matter of timing. Both types of war endings involve an explicit coming to terms; a refusal to negotiate because one hopes to obtain a capitulation is essentially a decision to delay this coming to terms until the enemy's situation has so deteriorated that he is willing to accept one's demand totally. The decision to negotiate is thus not so much a choice of a discrete alternative but rather the selection of one moment along an anticipated continuum of time in which the military situation constantly changes. The most important choice is apt to be between negotiation now and negotiation later, not between negotiating at all and trying to conclude the war some other way. It is only when a belligerent seeks to conclude a war through the less frequent alternatives of extermination, expulsion, or withdrawal that it is choosing not to talk at all.

Nevertheless, there are enough instances of a belligerent's apparently intending to do just that (even in wars eventually settled through negotiation) to make it worthwhile to note in which circumstances a government will seek to attain its goals without ever talking to the enemy. This is done in the next subsection, after which we return to the central issue of the timing of offers to negotiate.

Negotiated Settlement Versus Direct Achievement

Whether a government attempts to use armed force to achieve its objective directly, rather than through the acquiescence of the en-

---

[1] Fred C. Iklé, *How Nations Negotiate*, pp. 43–58.

emy, depends on three general considerations. Any one of the three may provide sufficient grounds to reject attempts at direct achievement and to accept an eventual negotiated settlement.

The first is the nature of the objective. Some war aims can be achieved only through agreement, because they require the continued existence and willing cooperation of the other side (e.g., to regulate some peacetime activity such as trade in a certain way). Other objectives, however, such as the retention or capture of a piece of territory, might be attainable by exterminating or expelling the enemy rather than by reaching an agreement with him. The North Koreans, for example, although eventually having to accept a negotiated settlement to the Korean War, evidently were at first intent on driving their enemy right off the peninsula. The Communists showed not the slightest interest in peace negotiations until after the successful amphibious operation of the United Nations Command (UNC) at Inchon in September 1950 had put them on the defensive.

The second consideration is the belligerent's capability to attain its objective. Even if the war aim is suitable for direct achievement, the means to attain it may be lacking. The FLN in Algeria had an objective similar to that of the North Koreans—gaining complete control over a piece of territory. But, unlike them, the Algerian rebels never had any apparent chance of using military force to drive their enemy into the sea. Of all the belligerents in the five major cases, the FLN was the one that was consistently in the weakest military position throughout its war. It was also the one that was most consistently disposed to negotiate. In a statement of war aims that it issued when it launched its insurrection on 1 November 1954, the FLN explicitly stated its desire for a negotiated settlement.[2] From then until the peace agreement was signed at Evian more than seven years later, the FLN never entertained the idea that the war would end any other way.

While the nature of an objective cannot change during the course of a war (although objectives themselves can), the capability to achieve an objective sometimes does. Defeats or the exhaustion of resources make what once seemed possible now appear impossible; successes or the availability of new resources have the opposite effect. Changes in the perceived possibility of direct achievement may account for changes in the readiness of governments to negoti-

---

[2] Text in Philippe Tripier, *Autopsie de la Guerre d'Algérie*, pp. 567–570.

ate. A willingness on the part of the Communists to negotiate a compromise peace in Korea followed—on two separate occasions—a dashing of hopes to accomplish their goals without talking to the enemy. The first occasion was the reversal in September 1950 of the North Korean invasion. The second occurred the following spring, when another Communist invasion of the south, this time led by the Chinese, was stopped. The failure of a major Communist offensive in late May demonstrated once and for all the inability of even a huge human wave assault to push the well-equipped UN army off the peninsula.[3]

It should be noted that the question of what is or is not possible extends not only to the attainment of an objective without an agreement, but also to its attainment *with* an agreement. Just as a decision-maker may write off direct achievement as being impossible, so too may he write off, at least for the time being, a negotiated agreement as impossible. He might still see no harm in indicating his readiness to make peace, even if he expects no negotiations to result. But he would be less likely to take any conciliatory action that seemed to entail significant risks or costs. President Johnson's perception of Hanoi's unwillingness to negotiate shaped his decisions in this way during the prenegotiation phase of the Vietnam War. Although Johnson never withdrew an offer to negotiate that he had made in 1965, he rejected later proposals from his advisers to halt the bombing of North Vietnam (most significantly a recommendation from Secretary of Defense McNamara in November 1967) because he did not think the enemy was ready to talk. The reports at that time of a coming enemy offensive convinced him, he later wrote, that "we would have to wait until the Communists realized that their military ambitions were unattainable before we could hope to get peace talks started."[4]

If a government deems it possible to achieve its goals either with or without agreement, it must then rest its decision on the third consideration: the costs and benefits of using each method.

The costs of attaining an objective—by either method—include the casualties, expenditures, and other continuing costs of warfare. They also include the delay in reaching the objective; that is, the value of the goal is discounted as it recedes into the future. Higher anticipated costs of direct achievement imply a greater inclination to

[3] David Rees, *Korea: The Limited War*, pp. 255–256.
[4] Lyndon B. Johnson, *The Vantage Point*, p. 377.

accept negotiations. This is consistent with the common view that the more difficult and costly a continued war appears to be, the more willingly a belligerent will make peace. The costs of direct achievement are only part of the equation, however. The same types of costs will be incurred in trying to reach an objective through a negotiated agreement. A belligerent may be discouraged from seeking negotiations if it expects that the costs of war required to induce the enemy to come to an acceptable agreement will be too great, or the delay before agreement too long. During the Vietnam War, the fear of repeating the Korean experience of a protracted negotiation led some American policy-makers to anticipate peace talks with trepidation, and may also have helped to discourage President Johnson from taking any more steps than he did to get talks underway.[5]

Like the perceived possibility of direct achievement, anticipated costs can change during the course of a war and thus may account for changes in a government's willingness to negotiate. The anticipated benefits, or value, of each method of obtaining a war aim may also change. The value of an objective achieved directly may change if, for example, a contested territory becomes so devastated by the war itself that the benefit of possessing it is less than when the conflict began. But what is more likely to change is the expected value of a negotiated agreement. This is because the result of a negotiation is not just *an* agreement; it is one out of several—usually many—possible agreements. Expectations concerning which possible agreement will result from a negotiation change during a war because they depend heavily on the military situation, which itself changes.

If we assume that a government perceives a positive relationship between the degree of its military success and the value to it of the agreement that would result from a negotiation, it follows that, *ceteris paribus,* it will be more likely to seek negotiations when the military situation is favorable. If this is counter-intuitive, it is because we tend to focus our attention more on the impact that changes in the military situation have on the possibility of achieving objectives directly. Such a focus is consistent with a view of war outcomes as wins and losses rather than as bargains; a belligerent acknowledges defeat when it recognizes that its forces cannot cap-

---

[5] The Korean precedent was cited in a memorandum to the President in April 1966 from Maxwell Taylor, who had been the last commander of UN ground forces during the Korean War. *Pentagon Papers,* Vol. 4, p. 97. See also *New York Times,* 19 January 1966, p. 1.

ture or retain the military objective, and it becomes the first to ask for peace. This view does contain an element of truth: as already noted, the possibility of direct achievement is one ingredient in the decision whether to seek negotiations. But it is only one. We now see why changes in military fortunes do not always shape this decision in a simple and easily predictable way: an improvement in the military situation might decrease the incentive to negotiate because it makes agreement less necessary, but alternatively it might increase the incentive to negotiate because any agreement that results is likely to be better than it would have been before.[6]

The latter type of change is exemplified by American policy toward a Korean settlement in the spring of 1951. The UNC's retreat that had begun after the Chinese intervention the previous autumn ended in January, after which General Ridgway's army steadily pushed the Communists back to the 38th Parallel. By the time it reached the Parallel in March, the prospects for further progress were good. Yet, it was precisely this turnabout in the military situation which, because it was expected to make possible a more favorable agreement, led Washington to seek negotiations for the first time in the war.[7]

Timing

This last point brings us back to the central question of *when* a belligerent offers to negotiate. It is precisely because there are not one but many possible settlements that a peace negotiation could produce, and because the probability of each depends on military conditions which are constantly in flux, that the timing of such an offer is critical. Decisions on timing depend largely on the prospects for future military success or failure.

A government that has suffered military setbacks but expects to be able to reverse them in the future will probably seek to delay

---

[6] This is somewhat of an oversimplification, because it assumes unidimensional military outcomes. Military activity aimed at gaining an objective directly may be different in type and locale from military activity aimed at softening the opponent's negotiating position. Success in one of these endeavors does not necessarily entail success in the other. Usually, however, the two are associated.

[7] Nevertheless, because it meant passing up an opportunity to exploit military successes, the decision to seek a compromise settlement near the 38th Parallel was not endorsed throughout the U.S. Government. The Joint Chiefs of Staff, in particular, accepted it only reluctantly. See J. Lawton Collins, *War in Peacetime*, p. 303. Collins was Army Chief of Staff during the war.

talks. This is a recurring pattern, particularly with the larger of two warring states, since its leaders see their superior manpower or material resources as being decisive in the long run. During the first weeks after North Korea launched its assault across the 38th Parallel in June 1950, the United States and other Western powers rebuffed attempts at a political settlement made by, among others, the UN Commission on Korea and Prime Minister Nehru of India.[8] Western leaders believed that any political discussions would have to await an improvement in the military situation. The same view prevailed within the United States government during the early phase of the Vietnam War, in late 1964 and early 1965, before the deployment of a half million U.S. troops halted the military deterioration in South Vietnam.[9] Such thinking is not limited to the beginning of a war. As late as November 1953—after seven years of warfare against the Viet Minh—the then French commander in Indochina, General Henri Navarre, urged his government to delay negotiations because he expected the military situation to be better the following summer.[10] Although most members of the French government had already come to favor negotiations, Navarre's optimism discouraged the government from responding directly to an offer of bilateral talks made by Ho Chi Minh in an interview published in the Swedish newspaper *Expressen* in November.[11]

One does not need a larger economy or population to anticipate future military success. The leaders of the Viet Minh—later becoming the leaders of the Democratic Republic of Vietnam (DRV)—in their wars against both France and the United States propounded the idea that the passage of time would strengthen their own cause while weakening that of the enemy, largely because the enemy's morale, finances, and international position would deteriorate. This was the doctrine of the "long-term resistance war." "Time works for us," wrote Truong Chinh, one of the Viet Minh's chief ideologues. "Time will be our best strategist, if we are determined to pursue the resistance war to the end."[12]

[8] Leland M. Goodrich, *Korea: A Study of U.S. Policy in the United Nations*, pp. 122–123.

[9] *Pentagon Papers*, Vol. 3, pp. 204, 331–332.

[10] Ely, *L'Indochine dans la Tourmente*, p. 34.

[11] R. E. M. Irving, *The First Indochina War*, pp. 117–118.

[12] Truong Chinh, *The Resistance Will Win*, facsimile edition in *Primer for Revolt*, p. 112. See also Vo Nguyen Giap, *People's War, People's Army*, pp. 100–101.

Conversely, the expectation of future setbacks is a reason for hastening peace negotiations. When President Theodore Roosevelt made the arrangements (for which he was to win the Nobel Peace Prize) for a peace conference at Portsmouth, New Hampshire, to end the Russo-Japanese War in 1905, he was acting in response to a request for mediation from Japan, which had compiled an almost unbroken string of military and naval victories over the Russians. The Japanese made their request because, however glorious their campaign had been until then, they anticipated that Russia's greater financial and other resources would work against them if the war continued. The Russian commanders also expected that the military tide would turn in their favor. What led the czar, despite this optimism, to accept a peace negotiation at that time was his desire to hold the conference before he suffered one last defeat—viz., the capture of Sakhalin, which would be the only loss of Russian territory in a war that had been fought mainly in Manchuria.[13] Thus both sides agreed to negotiate, and the conference took place when it did, because both sides feared future failures.

Side-Effects

As noted earlier, a belligerent may seek negotiations with the enemy for other reasons besides obtaining a peace agreement. The desired side-effects of a peace negotiation can include any of the same ones often sought in other kinds of negotiations, of which Iklé has provided a general discussion.[14] But, in a peace negotiation, there is a special interest in trying to alter the balance of strength in the current war. To do this, a belligerent may use peace talks to encourage some specific event that would help its war effort—e.g., drawing an ally into the war, which was the reason that Britain agreed to participate in ultimately unsuccessful negotiations at Vienna during the Crimean War.[15] More commonly, the aim is to undermine in a more general way the enemy's domestic and international support and to bolster one's own. Peace negotiations can thus

---

[13] John A. White, *The Diplomacy of the Russo-Japanese War*, pp. 201–205; and Denis Warner and Peggy Warner, *The Tide at Sunrise*, pp. 524–527.

[14] Iklé, *How Nations Negotiate*, pp. 43–58.

[15] Treaties provided that Austria, then a nonbelligerent, would enter the war on the Anglo-French side if peace negotiations failed. Vernon J. Puryear, *England, Russia, and the Straits Question, 1844–1856*, pp. 364, 405–406.

be used as an extension of combat, a nonviolent way of bringing about some of the results of combat such as the attrition of the enemy's strength and the sapping of his morale.

This has been a major part of peace negotiations only in the twentieth century—specifically, since the Bolsheviks introduced revolutionary diplomacy at Brest-Litovsk in 1918, distributing leaflets to the German soldiers and using the conference as a propaganda forum to encourage revolution in Central Europe.[16] The Bolsheviks' revolutionary socialist heirs, though not always attempting to incite the overthrow of an enemy government, have been the foremost practitioners of this combative use of peace negotiations. A Vietnamese People's Army general, speaking at a party congress in 1966, explained negotiations during the Vietnam War this way:

> Fighting while negotiating is aimed at opening another front, at making the puppet army more disintegrated, at stimulating and developing the enemy's contradictions and thereby depriving him of propaganda weapons, isolating him further, and making those who misunderstand the Americans clearly see their nature.[17]

If negotiations work to the advantage of one side in this way, they work to the disadvantage of the other. Thus a concern over side-effects can discourage, as well as encourage, an offer to negotiate. The fear that peace talks would crack the fragile morale of an army or an ally has often led governments to reject negotiations. Preserving the morale of the French Expeditionary Force and avoiding panic among the Vietnamese were reasons that the French government gave the National Assembly for not negotiating with Ho Chi Minh in 1952.[18] Twelve years later, the avoidance of demoralization in Saigon was again cited as a reason for not negotiating with Ho, this time by the United States in rebuffing an attempt by U Thant to arrange peace talks in Rangoon to end the Vietnam War.[19]

---

[16] The increased use of negotiations as an adjunct to combat is a subsidiary reason for the change from post-armistice to pre-armistice negotiations discussed in the previous chapter. The belief by either side that negotiating while fighting will improve its military posture, which in turn will improve its subsequent bargaining position, leads it to reject a preliminary cease-fire.

[17] Quoted in Dennis J. Duncanson, *Government and Revolution in Vietnam*, p. 374.

[18] Irving, p. 85.

[19] Accounts of the Thant initiative are in George McT. Kahin and John W. Lewis, *The United States in Vietnam*, pp. 163–164; and David Kraslow and Stuart H. Loory, *The Secret Search for Peace in Vietnam*, pp. 97–109.

The Opening of Peace Negotiations as a Bargaining Problem

The discussion to this point should be sufficient to show that any decision on whether or not to open peace negotiations is complex. The decision depends on the degree of one's military success, but not entirely on it, and not in any simple and easily describable way. The picture becomes even more complex when we realize that *both* sides must weigh the considerations discussed above in deciding whether a negotiation would be advantageous. Since the agreement of both sides is required to begin a negotiation, each must consider when the other would be receptive to a conference, and this adds an entirely new dimension to its decision. One aspect of this was noted earlier: the belief that the other side is not ready to negotiate can discourage a decision-maker from taking steps aimed at getting talks started, as was true of President Johnson during the Vietnam War. Conversely, negotiations may be accepted at an otherwise unfavorable time because the enemy *is* willing to talk but, it is feared, may become unwilling in the future. This entered into the French government's thinking in early 1954 when it accepted a Geneva conference on Indochina despite the unpropitious military conditions within Indochina and General Navarre's forecast of improvement in later months. The Viet Minh were prepared at that time to negotiate a peace partly because of several conditions (including the interests of their benefactors, the Soviet Union and China) that might quickly change. French leaders believed the opportunity to negotiate a peace had to be seized or else it would be lost.[20]

This last example is one of a peace conference finally opening by virtue of the sensitivity of one side to the decision calculus of the other. The fact that this kind of sensitivity was needed at all points to another implication of the requirement that both sides be willing to negotiate before negotiations can begin. Most of the factors discussed so far in this chapter, if they are reasons for one side to welcome negotiations at a given time, are reasons for the other side to shun them at the same time. That is, they are zero-sum: what strengthens the bargaining position of one belligerent weakens that of its enemy. If each side's concern for its own bargaining position exceeds its sensitivity to that of the other—and it usually does—the attitudes of both toward negotiations may shift with the changing

[20] Ely, *L'Indochine dans la Tourmente*, p. 47. At that time Ely was chief of the combined staff in France.

fortunes of war while remaining divergent: when one wants to talk, the other does not.

The Korean War is a good illustration. The goals of each side expanded and contracted drastically several times during the first year of the conflict, yet at no moment during this period were both prepared to negotiate. Figure 2 represents schematically each side's attitudes toward negotiations during the first year of that war. At the risk of oversimplification, each side's position at any time is located on one of three tracks. The left-hand track is one of resistance to negotiations growing out of an unfavorable military situation. Negotiations are delayed in the belief that the war map must first be improved. The right-hand track is one of resistance to negotiations growing out of a military situation that is too favorable. Negotiations are rejected because the eventual extermination, expulsion, or capitulation of the enemy appears possible. The middle track is the one of

FIGURE 2. Attitudes toward negotiations in the Korean War.

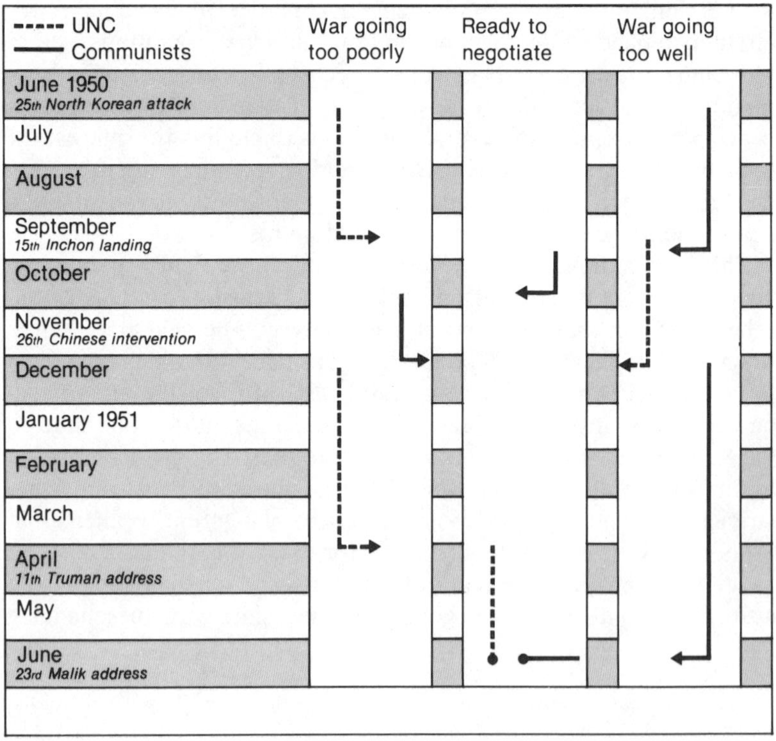

willingness to negotiate. Only when both sides are on this track, and realize they are, can talks begin. Neither side was on the negotiation track initially—not the Communists because their invasion was going too well, and not the UNC because the dire military situation first had to be improved. The UNC landing at Inchon in September turned the war around so suddenly that the United States/UNC policy[21] switched directly to one of destroying the North Korean regime without touching the negotiation track on the way. Following this reverse, the Communist powers made some efforts, principally in the form of accelerated Soviet activity at the UN, to arrange an armistice negotiation. Sometime in October, after UNC forces had moved across the Parallel, the Chinese made their decision to intervene in the war.[22] The efforts to arrange talks gave way to China's threats of military escalation. The Chinese intervention in force in late November turned the tide as quickly as Inchon had. The subsequent Communist hard line reflected the rapidity of their southward advance, while the United States decided that negotiations would have to await an improvement in the military situation.[23] The United Nations forces finally halted the Chinese advance in mid-January. As the front line slowly moved back northward to the 38th Parallel, the Truman administration came to see that the time was increasingly ripe for negotiations. It made no direct offer of talks, but on 11 April, in the radio address in which he announced the firing of MacArthur, President Truman declared his readiness to negotiate. The Communists continued to hope for a new southward push until such hopes died with the failure of their May offensive. The Communist side then announced on 23 June, through a UN radio broadcast by Soviet Ambassador Malik, its readiness to negotiate. This led to an exchange of messages between the military commanders, setting up the truce talks which began at Kaesong in July.

Both sides in the Vietnam War were willing, early in that conflict, to negotiate a peace, but again no conference convened until much later because the two sides were not amenable to talks at the same time. Planners within the United States government had, by the spring of 1964, come to see eventual negotiations with Hanoi as

[21] Actually, it was more a lack of policy, which had the effect of giving a free hand to MacArthur, who on 1 October broadcast an ultimatum demanding North Korea's unconditional surrender.

[22] Allen S. Whiting, *China Crosses the Yalu*, p. 94.

[23] Truman, *Years of Trial and Hope*, p. 398; and Dean Acheson, *Present at the Creation*, p. 475.

inevitable,[24] but the Johnson administration remained unreceptive to talks for another year in the face of the unfavorable military situation in South Vietnam. During this period the United States turned aside several peacemaking efforts, including the one by U Thant to arrange a meeting in Rangoon and a Soviet suggestion, relayed by the British, to reconvene the Geneva conference.[25] President Johnson finally announced American willingness to negotiate on 7 April 1965—after Rolling Thunder, the program of sustained bombing of North Vietnam, was well underway—in an address at Johns Hopkins University, when he offered "unconditional discussions" with the enemy.[26] Earlier, during the period of American reticence, the Communists had displayed a willingness to talk. In July 1964, for example, Hanoi as well as other Communist powers responded positively to Thant's suggestion that the Geneva conference reconvene.[27] But by the time Johnson delivered his Johns Hopkins address, the North Vietnamese had changed their minds. The change probably reflected a belief both that the short-term prospects for toppling the Saigon regime by force remained good (U.S. ground combat forces were not introduced into South Vietnam until mid-1965), and that the United States, having now begun bombing and having insisted on the preservation of the Saigon regime, would not be a very pliable negotiating partner.[28] It was to be three more years before direct talks would finally begin.

The Korean and Vietnam conflicts were not exceptional in demonstrating how difficult it can be to agree on a time to open peace negotiations. The pattern is common because of the discontinuous nature of military actions and outcomes. If each belligerent had an infinite number of military options open to it, ranging from no effort to all-out effort, it would be easier for one party to slide onto the

---

[24] *Pentagon Papers,* Vol. 3, p. 156.

[25] *Ibid.,* pp. 325–330.

[26] Text in *Department of State Bulletin,* 26 April 1965, pp. 606–610.

[27] Kahin and Lewis, pp. 155–156.

[28] The DRV's outlook became apparent in March 1965, when J. Blair Seaborn, Canada's representative on the International Control Commission, visited Hanoi in March 1965. The two sides had used Seaborn during the previous year as a private channel of communication (the first such in the war). But now he discovered that Hanoi's interest in the channel had vanished. Vietnam Task Force, Office of the Secretary of Defense, *United States-Vietnam Relations, 1945–1967* [hereinafter *U.S.-Vietnam Relations*], Vol. VI.C.1, p. 6. This is one of four unpublished volumes of the Pentagon Papers study, on settlement of the war, which were declassified, with deletions, later than the other volumes.

negotiation track without knocking the other one off. But the selection of military options rarely looks like that; a government often must choose from among a limited number of discrete alternatives. A decision to act in a bolder or costlier way commonly implies a large and sudden—not a small and gradual—change in the level, locale, or type of violence. If this is sufficient to alter one side's attitudes toward negotiations, it usually alters that of the other side as well. A particularly large and distinct threshold is crossed whenever a nation that had not previously been actively involved in a war enters combat. The American and Chinese entries into the Korean War and the American entry into the Vietnam War all were intended to reverse military trends deemed too unfavorable to permit immediate negotiations. All succeeded in doing so, but they also postponed negotiations still further by raising the possibility of direct achievement by the intervening nation, or by leading the enemy to conclude that now it must reverse the course of military events before negotiating.

Warring states thus have conflicting interests in determining exactly *when* peace negotiations will open. But because both are enduring the continuing costs of warfare, they also have a common interest in seeing that negotiations *do* open. The presence of both these elements means that the opening of peace negotiations, like the conclusion of a peace agreement, is a bargaining problem. Many of the attributes of bargaining over a peace agreement during warfare, to be examined in subsequent chapters, therefore apply as well to bargaining over the opening of negotiations. There are, however, several significant differences: (1) Agreeing to negotiate does not immediately end the costs of war; it is only a first step in reaching an armistice that will end them. (2) The process of reaching agreement is different. Instead of making incremental concessions to converge on a final outcome, as is characteristic of face-to-face negotiation over a peace agreement, the parties simply indicate their willingness or unwillingness to negotiate.[29] Agreement (i.e., the opening of talks) results whenever both sides are simultaneously willing. (3) The value of the outcome to each side is more dependent on time. In fact, one can say that time *is* the outcome. (4) The outcome is usually more easily revoked. Revocation means not the start of a new war, as with an armistice agreement, but merely the breaking

---

[29] Conditions, however, may be attached to offers to negotiate. These will be discussed later in this chapter.

off of negotiations. (5) The value of the outcome to each side is less certain. Instead of being a written agreement which specifies how the issues are resolved, which is true of the armistice accord itself, the outcome of bargaining over the opening of negotiations is only a procedure. The ultimate value of that procedure to each belligerent depends on whether an armistice agreement results from it, how long it takes to write that agreement, what the provisions of it are, and what the side-effects of the negotiations are.

This last attribute—the uncertain future of a peace negotiation—can inhibit the opening of talks if the parties are excessively pessimistic about the results of the negotiation. But this very uncertainty more often facilitates agreement on the opening of talks. Vagueness or ambiguity in any sort of agreement generally eases bargaining, because the bargainers do not have to resolve their disagreement completely. Uncertainty about the results of a negotiation provides a functional equivalent to vagueness; the parties can enter the conference each hoping and expecting to obtain more than the hopes and expectations of the other would allow. Both sides evidently entered the long Vietnam negotiations, for example, with incompatible expectations regarding the central issue of whether the regime of Nguyen Van Thieu would be permitted to survive. It was not until Henry Kissinger and Le Duc Tho unsuccessfully concluded a series of secret meetings in September 1971 (their last such meetings before the large Communist offensive of the following spring) that they each finally realized that the other side was not, after all, prepared to concede on this point.[30]

When Negotiations Open

Belligerents disagree on when to open negotiations when they disagree about military trends—about which side the tide of battle favors—or, more precisely, about the reversibility of such trends. A government declines to negotiate when it believes that it can reverse an unfavorable trend that the enemy apparently sees as irreversible. It also declines to negotiate when it sees a favorable trend as irreversible but the enemy evidently believes it can be reversed. In either case, it does not expect to receive through a negotiation what it would receive if the war first continued long enough to induce the enemy to see things the same way it does. In short, disagreement

---

[30] Marvin Kalb and Bernard Kalb, *Kissinger,* pp. 183–184.

persists, and negotiations do not open, as long as the two sides hold differing long-term expectations about a continued war.[31]

It follows that negotiations are more likely to open once the parties arrive at a common view of the future course of the war and both become aware that they hold such a common view. This occurs when the ability (or inability) and willingness (or unwillingness) of each side either to maintain or to reverse the current course of the war become obvious. This can happen when one side's resources for expansion of the war are exhausted, or one side demonstrates that it cannot push or punish the enemy beyond a certain point, or one side finds new resources that promise to exceed any available to the other side.[32]

A review of the circumstances in which negotiations opened in each of the five major cases demonstrates the principle, and also permits some further observations on when belligerents usually offer to talk.

In the War of 1812, the United States was the party consistently more willing to open peace negotiations. It was the smaller of the two states and had declared war while the British were devoting most of their energies to the struggle against Napoleon. The Americans were clearly in a more advantageous position while the European war continued than they would be after Britain was no longer distracted by it; this was reason enough to seek early negotiations and to avoid the risk that their own war would still be in progress when peace came to Europe. The Anglo-American war was hardly underway, in fact, when President Madison empowered the U.S.

---

[31] R. Harrison Wagner, in "On the Unification of Two-Person Bargaining Theory," p. 79, argues from a game theoretical perspective that the crucial aspect of any bargaining problem is how the bargainers might establish convergent expectations about the consequences of stalemate.

[32] Kecskemeti has advanced a similar idea which he calls the "irreversibility principle." See his *Strategic Surrender,* pp. 8–9, and "Political Rationality in Ending War," pp. 108–109. Kecskemeti's formulation differs from the present one in two respects, however. First, he focuses specifically on attrition (rather than on any other possible measure of a military trend, such as capture of territory) and on the decision of the disadvantaged side to quit (rather than on the simultaneous decisions of both sides). Second, he contends that irreversibility of the current trend is the crucial condition. The present contention is that what matters is not that the trend be irreversible, but rather that the parties agree on whether or not it is. Agreement is in fact most frequent with an irreversible trend; it makes forecasting the future course of the war simpler and easier. But it may also occur in the presence of one side's obvious capacity to change the course of the war. Something like this happened in the War of 1812, discussed below.

chargé in London to arrange a peace if the maritime issues which constituted the principal *casus belli* could be satisfactorily resolved.[33] And when the Russian czar offered to mediate a settlement in March 1813, the United States quickly accepted. The British government, apart from an initial attempt to nip the war in the bud,[34] remained cool to the idea of negotiations throughout the first fifteen months of the war, a period of fluctuating military fortunes in North America and uncertainty over the final outcome of the European war. The proposal that finally led to the peace conference at Ghent was a British offer of direct negotiations in November 1813. Although, as will be explained later, this offer was indirectly related to the earlier Russian offer of mediation, its timing was largely the result of military events in Europe. It was extended shortly after the battle of Leipzig, the great allied victory that made the collapse of Napoleon's empire inevitable. The same ship that carried the news of the battle to America also carried the British offer, which Madison and Monroe promptly accepted.[35] Negotiations could open because the future course of a continued Anglo-American war now seemed clear. Within a few months, thousands of Wellington's seasoned veterans would be available to give Britain a marked superiority in the fight against the upstart republic. The fact that such visions were not to materialize fully—mainly because of unanticipated frictions among the allies at the Congress of Vienna and superior American naval skill at the battle of Plattsburg—did not make them seem any less realistic at the time to statesmen on both sides of the Atlantic. The point is not that the American leaders now saw themselves in a hopeless situation; in fact, they continued to place considerable hope in advantages that they still enjoyed, including what they be-

[33] Monroe to Russell, 26 June and 27 July 1812. *American State Papers*, pp. 585–586.

[34] Less than three weeks after the declaration of war (and before it was known in London), Britain had removed one of America's grievances by repealing the Orders-in-Council which had restricted neutral commerce to French-controlled ports. Hopeful that this would induce the United States to call off the war, the British government instructed its naval commander in Halifax to propose an armistice. Secretary of State James Monroe rejected the proposal on the grounds that Britain would also have to agree to stop impressing American seamen before hostilities could cease. Warren to Monroe, 30 September 1812, and Monroe to Warren, 27 October 1812. *American State Papers*, pp. 585–587.

[35] Henry Adams, *History of the United States of America During the Administrations of Jefferson and Madison*, pp. 370–371; and Bradford Perkins, *Castlereagh and Adams*, pp. 22–23.

lieved to be the support of most neutral nations. The point is rather that with the uncertainty over Britain's European commitments apparently dissolved, both sides had less hope of changing the enemy's expectations through continued warfare. Note also that no irreversible trend in the war had yet been established; Wellington's troops were still several European battles and a long ocean voyage away from action in North America. What was important was that both sides expected such a trend.

The events and attitudes during the first year of the Korean War were reviewed earlier. During that period of ebb and flow, the two sides held incompatible expectations. The North Koreans initially expected to sweep their foes off the peninsula, while the United States government had contrary intentions. The United States later expected to eradicate the Communist regime in North Korea without a Chinese intervention, while Peking had contrary plans. The only time during this year that the two sides came close to having a common vision of a continued war was in December 1950 and January 1951, when the Truman administration feared that the Chinese might succeed in their apparent goal of overruning South Korea. This gloom vanished once the front stabilized in mid-January. For the next several months, expectations were again divergent: the UNC was confident of staying in Korea, while Peking evidently did not give up the hope of driving it out until its May offensive failed. That failure marked the end of contradictory expectations. Each side now knew—and knew that the other knew—that the Communists could not push the UNC out of Korea. It was also fairly clear that the UNC was capable of advancing farther north, but only at the cost of heavy casualties.[36] When negotiations opened, each belligerent had shown how much it could and would invest in the struggle.

The Geneva conference that ended the Indochina War was arranged at a four-power meeting in Berlin in February 1954, but both belligerents had expressed their willingness to negotiate during the previous year. For the French government and people the war had been a long descent from the initial high hopes in 1946 of quickly stamping out the Viet Minh into what seemed, by 1953, like a bottomless pit. In a policy statement to the National Assembly on 27 October 1953, Premier Joseph Laniel, though making no explicit

---

[36] Although they phrased their estimates differently, this was the opinion later expressed by both of the last two UNC commanders. Matthew B. Ridgway, *Soldier: The Memoirs of Matthew B. Ridgway*, pp. 219–220; and Mark W. Clark, *From the Danube to the Yalu*, pp. 100–101.

offers, revealed his government's readiness to talk.[37] A few weeks later came Ho Chi Minh's *Expressen* interview. The Viet Minh leadership had undoubtedly believed for at least the past four years that the tide of war was running inexorably in their favor. Now they could see that this had also become the prevailing view in Paris. They could open talks with an enemy who had shed his earlier aspirations and would be sufficiently pliable to make a peace conference worthwhile.[38]

The FLN in the Algerian War, like the United States in the War of 1812, had been prepared to negotiate a peace from the very beginning of the conflict. It was a change of attitude on the part of France, or more specifically on the part of President de Gaulle, that led to the opening of talks. The Algerian insurrection was different from the other cases in that the events which made possible a shared expectation were political, not military. The FLN's armed strength and activity within Algeria had peaked by 1958. Over the next two years, the French army succeeded in reducing rebel violence to scattered acts of terrorism while keeping most of the FLN's troops behind barriers constructed along the Moroccan and Tunisian borders. France had already managed to reverse the earlier military successes of the FLN; de Gaulle now hoped to reverse its political success by driving a wedge between the FLN and most of the Moslem population and by fostering a "third force" which would win Moslem support while favoring a continued association with France. His hope vanished during a visit to Algeria in December 1960, when the FLN staged demonstrations and disorders so widespread that he instantly became convinced that he could not divest the rebels of their popular support.[39] One French officer, comparing the demonstrations to France's greatest military defeat in the Indochina War, described them as a "diplomatic Dienbienphu."[40] Shortly afterward, de Gaulle initiated secret contacts which led to the first formal, substantive peace negotiations with the FLN in May 1961. Talks opened when the result of any prolonged conflict had become

---

[37] Text in Allen W. Cameron (ed.), *Vietnam Crisis, A Documentary History,* Vol. 1, pp. 209–214.

[38] The opposition to talks at that time which persisted among some on the French side, including the field commander, General Navarre, rested on the belief that the military trend *was* reversible.

[39] Louis Terrenoire, *De Gaulle et l'Algérie,* pp. 215–217; and Joseph Kraft, *The Struggle for Algeria,* pp. 245–246.

[40] Quoted in Tanya Matthews, *War in Algeria,* p. 119.

clear—continued French military hegemony but with a continued accretion in popular support for the FLN—and neither side had any hope of changing it.

The Paris peace talks on Vietnam opened when Hanoi, in April 1968, indicated its readiness to negotiate with the United States, whose own offer to talk had lain on the table for three years. Hanoi's move followed on the heels of two others. The first was the assault on South Vietnamese cities in January and February that became known as the Tet offensive. The second was President Johnson's televised address on 31 March, in which he announced the cessation of bombing over most of North Vietnam and his decision not to seek re-election. Taken together, these events gave Hanoi reason to believe that the enemy shared with it a common perception of the future course of the war. The precise purposes of the DRV leadership in launching the Tet offensive are not entirely clear. It may have been designed from the outset as a way of launching a period of negotiating while fighting. But there is also evidence that General Giap conceived of the offensive not as an adjunct to negotiations, but rather as a militarily decisive campaign that would precipitate a popular uprising against the Thieu regime and cause ARVN (the South Vietnamese army) to disintegrate.[41] Perhaps the thinking in Hanoi was a combination of the two; either way, the result of the offensive would have made Hanoi more inclined to negotiate. The assault did not incite an uprising or shatter ARVN; thus it dispelled any hope that the Communists had of gaining their objective in the near future through military effort alone. But it did splatter the war over front pages and television screens in the United States, demonstrate that the American effort had not succeeded in creating a truly secure area in South Vietnam, sap the American people's will to continue the war, and therefore weaken the U.S. bargaining position in any negotiations. On both counts, the offensive removed obstacles to the convergence of expectations. It destroyed any belief in Hanoi—not shared in Washington—that Communist forces could topple Thieu unilaterally and also any belief in Washington—not shared in Hanoi—that the American public would tolerate the war indefinitely. Put in this context, Johnson's address must have appeared to Hanoi as a confirmation and acknowledgment of the new

---

[41] The first interpretation is offered by Patrick J. McGarvey, *Visions of Victory*, p. 50. The second is made by Douglas Pike, *War, Peace, and the Viet Cong*, pp. 125–128.

shared expectation. It not only seemed to reflect the change in mood of the American populace, but it also indicated that the President was calling off the contest in escalation.[42] With the end of Tet, the Communists had finished, for the time being, trying to redirect the course of the war. Now the Americans had finished trying as well. Three days after the President spoke, the DRV said it was ready to talk.

Besides demonstrating the importance of shared expectations in the opening of peace negotiations, this review of the five major cases permits an additional observation about the circumstances in which individual governments tend to offer, or accept an offer, to negotiate. Of the ten decisions to become available to negotiate (two in each war, disregarding any early ones which were later retracted), only three (the Communists in Korea, France in Indochina, and France in Algeria) were responses to a worsening situation. And one of these three—France in the Algerian War—was a response to political, not military, failure. In two instances (the United States in the War of 1812 and the FLN in Algeria), a belligerent was ready to negotiate from the beginning of the war. Four of the remaining five decisions (Britain in the War of 1812, the UNC in Korea, the Viet Minh in Indochina, and the United States in Vietnam), and probably the fifth as well (the DRV in Vietnam), were taken when the war was following a favorable course; they were instances of one side's having waited until events had strengthened its bargaining position before it became willing to talk. It is therefore erroneous to consider a willingness to treat with the enemy as a "suing for peace," an action that befits a "loser" but not a "winner." By their own actions, governments have demonstrated that the opening of a peace negotiation has as much to do with the bargains that have yet to be struck as with the battles that have already been fought.

Barriers to the Opening of Negotiations

Disagreement over the best time to open negotiations is not the only reason for difficulty and delay in getting peace talks started. After all, an agreement to negotiate neither stops the war nor commits either party to specific peace terms. The difficulty results as well from certain other barriers that must be overcome before initiat-

[42] Cf. McGarvey, p. 55.

ing diplomacy with an enemy during wartime. The three most important barriers are: (1) the deliberate exaggeration by governments of the extent to which interests conflict; (2) the hesitancy of belligerents to take the first overt steps toward a peace settlement; and (3) the imposition of conditions to the opening of talks.

The Exaggeration of Hostility

Besides managing combat and conducting diplomacy, governments at war are also in the business of creating images—images of themselves, their policies, the enemy and his policies, and the issues at stake. A government may find it advantageous to nurture a false image. Specifically, governments at war usually attempt to portray the underlying conflict of interest as high, and their own willingness to compromise with the enemy as low. Sometimes governments use such image-building efforts to convince the enemy of their determination and confidence, thus discouraging the enemy from holding out for a favorable bargain or from attempting to play upon divisions within the other side. More frequently, the object is to nurture such images among one's own troops and population, in order to justify the sacrifices demanded of them. Most soldiers do not understand why they should die so that their government can strike a better rather than a worse bargain, or reach one compromise rather than another. They find it easier to understand—and accept—dying if they think it is needed to preserve their way of life, to make the world safe for democracy, to launch the age of eternal peace, or for any of the other simplistic rationales that governments have used to inspire their subjects to pay the costs of war. Soldiers, and their civilian compatriots, also have difficulty understanding why they should continue to exert themselves to defeat the enemy if their leaders are already talking of reaching an accommodation with him. They are more likely to maintain their own determination to prosecute the war if they believe that the leaders are maintaining theirs. In short, the need for continued support and effort from their own citizens leads governments to understate the chances for a negotiated peace, the desirability of one, and their own willingness to make one. The requirements of the military struggle produce a distorted picture of the diplomatic opportunities.

Such bellicose posturing can delay the opening of peace negotiations by affecting the enemy's view of the prospects for peace. Each side examines the statements of the other, including those intended for internal consumption, for clues of its intentions. Statements designed to bolster internal morale by showing the leadership's determination thus risk diminishing the other side's estimate of the possibilities for an early negotiated settlement. This was less of a problem before the advent of modern communications, when politicians and generals could speak to one audience with less chance that their remarks would be reported to another. But now a leader is just as likely to exploit modern communications by ostensibly addressing one audience while actually sending a message to another (e.g., Johnson's speech at Johns Hopkins). Because of this possibility, the other side can ill afford to dismiss an opponent's statement as nothing more than internal propaganda that implies nothing about diplomatic opportunities.[43]

Because both sides in the Algerian War had serious morale problems among their troops, this demonstrated clearly how statements intended to bolster morale can retard peace negotiations. The bellicose declarations which the FLN's government-in-exile issued in an effort to restore the flagging spirits of its guerrillas contrasted sharply with the line it took in private diplomatic initiatives, and thus lessened the credibility and effectiveness of those initiatives.[44] For his part, President de Gaulle faced simmering discontent and opposition to compromise within the French army, which was to boil over in the form of a generals' coup in Algiers in April 1961. The fact that even such a master of ambiguity as de Gaulle could not placate one audience without provoking another demonstrates the extent of the difficulty. In early 1960 he visited military installations in Algeria on what became known as the "tour of the mess halls." His reported statements during the tour—such as "there will be no Dienbienphu in Algeria" and "France must not depart"—may have pleased the French officers, but they angered and distressed the FLN leaders in Tunis. The rebels abandoned the conciliatory line that they had taken during the preceding weeks, accused de Gaulle of "slamming the door on negotiations," and scuttled, for a time, the chances of a peace conference.[45]

---

[43] On how this problem pertained to U.S. statements during the Vietnam War, see Wallace J. Thies, *When Governments Collide,* pp. 285–286.

[44] Tripier, pp. 286–290.

[45] Dorothy Pickles, *Algeria and France,* pp. 72–73; and Anthony Hartley, *Gaullism,* pp. 173–175.

The Reluctance to Move First

A government's offer to negotiate is not only a step which may lead to a peace conference, but also an action which others—including the enemy, allies, and its own soldiers and citizens—may use as more general evidence of its intentions, plans, aspirations, and morale. The *act* of proposing talks, in other words, has implications and effects besides making negotiations possible. Sometimes a government believes that if it makes an offer skillfully, these effects will be, on balance, beneficial. Like peace conferences themselves, peace feelers or initiatives can have advantageous side-effects, such as dividing the enemy or undermining his domestic support, and their use for this purpose will be further discussed in the next subsection. But an unambiguous proposal for peace negotiations, if it is not a response to an earlier proposal from the enemy, is far more frequently viewed as an act to be avoided. The pervasive notion that an initial offer to negotiate is a "suing for peace" leads governments to resist making such offers for fear of being considered the defeated party and thereby encouraging the opposition to drive a harder bargain. In short, being the *first* to move toward peace negotiations is shunned because it is considered equivalent to crying "uncle." Jean Letourneau, the French Minister for Indochina, expressed this sentiment candidly during the Indochina War when he said in 1952, "France does not refuse to talk with the Viet Minh, but we will not take the first step."[46] Since someone has to take the first step before talks can begin, such reluctance is another barrier to the opening of peace negotiations.

Although the militarily less successful party is more likely to exhibit this unwillingness to take the first step, the more successful one may do so as well. Even after the Japanese cabinet decided in April 1905, at the height of Japan's successes in the Russo-Japanese War, that the time was ripe for negotiations, it refrained from making any immediate moves out of the belief that it would be improper for the victorious nation to act first.[47] This concern may even shape the dialogue of representatives who are already seated at the conference table. This was true, for example, of the allied generalissimo Mar-

[46] Quoted in Joseph Buttinger, *Vietnam: A Dragon Embattled*, Vol. 2: *Vietnam at War*, p. 800.
[47] Shumpei Okamoto, *The Japanese Oligarchy and the Russo-Japanese War*, pp. 116–117.

shal Foch when he met German negotiators in a railroad car at Rethondes to conclude the World War I armistice on the western front. Listening to his words, an observer might have guessed that the meeting had occurred by accident. "What brings these gentlemen here?" he asked. "What do you wish of me?" When the German representative said he awaited proposals on an armistice, Foch replied that he had no proposals to make. Only after the Germans indicated that *they* sought an armistice did Foch present the Allied demands.[48]

The unwillingness to move first is even more apparent, however, on the side that is worse off militarily. The party that most fears the label of loser is the one that already looks most like a loser. It resists asking for negotiations lest this be taken as a sign of weakness.[49] The reluctance to move first under such circumstances thus reinforces the reasoning, discussed in the previous section, whereby a peace negotiation may appear undesirable if military trends are unfavorable.

This reluctance impedes the opening of peace negotiations in two specific ways. First, it may lead a government to delay making any peace offer at all, whether its side is currently successful, as Japan was in April 1905, or unsuccessful, as the United States was in Korea in December 1950.[50] Second, when it does offer negotiations, it often does so in such an ambiguous and circumspect way that its offer can easily be misinterpreted. The misinterpretation may or may not be deliberate. When the Viet Minh proposed a cease-fire in Indochina in early 1947, through a delegation that Ho Chi Minh had

[48] Harry R. Rudin, *Armistice 1918,* p. 388.

[49] This fear is well founded insofar as loud or repeated expressions of a desire to make peace do create an image of despair. The North Vietnamese may well have viewed President Johnson's repeatedly proclaimed desire to go anywhere, any time, to negotiate an end to the Vietnam War as an indication of weakness. Johnson himself later came to this conclusion (Johnson, p. 250). This was particularly true of the American peace blitz undertaken during the bombing pause in December 1965 and January 1966, when U.S. envoys fanned out over the globe to convince everyone who mattered, and many who did not, that the United States wanted to end the war. More subtle and less energetic initiatives need not have this effect, but governments suffering military setbacks commonly fear that they will.

[50] It was the implications of the act of proposing an armistice during that gloomiest period of the Korean War, as well as more general expectations of the weakness of its bargaining position in any peace conference that took place at that time, that caused the Truman administration to decide against such a proposal. See especially the arguments in a memorandum prepared at Secretary Acheson's request by George Kennan on 3 December, in George F. Kennan, *Memoirs,* Vol. 2, pp. 26–33.

left in France following earlier negotiations, French Prime Minister Paul Ramadier dismissed the proposal as not authentic, making the feeble excuse that the message had come from within France and had not been signed personally by Ho.[51] When the Viet Minh again extended peace feelers in late 1953, they were once more met with expressions of skepticism in Paris, except that this time the French government was interested in talking and the skepticism was genuine. The Viet Minh willingness to negotiate was not clear at the time because the feelers were vague; they came through circuitous channels (such as foreign newspaper interviews and reports circulated in Communist capitals); and their timing suggested that the Communists were merely trying to capitalize on the investiture of a more nationalistic premier in Saigon.[52]

Conditions

An offer to negotiate is not a simple either-or proposition, because it may have conditions attached. Conditions applicable to the opening of peace negotiations may cover any of three subjects: (1) the negotiation itself, including such details as the site and the level of representation; (2) the conduct of the war while negotiations are in progress; and (3) the substance of the peace agreement. The opening of a peace conference always entails some conditions of the first type, since the parties must at least agree on a meeting place and a time for the conference to occur. The other two types of conditions may or may not be part of an offer, or acceptance of an offer, to negotiate.

All three types affect the value of a prospective negotiation to each belligerent. They influence, first of all, the shape of the armistice agreement that finally emerges. Restrictions on the substance of the agreement do so directly; the other two types influence it indirectly by strengthening or weakening each side's bargaining position. Conditions covering the negotiation itself determine what the side-effects will be. All three types help to determine how long it will take to reach agreement. And restrictions on the conduct of the war affect the extent of the costs as long as disagreement persists and the ability of each side to continue the war should talks fail. These considerations weigh upon any decisions to offer to negotiate, what

---

[51] Ellen J. Hammer, *The Struggle for Indochina*, p. 196.
[52] Melvin Gurtov, *The First Vietnam Crisis*, p. 18.

conditions to attach to the offer, and whether to accept conditions demanded by the other side.

Although governments at war often attach conditions to their offers, peace conferences usually open with no agreed conditions beyond those covering the negotiation itself. Of the five major cases, Vietnam was the only one in which the agreement to talk included a restriction on military activity.[53] Restrictions on the substance of the peace agreement played some role in the opening of negotiations in the War of 1812 and the Korean War, but, as we will see shortly, they were so imprecise that the two sides did not fully agree on what those restrictions were. The major reason governments so often fail to make their preferred conditions part of an agreement to negotiate is that conditions remove some of the advantage of uncertainty. Conditions, especially those pertaining to the substance of the agreement, make it less likely that the parties can begin talks despite incompatible hopes or expectations. Opening a conference without conditions that restrict future options or possibilities is thus the path of least resistance for two governments that seek a negotiated peace.

Nevertheless, attaching conditions to an offer to negotiate has several uses. One of the most common is to avoid talks when no talks are desired; one side insists on conditions that it knows will be unacceptable to the enemy and thereby prevents or delays a peace conference without incurring the odium that comes from refusing one outright. The French government responded in this way to Viet Minh proposals for peace negotiations during the early months of the Indochina War, laying down severe conditions that included the surrender of large quantities of war materiel. France's military commander in Indochina, General Valluy, when warned that the terms would be unacceptable to the other side, replied, "I hope so."[54] But this tactic can backfire because severe terms themselves—not just a refusal to negotiate—can antagonize third parties and stiffen the other side's resolve. As the Chinese Communists were throwing the UNC forces southward in Korea in December 1950, the harsh terms which Peking demanded for an opening of peace talks—a UN withdrawal from Korea, a United States withdrawal from Formosa, recognition of Peking, and an end to all Western rearmament—tended to increase support within the UN for the American-led military

[53] This does not include the establishment of small neutral zones for holding talks, such as the one around Panmunjom and Kaesong in Korea.

[54] Irving, p. 46.

effort.[55] This opened the way for the United States to employ a variant of the tactic of making an offer the other is expected to refuse. In January the United States government accepted resolutions in the General Assembly which went beyond the concessions that it was actually prepared to grant (particularly on the issues of Formosa and the China seat at the UN), estimating correctly that the Communists would reject them anyway. The United States thus preserved the unity of the anti-Communist coalition and placed the blame for continued fighting at the feet of the enemy.[56]

Attaching conditions to offers to negotiate enables a belligerent to straddle the fence between willingness and unwillingness to talk; it is in a position to jump to one side or the other, depending on the enemy's responses. In addition, this approach offers the chance to profit from the side-effects of peace feelers without committing oneself to negotiations that may be inopportune. The North Vietnamese, during the pre-negotiation phase of the Vietnam War, were enthusiastic practitioners of the art of the conditional peace feeler. Believing that they were cheated out of total control of Vietnam at the multilateral Geneva conference in 1954, and wishing to delay even bilateral talks until after the Johnson administration had abandoned the Ky-Thieu regime, the leaders in Hanoi remained basically antipathetic to negotiations until after the Tet offensive and the partial bombing halt in 1968. Nevertheless, by skillfully dangling the juicy plum of peace while calling for a reduction of the U.S. military effort—particularly a halt to the bombing of North Vietnam—they could portray themselves as peace-lovers, encourage anti-war forces in the United States, and make it appear that the Johnson administration was deliberately passing up opportunities for negotiations. Moreover, the North Vietnamese might induce the United States to reduce its military effort, and they stood ready to respond in case the enemy's will weakened sooner than expected.

Hanoi's responses to the several pauses in U.S. bombing of North Vietnam revealed these intentions. The first of these was a six-day pause in May 1965, the month after the Johns Hopkins speech. During the pause, the Communists made no positive response and even refused to accept delivery of an American note at their Moscow embassy.[57] But several hours *after* the bombing resumed on 18

---

[55] Robert Leckie, *Conflict: The History of the Korean War, 1950–53*, p. 236.

[56] Acheson, p. 513; and Goodrich, p. 175.

[57] Johnson, p. 137.

May, the head of the DRV delegation in Paris, Mai Van Bo, made an urgent request to the French Foreign Ministry to relay to the United States a message which hinted that negotiations were possible.[58] The timing was close enough to make it appear that the bombing pause had been a bit too short, that a trigger-happy Johnson administration had spoiled a chance for peace by being overanxious to resume the attacks.[59] The DRV used the same tactic during the next bombing pause, even though this one lasted not six days but thirty-seven, from Christmas Eve 1965 to the end of the January 1966. In addition to its public peace offensive, the United States attempted to get negotiations started through secret channels, the most promising of which was between the U.S. and North Vietnamese ambassadors in Rangoon. An American note was accepted, but again there was no reply during the bombing halt, which Hanoi publicly scored as a "trick."[60] Again, a response finally came a few hours *after* the bombing resumed. The reply was so rushed that when the U.S. ambassador arrived at the North Vietnamese embassy to receive it, the aide-memoire was still in the typewriter.[61]

Perhaps there were times between the spring of 1965 and the spring of 1968 when Hanoi was prepared to talk. One of those times could have been late 1966, when numerous exchanges (which acquired the code name Marigold) between the Polish ICC representative, Janus Lewandowski, and Ambassador Lodge in Saigon appeared to come close to setting up a bilateral meeting between the United States and the DRV in Warsaw. But if negotiations were seriously considered by Hanoi, it was only one possible route to follow, depending on the responses of the United States. If Lewandowski's meticulous probing revealed that American will had weakened and that the United States government would agree to a conference under circumstances favorable to the Communists, preferably with a total bombing halt or other unreciprocated restrictions on American military activity as conditions, there might be no harm in talking. But the more likely course was to break off the contact on some convenient pretext and once again to accuse the Americans of wrecking the chances for peace. In Marigold, that pretext came

[58] *U.S.-Vietnam Relations,* Vol. VI.C.1, p. 69.

[59] Even careful scholars such as Kahin and Lewis (writing before the release of the Pentagon Papers study had revealed the details of this and later North Vietnamese peace ploys) concluded that the pause had been too short. Kahin and Lewis, p. 214.

[60] *New York Times,* 5 January 1966, p. 2.

[61] *U.S.-Vietnam Relations,* Vol. VI.C.1, p. 130.

when U.S. aircraft bombed targets near the center of Hanoi for the first time in several weeks in early December, as the Warsaw contact was in preparation. (The timing of the attacks was determined by the weather.) The North Vietnamese broke off the contact and refused to renew it although the United States then instituted bombing restrictions around Hanoi that went beyond what even the Poles had recommended earlier. For Hanoi, Marigold had served its primary purpose of providing material for future propaganda; to have resumed the contact would only have reduced the propaganda advantage.[62]

Throughout the three years preceding the opening of the Paris peace talks, Hanoi appeared more eager to profit from the side-effects of conditional peace feelers than to get a conference underway. Whenever a promising exchange hit a snag, the North Vietnamese, instead of preserving the contact's secrecy and thus its future usefulness, soon leaked their own version of it. In fact, their private written communications were evidently drafted with subsequent publication in mind.[63] They confused matters by sometimes making a distinction between "talks" and "negotiations" without ever clarifying that distinction enough for the other side to know what they meant.[64] And until the end of 1967, they had not committed themselves to negotiations even if the United States halted its bombing of North Vietnam completely; such a halt only "could"— not "would"—bring negotiations.

Thus a belligerent can advantageously manipulate conditions, but conditions also create barriers to the opening of negotiations. The general reason they do so is the same reason that most agreements to negotiate entail few conditions: they reduce the advantage of uncertainty and force the parties to resolve issues sooner rather than later. There are also several more specific ways in which conditions present obstacles to the opening of a peace conference.

Conditions covering the negotiation itself—the kind necessarily included in any agreement to talk—impede the opening of a confer-

---

[62] A complete account of Marigold is in *U.S.-Vietnam Relations,* Vol. VI.C.2. Published accounts are in Chester L. Cooper, *The Lost Crusade,* pp. 333–342; Kraslow and Loory, pp. 3–88; Wallace J. Thies, "Searching for Peace: Vietnam & the Question of How Wars End"; and Thies, *When Governments Collide,* esp. pp. 146–147.

[63] Ambassador Llewellyn Thompson made this observation about a message received through the Moscow embassy in January 1967. *U.S.-Vietnam Relations,* Vol. VI.C.3, p. 46.

[64] *Ibid.,* p. 12.

ence when they are inherently related to the substantive issues at stake. This commonly occurs when the status or legitimacy of one of the parties is itself an issue. When it is, matters of representation and protocol, which must be resolved before negotiations can commence, become matters of substance. Early efforts to arrange negotiations in the Algerian War stumbled on the differing views of the status of the FLN, which considered itself an alternative government (it already had formed a "Provisional Government of the Algerian Republic") that was the sole legitimate representative of the Algerian people, but that the French government considered to be at best an insurrection and at worst a band of criminals.[65] Preliminary talks at Melun in June 1960, which were supposed to make arrangements for later substantive negotiations, failed partly because de Gaulle was simply not yet ready to negotiate but also because of these differing attitudes regarding the FLN's status. The FLN wanted political negotiations between their own top leaders and a high-ranking French political figure, preferably de Gaulle himself, whereas the French would only agree to a low-level military parley. The later conference at Evian almost collapsed before it began when France's chief negotiator made a remark which suggested (incorrectly) that he would also negotiate with a rival nationalist organization, the Mouvement National Algérien.[66] The FLN refused to talk if this were true; to do so would concede their claim to be the Algerians' "sole legitimate representative." The Indochina and Vietnam peace conferences each came close to foundering at the outset over procedural disagreements that reflected disagreement over the status of rebel organizations within Indochina. At Geneva in 1954, the question was whether the Communist movements in Laos and Cambodia were to be permitted representation (they were not). At Paris in late 1968, the disagreement was over the shape of the conference table, an issue that symbolized the question of whether or not the Viet Cong were independent of the DRV.

Among conditions restricting military activity, the most far-reaching would be to demand that it end completely—i.e., to demand a preliminary cease-fire. This was discussed generally in the last chapter, and some reasons the two sides may disagree over a cease-fire

---

[65] In fact, the French had imprisoned Ahmed Ben Bella and four other FLN leaders in 1956 when an airplane in which they were flying from Morocco to Tunisia was tricked into landing at Algiers. They remained in captivity until the end of the war.

[66] Yves Courrière, *Les Feux du Désespoir*, p. 249; and Edward Behr, *The Algerian Problem*, pp. 185–186.

will be mentioned below. But the present concern is how insistence on more limited and specific restrictions on wartime activity may impede the opening of negotiations. For one thing, belligerents may disagree over whether particular means of prosecuting the conflict are legitimate usages of war. These need not be strictly military means; in fact, disagreement over their propriety is more likely when they are not. In response to Britain's early efforts to persuade the Americans to call off their war in 1812 after the repeal of the Orders-in-Council, Secretary Monroe replied that because the impressment of seamen was an "outrage," it must cease before negotiations could begin. At the same time, Monroe defended the continuation of an American law prohibiting trade with Britain; it was a legitimate "engine of hostility," he said, and would continue as long as the war did.[67] The British, who had no pre-war commercial grievance against the United States but who saw impressment as a necessary means of recovering deserters and maintaining the manpower of the Royal Navy, took a different view. The unconventional nature of the FLN's activity in Algeria (because the rebels were powerless to do much else, they concentrated on terrorism against civilians) and de Gaulle's view that this activity was criminal rather than military lay behind the French President's insistence until late 1960 that the terrorism would have to stop before he would discuss the political future of Algeria with the FLN. In de Gaulle's words, the rebels would have to "put the knives in the cloakroom" before he would negotiate.[68] One belligerent's outrage is another belligerent's engine of hostility.

These differences of view on the propriety of certain hostile acts are largely unavoidable consequences of the different needs and capabilities of each side. What hinders agreement on negotiations even more, however, is the kind of slippery manipulation of conditions that Hanoi practiced during the Vietnam War, when it dangled vague peace feelers while attempting to link negotiations to a halt in the bombing of North Vietnam. Quite apart from the overall disagreement on the future course of the war and Hanoi's interest in delaying talks until it believed that the Americans had lowered their aspirations, the North Vietnamese tactics hindered the opening of a peace conference in several ways.

---

[67] Monroe to Warren, 27 October 1812, *American State Papers,* pp. 586–587; and Irving Brant, *James Madison: Commander in Chief,* p. 14.

[68] Terrenoire, p. 192.

In the first place, they reduced the credibility of Hanoi's statements about what was necessary and what was sufficient for negotiations to commence. On one hand, the DRV's apparent willingness to talk during Marigold undercut their insistence that the bombing first had to end before they would discuss a peace agreement (and incidentally increased doubts in Washington about Hanoi's determination to continue the war).[69] On the other hand, the DRV's rude responses to the earlier bombing pauses and its lack of concern for preserving the usefulness of private channels lowered American confidence that a bombing halt would in fact be sufficient to get a conference started. Johnson's March 1968 decision was a response not so much to improved diplomatic prospects[70] as to the realization that the military effort was not accomplishing what it was supposed to.[71]

The latter problem was exacerbated by Hanoi's attempt to get a bombing halt not just to end destruction in its territory, but to force the United States to make a major unreciprocated concession. The North Vietnamese repeatedly insisted on an *unconditional* bombing halt; if it obtained one, the United States would lose face, would appear to have lost its determination, and would consequently be on the defensive in any subsequent negotiation. The United States government attempted to obtain at least a private assurance that Hanoi would not take advantage of a bombing halt. Hanoi's response was that any such assurance would be a "condition" and hence was unacceptable.[72] The United States faced a quandary: it could not be confident, without assurances to that effect, that an unconditional bombing halt would lead to negotiations but the assurances would mean the halt was not unconditional.

Another reason for American reluctance to attempt a bombing halt was the fear that, placed in the context of Hanoi's statements on preconditions for negotiations, it would be interpreted as a concession on substance as well. Hanoi's substantive position was embodied in its "Four Points," first presented in an address by Premier

---

[69] *U.S.-Vietnam Relations,* Vol. VI.C.2, p. 14.

[70] Although he later wrote that this did play a part in his decision. Johnson, p. 396.

[71] Hoopes's *The Limits of Intervention* is an excellent account of the background of this decision.

[72] This subject was covered most extensively in a channel (code-named Pennsylvania) which was active in the summer and autumn of 1967 and involved a private American citizen (Henry Kissinger), two Frenchmen, and Mai Van Bo in Paris. See especially the report of Bo's conversation with the Frenchmen on 30 September in *U.S.-Vietnam Relations,* Vol. VI.C.4, p. 230.

Pham Van Dong in April 1965.[73] The North Vietnamese did not consistently make acceptance of the "Four Points" a condition for the opening of negotiations; often they used some other formulation, such as that the "Four Points" were the "soundest basis" for a political settlement of the war. But even when employing this softer phraseology, the DRV insisted that a settlement would require the United States to demonstrate its acceptance of the "Four Points" through its "deeds."[74] Coupling this with Hanoi's unceasing demands for a bombing halt, American decision-makers concluded, correctly or incorrectly, that such a halt would be a "deed" which would imply acceptance of Hanoi's position.[75]

Finally, manipulation of conditions reduces the future flexibility of the manipulator. Following the partial bombing halt of March 1968, the DRV agreed to meet with U.S. representatives in order, in its words, "to decide with the U.S. side the unconditional cessation of bombing and all other war acts against the DRV so that talks could begin."[76] In the wake of Tet and the change in the course of American policy, Hanoi was finally prepared to discuss a political settlement. But having insisted so long and so strenuously that there must first be an "unconditional" bombing halt, it could not now agree to an expanded political conference prior to such a halt without suffering a severe loss of face and/or credibility. There were indications in the summer of 1968 that Hanoi was attempting, through a battlefield lull and very oblique references to it, to signal its willingness to reciprocate militarily and to negotiate seriously if the United States did halt the bombing.[77] Its inability to convey a clear and direct message to that effect probably delayed the opening of the four-sided Paris negotiations by several weeks or months.

How Barriers Are Overcome

Despite these barriers, peace negotiations do take place; they took place in all of the wars from which the illustrations in the

[73] Text in U.S. Senate, Committee on Foreign Relations, *Background Information Relating to Southeast Asia and Vietnam* [hereinafter *Background Information*], pp. 579–580.

[74] See, e.g., a North Vietnamese broadcast of 1 February 1966, text in *U.S.-Vietnam Relations*, Vol. VI.C.1, pp. 132–138.

[75] See a State Department memorandum dated 26 April 1966, text in *ibid.*, pp. 171–172.

[76] Johnson, p. 495.

[77] See reports in the *New York Times*, 10 August 1968, p. 1.

previous section were drawn. Several procedures enable belligerents to surmount the barriers.

Overcoming the Reluctance to Move First

To offer negotiations without suggesting that it is weakening, a government may couch its offer as a *response* to a request, real or hypothetical, from the other side. Jacob Malik's radio address and some diplomatic exchanges that followed it convinced the Truman administration that the Communists were ready to talk peace in Korea in June 1951, but the Chinese and North Koreans had still made no explicit offer to that effect. Nevertheless, when the UNC commander, General Ridgway, sent a proposal to his enemy counterpart on 29 June, his message was phrased as a response, not an initial offer. "I am informed," it began, "that *you may wish* to discuss an armistice. . . ."[78] Ho Chi Minh's offer of talks in *Expressen* in November 1953 was similarly phrased: ". . . if *the French Government has drawn a lesson* from the war they have been waging these last years and *want to negotiate* an armistice in Vietnam and to solve the Vietnam problem by peaceful means, the people and Government of the DRV are ready to meet this desire."[79]

A judicious choice of words, however, can go only so far. Even though they had made no explicit offers, it was already clear that the Communists in June 1951 and the French in November 1953 desired negotiations. When the likely response of the other side is less obvious, the parties must use less direct means to establish contact. Contacts that occur for reasons other than negotiating a peace settlement may provide suitable opportunities. The most common such contact concerns the handling of prisoners of war. POWs are an almost inevitable byproduct of war and are often the subject of discussions between warring governments that are not otherwise on speaking terms. Furthermore, an exchange or release of prisoners enables a belligerent to demonstrate its good will while retaining the option of describing its action as a humanitarian deed rather than a diplomatic signal. The United States and Britain used their prisoner

---

[78] Quoted in Leckie, pp. 294–295. Emphasis added. When the armistice talks began in July, the Communists did their best to make it appear that the UNC was entering them as supplicant. Their propaganda machine disseminated photographs of UNC vehicles arriving at the conference site with white flags flying, interpreting the flags not as the symbols of a local truce that they were, but as symbols of surrender.

[79] Text in Cameron, pp. 223–224. Emphasis added.

agents in each other's country as channels of communication in the War of 1812. During the Indochina War, the first open and direct contact between France and the Viet Minh, as distinct from their participation in the multilateral Geneva conference, was between military commanders in the field early in July 1954 for the purpose of exchanging prisoners.[80] And during the Korean War, a six-month recess in the armistice talks ended when an exchange of sick and wounded prisoners in April 1953 ("Operation Little Switch") offered an opportunity for the two sides to renew contacts.[81]

Action by a nonbelligerent provides an even better opportunity. A suitable proposal by a third party eliminates the need for either belligerent to move first in offering negotiations. Both sides' indications of readiness to make peace become responses to someone else's proposal, and thus are less readily interpreted as signs of weakness. Czar Alexander's offer of mediation was instrumental in getting negotiations started to settle the War of 1812, even though the eventual peace conference was unmediated. It was in response to the czar's offer that the United States, the party that was then more desirous of talks, first sent a peace commission across the Atlantic. Moreover, a third party need not be genuinely neutral in order to feel more free to act than the belligerents. During the Korean War it was the Soviets, whose own complicity in the war was fairly clear despite their professions of neutrality, who led the Communist diplomatic efforts in the autumn in 1950 and again in June 1951. This partly reflected their access to the United Nations, but it also was because, as a nonbelligerent, it was not the Soviets' strength or weakness, but that of the Chinese and North Koreans, that was most important.

An effort by a third party to arrange peace negotiations forces belligerents to indicate whether or not they are ready to talk. Demonstrating peaceful intentions and avoiding the blame for continued hostilities may be reason enough for a government to respond positively to such an effort, even if it prefers to delay negotiations or does not believe that the effort will produce any results. Britain's offer to negotiate directly with the United States in November 1813 was an indirect result of the earlier Russian offer of mediation. The British opposed Russian involvement for the same reason that the Americans welcomed it: Russia seemed likely to support the U.S.

[80] Buttinger, p. 837; and Edgar O' Ballance, *The Indo-China War, 1945–1954,* pp. 245–246.

[81] Clark, pp. 240–247; and Rees, pp. 406–407.

position on the disputed maritime issues.[82] Besides, with the European struggle still in the balance, Britain was not yet ready to negotiate with the United States in the spring of 1813. Even in the autumn, London would have preferred to wait somewhat longer, as indicated by British foot-dragging tactics that delayed the start of the peace conference in Ghent until the following August. But the czar's offer, the dispatch of the American peace commission, and the importance of preserving the anti-Napoleonic coalition forced Castlereagh's hand and led him to propose direct talks as an alternative to a mediated settlement. His action was designed as much to placate Alexander as to accomplish anything else. The responses of the United States to third party efforts to open a channel to Hanoi during the Vietnam War, although they did not bear fruit as long as the North Vietnamese were unwilling to talk, reflected similar thinking. The United States was careful to cooperate with these efforts even when it was pessimistic about the outcome or less than satisfied with the middleman, because to do otherwise would suggest that it did not want to make peace. This was true of the responses both to Lewandowski's efforts during Marigold and to a Canadian proposal in early 1966 to dispatch Chester Ronning, a retired diplomat known to be critical of American policy, on a peacemaking mission.[83]

Overcoming Distrust and Exaggerated Perceptions of Hostility

Even an initiative by a third party does not lower another of the barriers to the opening of negotiations: the lack of confidence in the other side's willingness to make peace, fueled by the internally oriented rhetoric of war. Probably the most direct method of overcoming this distrust would be a face-to-face meeting between the top leaders of the two sides. This almost never happens during war, but the episode from the major cases that comes closest to it shows how important it is to remove distrust. This episode occurred in 1960 during the Algerian War, when a regional FLN commander named Si Salah, discouraged by the desperate conditon of his men, indirectly informed the French of his interest in making a separate peace. He was responding to an offer that de Gaulle had made in October 1958 of a "peace of the brave," which was essentially an invitation to the rebel soldiers to surrender honorably and a promise

---

[82] Frank A. Updyke, *The Diplomacy of the War of 1812,* p. 155.
[83] *U.S.-Vietnam Relations,* Vol. VI.C.1, p. 149; and Vol. VI.C.2, p. 17.

to conduct subsequent negotiations with the political arm of the FLN. Salah's initiative ultimately failed when some of his own subordinates betrayed him, but before that happened he had met secretly with French officials several times, the most important meeting being one which he and two of his associates had with de Gaulle himself in June. De Gaulle granted the interview not to transact any real business but rather to show his sincerity in offering an honorable peace. In doing so, he assumed a risk to his personal safety; the private meeting between the President, accompanied by two of his senior aides, and the three rebel chiefs was an opportunity for the FLN to carry out what would have been the most spectacular terrorist act of all. The rebels were not subjected to a body search because to do so would have destroyed the climate of confidence that the meeting was designed to create.[84]

Heads of warring governments do not hold summit meetings as a way of removing distrust because such a meeting presumes that the barriers to opening a negotiation have already been overcome. Moreover, the actions best able to cope with the problem of being the first to offer talks are not those that best demonstrate a sincere desire to make peace. Official, high-level contacts can most quickly dispel mistrust, but low-level or unofficial contacts are less likely to be seen as a sign of weakness. The ideal agent to be entrusted with a peace initiative is one who offers the advantages but minimizes the dangers of each approach. Such a person would be known to convey his own government's views and intentions accurately, but his activity could not be interpreted as a "suing for peace." An agent would fit this description if he had access to his government's leaders but currently occupied no official position himself, thus making his actions disavowable.

This is exactly the type of agent frequently used to discover if the enemy is ready to negotiate. The United States and the Soviet Union were able to confirm each other's desire for an armistice in Korea in early June 1951 through a pair of private meetings between George Kennan and Jacob Malik, arranged by Kennan at the request of Secretary Acheson. The Soviets could be assured that Kennan had access to the top decision-makers in Washington, but since he was then on leave from the State Department, he was not an official

---

[84] One of de Gaulle's aides, Bernard Tricot, denies that either he or the other aide was armed, although a security man with a submachine gun was standing behind a curtain in the Presidential office. Bernard Tricot, *Les Sentiers de la Paix*, p. 175. Other accounts of this affair are in: Courrière, pp. 79–110; and Tripier, pp. 438–456.

representative who could commit the United States. The purpose of
the meetings was not to negotiate, but to permit each side to understand the other's intentions and thereby discover if a basis for negotiations existed.[85] After deciding in December 1960 to negotiate a
political settlement with the FLN, President de Gaulle used Georges
Pompidou as his secret agent for the same kind of preliminary contact. Like Kennan, Pompidou was known to have direct access to
the top leadership in his country, in this case through his personal
association with de Gaulle. And also like Kennan, he was not then in
government and therefore would be a wholly unofficial representative. In February, Pompidou took a "winter sports vacation" in
Switzerland, where he conferred with FLN representatives in meetings that succeeded in sufficiently convincing each side of the sincerity of the other for formal negotiations to begin at Evian in April.[86] In
the unsuccessful secret contacts during the pre-negotiation phase of
the Vietnam War, the United States used the services of this kind of
agent several times. To follow up on Mai Van Bo's peace feeler after
the May 1965 bombing pause, the U.S. dispatched Edmund Gullion,
a former high-ranking Foreign Service Officer who was then a private citizen, to confer with Bo.[87] And in the indirect contacts with
Bo two years later, the American agent was Henry Kissinger, a
private citizen whose consulting work had given him access to the
leadership in Washington.

Overcoming Problems of Conditions

The imposition of conditions to negotiations can itself be one
means of overcoming barriers to the opening of talks, particularly
the reluctance to move first for fear of showing weakness. By
coupling an indication of readiness to negotiate with a demand that
the other side make a substantive concession, as Secretary Monroe
did in 1812 when he told the British that the United States was
willing to negotiate once Britain ceased impressment, a government
can broach the subject of peace talks without making it appear that it
is acknowledging defeat. But we saw earlier that conditions produce
barriers themselves. Some of these barriers, such as distrust and the
lowering of a government's credibility, can be handled through the
techniques already described. Other methods are required, how-

---

[85] Acheson, pp. 532–533; and Kennan, p. 36.

[86] Merry Bromberger, *Le Destin Secret de Georges Pompidou*, pp. 182–184.

[87] *U.S.-Vietnam Relations,* Vol. VI.C.1, p. 70.

ever, to cope with situations in which the two sides have committed themselves to incompatible positions regarding the conditions under which they will negotiate. Two such methods are available.

One is to initiate negotiations with an ostensibly limited agenda. By agreeing in April 1968 to discuss with the United States "the unconditional cessation of bombing and all other acts of war against the DRV so that talks could begin," Hanoi began formal meetings with the United States without explicitly backing down from its commitment not to negotiate a settlement prior to a total bombing halt. The bilateral meetings were officially only talks about talks.

The other device is to reach an agreement that is subtle or ambiguous enough for neither side to have to admit that it backed down. When the UNC broke off the Korean truce talks in October 1952, it announced it would return to Panmunjom only if the Communists accepted one of its proposals for handling unrepatriated prisoners. In other words, the UNC attached substantive conditions to the reopening of negotiations. When the talks did reopen six months later, following Operation Little Switch, it was through an exchange of messages that enabled the UNC to consider its condition to have been met without requiring the Communists to admit that it had. In agreeing to Little Switch, the Communist command proposed a reopening of the armistice negotiations, but without mentioning the issue of the repatriation of prisoners. In his reply accepting the proposal, the UNC commander, General Clark, stated that he took as "implicit" in the proposal that the Communists were prepared to accept one of the UNC plans on the handling of the prisoners or to make some comparable proposal of their own.[88] The same kind of unilateral understanding served to overcome the barrier to the opening of the four-sided peace talks on Vietnam in 1968 created by Hanoi's insistence on an "unconditional" bombing halt and by Washington's desire for assurances of military reciprocity before it did halt the bombing. After President Johnson announced a bombing halt on 31 October, Secretary of State Rusk asserted that the action was taken upon "specific expectations" that it would bring about a de-escalation of fighting on the ground. The United States, he said, was acting on "more than an assumption."[89] Yet, there is no indication that the DRV offered anything more in the way of assurances than some very vague hints to the American delegates in Paris that if the bombing did halt, certain "circumstances" would follow. There

[88] Clark, p. 243.
[89] *New York Times*, 2 November 1968, p. 1.

was no explicit promise of reciprocity. Instead, the United States had made a unilateral declaration—tacitly accepted by the North Vietnamese—that the bombing halt could not continue if the Communists carried out large-scale violations of the demilitarized zone or attacks on South Vietnamese cities.[90]

Unilateral understandings, unilaterally determined agenda, ambiguous agreements, and the like naturally have high potential for generating misunderstandings and frictions in the subsequent negotiations. But the more important point is that these devices, troublesome though they may be, do work: they make possible the opening of negotiations which do not promptly break down. In fact, it is rare for talks to break down due to disagreements over conditions even when the parties do not become aware of their disagreement until after negotiations are underway. In short, if both sides are willing to negotiate, then peace negotiations, once open, usually acquire sufficient momentum to survive many of the hazards that are capable of preventing them from opening in the first place. Disagreements over conditions that previously appeared as formidable obstacles tend to be shoved aside.

The peace conference at Ghent, the opening of which was marked by a disagreement over the agenda, is illustrative. Among the topics that the British commissioners, at the first session, said they wished to discuss were the making of peace with Britain's Indian allies and whether the privilege of drying fish on British shores in the North Atlantic (which the peace treaty of 1783 had granted to Americans) was to be renewed. Surprised to hear these subjects raised, the U.S. commissioners asserted they were not open for discussion because Castlereagh had not mentioned them in the letter proposing negotiations and neither one was germane to the issues which had caused the war.[91] But the Americans' protests could not prevent the British from discussing them; if one side says that a matter is in dispute, it is in dispute. Britain made the inclusion of the Indians in the peace a *sine qua non* for continued negotiations. This meant that until the Americans accepted a draft article on the Indians—which they did not do until mid-October, halfway through the conference—the negotiations had the same status as the two-sided Vietnam negotia-

[90] Robert Shaplen, *The Road from War: Vietnam 1965–1971*, pp. 236–242; Marvin Kalb and Elie Abel, *Roots of Involvement*, pp. 260–269; and Kahin and Lewis, pp. 384–388.

[91] American commissioners to Monroe, 12 August 1814, *American State Papers*, pp. 705–708.

tions in 1968: they were talks about talks, in which substantive exchanges on all topics but one were supposedly out of order. But the Americans felt just as free to discuss the maritime grievances and other issues which most concerned them as the British did in introducing the Indian and fisheries topics. The conference continued without interruption until a treaty was signed, even though disagreements over conditions—conditions concerning the subjects to be included in the peace agreement and the order in which they were to be resolved—were never directly removed.

Like the conference at Ghent, the Korean truce negotiations began with the parties suddenly discovering that they were in disagreement over a substantive condition. In discussing the agenda, the Communists proposed as the first item "the establishment of the 38th Parallel as the military demarcation line."[92] This was consistent with Malik's proposal in his radio address, but it contradicted the UNC's contention that the location of the demarcation line had not been agreed upon as a condition for holding the conference but rather was a substantive issue yet to be negotiated. (The line of contact, which was eventually agreed upon as the demarcation line, was by then north of the 38th Parallel in most places.) The Communists probably thought that Washington had played a trick, and were as surprised to learn that the Americans would not accept the 38th Parallel as the latter were irritated to hear the Communists injecting substantive matters into a discussion of the agenda.[93] But neither side broke off the talks because of the disagreement. Nor did the UNC break off the talks when they resumed following Little Switch, even though the Communist proposal on the prisoner issue fell well short of what the UNC had demanded.

Like the talks about talks at Ghent, the two-sided Vietnam negotiations starting in May 1968 were not limited to the one topic to which the agenda supposedly was restricted, in this case the bombing of North Vietnam. In fact, the Communist delegates themselves spoke on other substantive matters from the very beginning.[94] The United States neither resumed the bombing of the north nor broke off the talks when the Communists evidently violated the October "understanding" with a major offensive in February 1969 that included the shelling of cities and heavy action below the demilitarized

[92] William H. Vatcher, Jr., *Panmunjom*, p. 33.
[93] The American approach was actually the product of inadvertence, not trickery. See Acheson, p. 536.
[94] *New York Times,* 14 May 1968, pp. 18–19.

zone. Nor did the Communists respond when President Nixon later attempted to expand the "understanding" into a prohibition against any increase in the level of fighting in South Vietnam.[95] The fits and starts of the Vietnam negotiations, both public and private, reflected the contentious substantive issues in the negotiations, not any lingering results of disagreement over the conditions under which the negotiations opened.

Just because disagreements over conditions do not abort a negotiation does not mean that they pose no problems, however. The chief UNC negotiator during the first year of the Korean truce talks, Admiral C. Turner Joy, later complained about the misunderstanding concerning the demarcation line, noting the several frustrating weeks of negotiations that were required before the issue was resolved.[96] His complaint is understandable; he was the one who had to deal with the consequences at the conference table. But such unpleasantness may be a necessary price—and in retrospect, a small price—to pay for negotiations to begin at all.

A Preliminary Cease-Fire?

We saw in Chapter 1 why political settlements once were commonly separated from armistices but now rarely are. Beneath this overall pattern, however, the two parties to any one conflict frequently disagree over whether there ought to be a preliminary cease-fire. There are several possible reasons for this disagreement. One is that the side which relies more heavily on the infliction of pain and destruction, as opposed to the use of armed force to capture and retain objectives directly, is less disposed to accept an armistice during negotiations because its bargaining position is based on the continued use of violence to punish the opponent. This helps to explain why a belligerent such as the FLN, whose military capability in Algeria was almost entirely limited to the infliction of pain, opposed a preliminary cease-fire while its opponent favored one.

Each side's position on the cease-fire issue also depends, like its preference regarding the timing of negotiations, on its estimate of the outcome of continued fighting. The expectation of future success

---

[95] See especially Nixon's news conference of 10 December 1970. Text in *Weekly Compilation of Presidential Documents,* 14 December 1970, pp. 1650–1656.

[96] C. Turner Joy, *How Communists Negotiate,* p. 165.

is a reason for opposing a cease-fire, the expectation of future set-backs or stalemate a reason for accepting one. The main respect in which the decision on a cease-fire differs from that on the timing of negotiations is that the expectations which matter are shorter term: they concern the likely course of the fighting for the period that negotiations are in progress, not for an indefinite future. Military events which appear imminent are therefore especially likely to shape preferences regarding a cease-fire. Accordingly, the fear of a disaster at Dienbienphu, where a Viet Minh siege army surrounded an isolated French garrison in the spring of 1954 as the diplomats were gathering at Geneva, led some of the French side, including the field commander, General Navarre, to favor an immediate cease-fire as the first order of business at the conference so that the garrison might be saved.[97]

Like decisions on the timing of negotiations, however, decisions on a preliminary cease-fire are often not quite that simple. They share with the former two complicating elements. The first is that one side usually anticipates an event as well as the other, and the anticipation can be as important as the execution. Once the predica-ment of the garrison at Dienbienphu became clear, the damage to France's bargaining position had already been done. The actual fall of the garrison (on the day the conference on Indochina opened) was less a denouement than a conclusion which everyone had expected.

The second complication is that a decision regarding a cease-fire is really the product of two separate estimates. One is the prediction of events should combat continue; equally important is the prediction of events that would follow a cease-fire. A belligerent may oppose a preliminary armistice because the opponent could better use it to prepare for resumed hostilities. The threat of such a resumption would determine the strength of each side's bargaining position in the negotiations that take place while the armistice is in effect. This is most likely to influence the decision of the side that currently has the upper hand on the battlefield, as when the allies denied a French request for an armistice during the conference at Châtillon in 1814. They feared that a cease-fire would give Napoleon the opportunity to regroup and take the field later with a larger and better organized army.[98] In such a case, the expected drawbacks of granting the enemy a cease-fire usually only reinforce a decision based on ex-

[97] Henri Navarre, *Agonie de l'Indochine*, pp. 299–300.
[98] Henry Houssaye, *Napoleon and the Campaign of 1814*, pp. 83–84.

pected success in a continued campaign. What is less likely but nevertheless possible is that those drawbacks may outweigh the prospect of further *setbacks* in a continued campaign. In the Indochina War, it was the expectation that a standstill cease-fire would enable Viet Minh irregulars to continue their revolutionary effort through infiltration and economic and political disruption in French-held territory that caused most members of the French government to be less anxious than Navarre to obtain a cease-fire before the fall of Dienbienphu. They continued to be wary of one after Dienbienphu, despite the prospect for further defeats in the Red River delta in the summer of 1954 and perhaps even the loss of Hanoi. They believed that France had erred in not establishing guaranties against a continuation of revolutionary activity in the agreements reached with the Viet Minh after World War II, and they did not wish to repeat the mistake.[99] An additional consideration is that for the party that is suffering military defeats, the act of asking for an immediate cease-fire entails the same risk as the act of asking for negotiations: it might be interpreted as a sign of weakness, as a yielding to force. This is why even Navarre, after Dienbienphu was lost, recommended that no attempt be made to obtain a quick truce.[100]

Disagreement over the desirability of a preliminary cease-fire may also arise when, as is often the case, one party seeks to preserve the status quo and the other seeks to change it. In the Algerian, Indochina, and Vietnam Wars, it was the revolutionaries who were most consistently and firmly opposed to a cease-fire during negotiations. If combat stopped, they would still be in half of a divided homeland, in exile, or in the bush. The enemy, meanwhile, though incurring some costs of disagreement, could at least boast that when the guns stopped firing it had not surrendered what was at stake in the war.

These sources of disagreement reinforce the point made in Chapter 1 concerning the likely rarity of political settlements separated from armistices. A disagreement over a preliminary cease-fire is the opposite of a disagreement over admissible subjects for discussion; only one side needs to raise a subject for it to be part of a negotiation, but both sides must agree before combat ceases. As long as either side sees an advantage in continuing to fight, the fight will continue.

[99] Ely, *L'Indochine dans la Tourmente*, p. 104; and Philippe Devillers and Jean Lacouture, *End of a War*, pp. 101–102.

[100] Ely, *L'Indochine dans la Tourmente*, pp. 106–107.

Conclusion

Evidence from past wars indicates that the opening of armistice negotiations is generally not the result of a "loser" "suing for peace." Indeed, we saw in the major cases that belligerents more often agree to talk when military developments are relatively favorable. The opening of peace talks, rather than culminating a "win" and "loss," is instead an important point in the process of striking a bargain to end the war, as well as being a subsidiary bargaining problem in its own right. Some differences between it and the main bargaining problem were noted, but there are also many similarities. Several of the points made in this chapter—such as that diplomatic decisions do not follow military actions in simple, obvious ways— thus foreshadow what we will find in bargaining during the negotiation period.

Once face-to-face negotiations begin, there has been some narrowing of the range of conceivable outcomes of the war. But typically that range is still fairly wide, with the two sides often holding markedly divergent views of an acceptable settlement. Although military trends are generally clearer than they were earlier in the war, the belligerents will continue to press whatever military advantages they have. In addition, they will now have greater opportunities to employ diplomacy, as the conference table becomes an extension of the battlefield—the subject to which we turn next.

CHAPTER THREE

The Dynamics of Concession

Negotiating peace while fighting a war entails the use of two different instruments—diplomatic and military—to pursue the same set of objectives. How a belligerent uses each of these instruments depends on how he uses the other, and also on how the enemy uses both of his. This chapter analyzes one aspect of this set of interactions: the effect of each side's diplomatic behavior on that of the other. The premise is that bargaining behavior at a peace conference is to a significant degree internally determined. That is, each party's offers are influenced in part by its own previous offers and those of its opponent. This does not imply that the internal dynamics of a peace negotiation are more important than external influences—only that they deserve attention as well.

The objective is thus to describe and explain any regularities in bargaining behavior which can be discerned while disregarding combat and other activity outside the conference room. This means focusing on those aspects of peace negotiations that most resemble other bargaining problems, including ones outside international relations in which the possibility of violence plays no part. Accordingly, the chapter draws extensively on the insights of those who have studied or theorized about other kinds of negotiations, or about negotiations in general. It puts these insights together in a manner not done elsewhere and uses the evidence from peace conferences to corroborate the resulting conclusions. The discussion is thus offered as an explanation of bargaining behavior not only in peace negotiations but also, to at least some extent, in negotiations of any kind.

The difficulties involved in generalizing about negotiating behavior emerge from the first section below, which enumerates the different ways in which bargainers may interpret each other's behavior. The next section attempts to bring some order out of the chaos, particularly by identifying the various phases of a negotiation. The subsequent three sections discuss these phases individually, with reference to the patterns of bargaining in the major cases.

The Meanings of Concessions

The fundamental diplomatic act in an international negotiation is a change in one's offer—a change in what a negotiator says he will accept as an agreement. It is, admittedly, not the only kind of diplomatic act one finds: informing, probing, warning, and threatening are all diplomatic actions which also occur in negotiations. But changes in offers are particularly important because: (1) it is the incompatibility of offers that gives rise to a bargaining problem in the first place; and (2) one or both sides must change their offers if an agreement is to be reached. Furthermore, it should shortly become clear how such processes as informing and probing can be considered within the context of a discussion of offers. Accordingly, this chapter focuses on the patterns of change in each side's offer, and particularly on how one side's offer may depend on changes in that of the other. More succinctly, it focuses on *concessions*. Most changes in offers are in fact true concessions, and true concessions are required to reach any agreement. Discussing concessions is thus a convenient way of discussing the patterns of offers in a negotiation, while recognizing that at any given time a negotiator might leave his offer unchanged (zero concession) or make a retraction (negative concession).

The central issue of this chapter may therefore be rephrased as: How does each side in a peace negotiation respond to concessions of the other? This depends on the further question of how each side interprets the concessions of the other. There is no single and obvious answer, for there are several possible interpretations of a concession, most of which are not mutually exclusive and several of which have provided bases for theories of bargaining. Evidence of each of these interpretations, furthermore, can be found in actual negotiations. What follows are seven possible interpretations of a concession which one negotiator (A) makes to his opponent (B), with the implications of each for B's (and A's) subsequent behavior.

1. A Cause of Change in B's Incentives

Among the influences on B's bargaining behavior at any moment are the relative utilities to him of his own last offer and that of his opponent. The greater the difference between the two, the larger is his stake in the negotiation, and the greater is his incentive to accept risks or costs in order to obtain an agreement closer to his offer than to A's. Conversely, the smaller the difference, the less is the risk or cost he is willing to accept in order to get his way. A concession by A raises the value of A's offer to B, thus diminishing the difference in value between the two offers and with it B's acceptable risk or cost. The implication is that any concession by A, because it changes B's incentives in this way, makes it more likely that B himself will concede. Concessions, according to this reasoning, tend to be reciprocated.

This reasoning underlies Frederik Zeuthen's abstract model of bargaining, the oldest such model and one that has since spawned variants. Zeuthen offered his work chiefly as an explanation of the bargaining between buyer and seller in bilateral monopoly, especially a contract negotiation between a company and a labor union. But like several other economic theorists who have addressed the subject, he claimed that his work was also applicable to other bargaining situations. In fact, he specifically mentioned international conflict, with war being the outcome of no agreement, as one such situation.[1] According to Zeuthen's reasoning, B determines his offer by weighing the expected benefits of holding out for his own preferred agreement against the risk that, in doing so, no agreement will be reached. If U_{xy} is the utility to X of Y's offer (with the utility of no agreement arbitrarily denoted as zero), and C_x is X's estimate of the probability that the negotiation will break down if he adheres to his own offer, then the expected benefit to B of holding out for his offer, rather than accepting A's, is $(1 - C_b)(U_{bb} - U_{ba})$. I.e., it is equal to the increase in utility that his own offer represents over that of his opponent, multiplied by the probability that the negotiation will not break down if he holds out for it. By holding out, he runs the risk of losing even the utility of A's offer should no agreement be reached. So he weighs the expected benefit against the expected cost, $C_b U_{ba}$. The greatest risk of a breakdown that it is advantageous

[1] F. Zeuthen, *Problems of Monopoly and Economic Warfare*, pp. 144–145. In discussing this and other economic models, the author's original terminology of "buyer," "seller," "company," "union," and the like is dropped in favor of one that is consistent with the present discussion, and notation is suitably modified.

for him to accept is one in which this expected cost equals the expected benefit—i.e., when

$$(1 - C_b)(U_{bb} - U_{ba}) = C_b U_{ba}.$$

Solving this equation for C_b yields

$$C_b = \frac{(U_{bb} - U_{ba})}{U_{bb}} \tag{1}$$

which indicates B's "critical risk" for any pair of offers.[2] This can be taken as a measure of B's inclination not to yield, which depends on the difference in the two offers relative to the value to B of obtaining any agreement at all. Any concession by A raises U_{ba}, thus lowering C_b and making it more likely than before that B himself will concede.

Applied to a labor-management negotiation, "no agreement" means a strike or lockout. Applied to a peacetime international negotiation, it could mean, in line with Zeuthen's own suggestion, the outbreak of a war. In a wartime negotiation it could mean the breakdown of a conference and a continuation of combat for some indefinite period. An alternative formulation, suggested by Robert Bishop, is to consider C not as the probability that a one-shot calamity will occur, but rather as the maximum time during which a bargainer is willing to endure warfare or some other continuing disagreement cost, suitably adjusted to reflect his discounting of future outcomes.[3] Bishop's version would be a more meaningful interpretation of the wartime bargaining problem; as the discussion in the previous two chapters indicated, the choice is usually between a peace agreement now and a peace agreement later, not between an agreement and an interminable war. Nevertheless, the logic being used here will henceforth be referred to as "Zeuthenian," simply because Zeuthen was the first to use this interpretation of concessions as the basis for a bargaining model.[4] In any event, in either Zeuthen's or Bishop's version, Equation (1) implies that a conces-

[2] *Ibid.*, pp. 104–114.

[3] Robert L. Bishop, "A Zeuthen-Hicks Theory of Bargaining." A similar approach is in Lucien Foldes, "A Determinate Model of Bilateral Monopoly." The dependence of bargaining behavior on the time which each side is willing to incur a continuing disagreement cost was first suggested in J. R. Hicks, *The Theory of Wages*, pp. 140–147.

[4] The meaning of "no agreement" is a central issue in formal bargaining theory. For a recent discussion of what different interpretations of "no agreement" imply for the validity of various models, see R. Harrison Wagner, "On the Unification of Two-Person Bargaining Theory," especially p. 84.

sion by A will soften B's negotiating position, with B becoming less tolerant of costs as the difference in utility between the two offers diminishes.

2. A Cause of Change in A's Incentives

Zeuthen moves from the reasoning given above to a description of the dynamics of a negotiation by postulating that the bargainer with the smaller critical risk always makes the next concession. He will concede enough, but only enough, to reverse the inequality of critical risks, thus inducing a concession from the opponent while giving up as little as possible. Concessions are reciprocated as the two bargainers take turns manipulating critical risks.[5]

One question which may be raised about this model is why the next concession should always come from the bargainer with the smaller critical risk. Some economic theorists who have accepted Zeuthen's other premises have rejected this one, contending that there is no necessary reason that probabilities which are derived mechanically from the utilities of offers should determine the sequence of concessions.[6] In the absence of other asymmetries, however, it seems intuitively plausible that the bargainer who is less tolerant of risks or costs would be more likely to concede. Moreover, John Harsanyi has shown that this postulate can be formally derived from four others: symmetry, perfect knowledge, monotonicity, and expected utility maximization.[7]

But even if the dynamic assumptions are accepted, they do not necessarily lead to a pattern of reciprocated concessions. Any concession reduces the critical risk of *both* bargainers. A's concession not only raises U_{ba} but also lowers U_{aa}. This in turn—reversing the subscripts in Equation (1)—lowers C_a. Thus A's concession causes a change in his own incentives; his own concession decreases his motivation to hold out for his own offer. This implies not reciprocity, as in the first interpretation of a concession, but the opposite. Reasoning by the bargainers which corresponds to Zeuthen's static

[5] Zeuthen, pp. 115–121.

[6] See, e.g., Pen, "A General Theory of Bargaining," pp. 33–40. Pen's own model involves a weighing of risks and benefits similar to that in Zeuthen's, but makes no assumptions about who concedes before whom, and consequently is indeterminate.

[7] John C. Harsanyi, "Approaches to the Bargaining Problem Before and After the Theory of Games: A Critical Discussion of Zeuthen's, Hicks's and Nash's Theories," pp. 149–151.

assumptions therefore has two possible contradictory effects. Which one predominates depends on what outcomes are available and how the parties value them. Later in this chapter, some conditions under which Zeuthenian bargaining behavior does and does not lead to reciprocated concessions will be described.

3. An Indicator of A's Incentives

A's concessions may be viewed not only as a cause of change in his incentives, but also as an effect. Each of A's decisions to concede or not to concede is the product of a calculation involving his toleration of disagreement, the value to him of each offer, and his estimate of B's determination—in short, all the elements of his bargaining position. As such, B can use A's behavior as an indicator of those elements—as evidence of aspects of A's thinking that might otherwise be obscure. B can then use this evidence to predict A's subsequent moves and to reach decisions about his own.

Precisely how A's concession, if used in this way by B, will affect B's behavior depends on how it compares with B's earlier estimates of what A would do. A might concede more quickly than expected, or more slowly. The concessions might be larger than anticipated, or they might be smaller. Considered in isolation, however—i.e., as a single change in A's offer, and not as part of an overall pattern of bargaining behavior—A's concession would make his position appear weaker than before. The effect, if any, on B's negotiating position would be to toughen it, not soften it. The concession would be a sign of weakness, or at least of weakening, and would not induce reciprocation.

4. A Basis for Projection of A's Future Bargaining Behavior

A fourth way to view A's concession is as a part of a pattern of offers from which A's future bargaining behavior may be extrapolated. This resembles the preceding interpretation insofar as it uses A's past and present actions to predict his future ones. It differs from it in that no conclusions are drawn about the underlying incentives. Rather than inferring causes from effects and using these to predict other effects, it is a simple matter of extending a trend. The two interpretations are distinct, even though in practice it would often be difficult to determine when one of these interpretations was being made rather than the other.

The use of the opponent's past concessions to project his future ones is the basis of John Cross's theory of bargaining. Cross assumes that each bargainer initially predicts the opponent's future concession rate. The bargainer then makes his own offer, with the intention of standing pat and waiting for the opponent to concede, at the expected rate, all the way to his position. He selects his offer by weighing the value of possible agreements against the costs of disagreement, each suitably adjusted to reflect his discount rate. A more extreme demand makes the eventual agreement more favorable, but it also means a longer delay before agreement is reached and thus greater total disagreement costs. The opponent's expected concession rate (not his initial offer) affects the bargainer's choice of a demand because he must consider the marginal costs and benefits of adjusting that demand upward or downward. The faster he expects his opponent to concede, the more extreme he makes his demand, because each unit of waiting time means a greater improvement in the value of the eventual agreement without increasing the rate at which he incurs disagreement costs. A bargainer changes his offer if the opponent concedes at a rate different from what was expected. If A concedes more slowly than B expected, B revises his estimate of A's future concession rate downward and consequently softens his own demand—i.e., he concedes. Conversely, if A concedes faster than expected, B makes his demand more extreme.[8]

As with the third interpretation, whether B reciprocates A's concession depends on how that concession conforms with his previous expectation. Although a concession can cause B to harden his position, a niggardly concession at a time when a large one was expected could have the opposite effect. A further complication is that B may not expect the pattern of A's concessions to be linear, as Cross assumes. He might instead anticipate an irregular sequence, such as a lengthy period without movement followed by rapid or large concessions.[9] Henry Kissinger once revealed, during the first year of

---

[8] John G. Cross, *The Economics of Bargaining,* Chaps. 3 and 4. Cross describes mathematically the relationship between one side's concession rate and the other side's demand on pp. 49–50. He assumes that a bargainer does not immediately change his prediction of the opponent's future concession rate to conform to the observed rate. Instead, he only partially alters his previous prediction; how much he alters it depends on how fast a learner he is.

[9] Alan Coddington, "A Theory of the Bargaining Process: Comment." Cross has since addressed such complications himself. See both his reply following Coddington's comment and his "Negotiation as a Learning Process."

the Nixon administration, that he anticipated North Vietnamese bargaining behavior would be something like that:

> The Vietnamese negotiate, or Hanoi negotiates, by adopting a posture of implacable ferocity. . . . If you look at the negotiations that have taken place with the Vietnamese over the years, you will see that every negotiation that succeeded has been preceded by a protracted stalemate that looked almost hopeless. . . . I am saying that the fact that there is a deadlock does not prove that they are not going to settle. . . .[10]

A bargainer who holds this kind of expectation but who otherwise behaves and reasons in a Crossian manner would leave his demand unchanged, at least for a time, despite his opponent's lack of movement. If he had assumed constant concessions, on the other hand, he would concede himself. But if we set aside these more specific questions of the kind of concession pattern that is expected, Crossian bargaining in general implies nonreciprocity, in the sense that more conciliatory behavior by one side induces less conciliatory behavior by the other. Softness begets toughness, and vice versa.

5. Conditionable Behavior

B values concessions by A; they bring the parties closer to the sort of agreement B desires. Therefore, he may respond to A's concession in a way that encourages more concessions. That is, he may attempt to reinforce A's conciliatory behavior by rewarding A with something he wants, just as the experimental psychologist conditions the behavior of a rat in a Skinner box by rewarding the proper responses with pellets of food. Attempts to condition another state's behavior are common in international relations, even in the absence of formal negotiations. Aid and trade, for example, frequently are used in this way. The interpretation of a concession as conditionable behavior implies reciprocity; the most direct way for B to reward A for his concession is to make a concession himself. At the very least, it discourages any obvious toughening of B's position. (Rewards may be bestowed in other ways, however, such as through de-escalation on the battlefield.)

---

[10] Quoted from a pirated transcript of a background briefing in David Landau, *Kissinger: The Uses of Power*, pp. 219–220.

6. A Signal

A concession can be used as a device for communication. Like a contract bridge player who uses a convention to convey information apart from the level and suit of his bid, a negotiator may concede in order to send a message or signal that goes beyond the substance of the concession. This can be useful in a peace negotiation because the problems, described in the previous chapter, that impose barriers to the opening of negotiations may persist to some degree after negotiations begin. Militant rhetoric continues, and the parties may still doubt each other's sincerity and willingness to make peace. Despite the existence of face-to-face negotiations, mistrust can impose barriers to communication as formidable as those between bridge players who are barred from table talk.

The most common message carried by concessions in a peace negotiation is "I am willing to reach an agreement with you." The concession becomes what is known as a good-will gesture. It differs from a convention in bridge not only because the signal is conveyed between participants who have partially conflicting interests, but also because the sender must make a sacrifice. Whatever else it may mean, his action is still a concession: he gives up something of substance. This is why it may be effective where words alone are not. Whether B, interpreting a concession by A as such a signal, will reciprocate depends on whether he shares A's belief that mistrust alone is preventing two willing parties from reaching a mutually beneficial agreement. If he does, he will reciprocate the concession. To do otherwise would be to signal his own unwillingness to settle.

7. An Act Which Obligates B to Concede

Possibly because several of the other interpretations of concessions imply reciprocity, or possibly because of more general considerations of fairness or mutuality, a norm has developed stipulating that it is right or just to reciprocate concessions. In his treatise on international negotiation, Iklé lists the reciprocation of concessions as a rule of accommodation, right alongside the rules against killing negotiators or telling flagrant lies.[11] The norm provides a reason to return concessions, or to appeal to another to do so, that is independent of the other interpretations. A concession, in this view, is an

[11] Iklé, *How Nations Negotiate,* Chap. 7.

act which engages the norm and obliges the opponent to concede in turn.

The effect of a concession depends not only on which of these interpretations is made, but also on the perceived importance or magnitude of the concession. The substance of the concession obviously goes a long way to determine this. But other circumstances contribute an aura of importance to particular issues, and hence to concessions on those issues, regardless of the actual substance. Lengthy discussion or wide publicity has such an effect. Japan's chief negotiator at the Portsmouth conference in 1905 saw this as having happened to two issues—the payment of an indemnity by Russia and the possession of Sakhalin—which Japan had originally viewed as secondary. In the closing week of the conference, when these issues were still outstanding, he advised his government that "since these two points have attracted the attention of the entire world since the beginning of the conference, and since in the last several sessions we have discussed them exclusively, it would greatly affect the honor of our Imperial nation if we should decide to withdraw them now."[12] It was precisely to avoid digging themselves into this kind of hole that the decision-makers in Washington during the Korean War directed General Ridgway not to stick too long to a UNC demand that the armistice line run north of the line of contact, thus placing the historically important city of Kaesong in the southern zone. Since it was probable that the Communists would stoutly resist the loss of Kaesong and that the UNC would eventually have to settle for the line of contact, it was feared that holding out for the more northerly line would only make their concession, once it came, seem that much more important.[13]

Patterns of bargaining behavior are further complicated by the fact that both bargainers are free to make their own interpretations of concessions. How A views his own possible concessions—or more precisely, how he expects B would view them—can influence the course of the negotiation as much as how B actually does interpret A's concessions, as the examples in the preceding paragraph illustrate. The fear that the opponent will employ the third interpretation and view one's own concessions as signs of weakness is especially

[12] Quoted in Okamoto, *The Japanese Oligarchy and the Russo-Japanese War*, p. 151.

[13] Walter G. Hermes, *Truce Tent and Fighting Front*, pp. 116–117.

likely to shape negotiating decisions. This fear can impede concessions, just as the similar fear concerning proposals for a peace conference can impede the opening of negotiations. Each bargainer's capacity to reflect on how the opponent is viewing his own concessions adds an extra dimension to his interpretations: A may interpret B's behavior as evidence of B's interpretations of his own behavior.[14] Accordingly, a tough bargaining stance by the opponent may be taken as evidence that the opponent has interpreted one's earlier concessions as signs of weakness. This was how the United States government interpreted Mexico's hard line during the early peace negotiations in the Mexican-American War. The Mexicans, thought Secretary of State Buchanan, "must attribute our liberality to fear," which was his government's reason for recalling the American negotiator and toughening its position.[15]

Patterns of Reciprocation

Given the different ways of looking at concessions and at bargaining behavior generally, one can, depending on which interpretations one selects, come to expect almost anything in a negotiation. It is only by adopting one, or at most a very few, of the alternative perspectives, as the economic theorists have done, that it is possible to arrive at more specific expectations.[16] So which perspective is correct? No single one is, in the sense of providing an exclusive truth. Governments and other bargainers interpret their own diplomatic behavior and that of their opponents in a variety of ways. Each perspective provides an insight that helps in understanding bargaining behavior, especially a bargaining situation as complex as a peace negotiation.

To use these insights without hopelessly complicating the analysis, the remainder of this chapter employs two devices.

One is to view bargaining behavior along a single overall dimension of toughness versus softness, and to inquire whether one party's behavior tends to be associated with similar or with opposite

[14] Cf. Jeffrey Z. Rubin and Bert R. Brown, *The Social Psychology of Bargaining and Negotiation*, pp. 276–278.

[15] Buchanan to Trist, 6 October 1847, quoted in George R. Rives, *The United States and Mexico, 1821–1848*, Vol. 2, p. 522.

[16] The resulting model, like Pen's, may still be indeterminate. See footnote 6 above.

behavior by the other. That was the purpose of pointing out the implications of each interpretation with regard to the reciprocation of concessions. The first, fifth, sixth, and seventh interpretations of a concession generally imply reciprocation, meaning that toughness induces toughness and softness induces softness. The second, third, and fourth interpretations generally imply the opposite.[17] From this perspective, the key question may again be rephrased to read: Do concessions tend to be reciprocated, or not?

The other device is a decomposition of peace negotiations into component phases, and a separate examination of the principles and perspectives which apply to each. This tool makes the analysis not only more tractable but also more valid, for there are several reasons to expect the pattern of bargaining to change during the course of a negotiation. The parties gain information and experience as they proceed, and perhaps alter their strategies as a result. And the settlement of some issues, bringing an agreement closer, may cause the parties to act differently in later stages of a negotiation from the way they behaved earlier. In fact, concession-making in laboratory bargaining experiments does tend to differ across phases of a negotiation; how subjects behave in the later phases is not readily predictable from their earlier actions.[18]

Several observers of negotiations outside the laboratory have also noted how bargaining behavior tends to change over time.[19] For example, Ann Douglas has described labor-management contract negotiations as passing through three phases: the first, "Establishing the Negotiating Range," an opening exchange of salvos during which the parties discover the outer limits of the territory within which they will contend; the second, "Reconnoitering the Range," generally a lengthy trial of strength; and the third, "Precipitating the Decision-Making Crisis," in which the bargainers must make their

[17] These two clusters of outlooks correspond to Sir Harold Nicolson's dichotomy of diplomacy into "warrior" and "mercantile" schools. The second stresses reciprocation of concessions, while the first does not. Nicolson describes the two schools as the mentalities of two castes—the soldiers and the shopkeepers—but it is perhaps equally valid to view them as the products of two bundles of perspectives which are each applicable to a variety of human endeavors. Harold Nicolson, *Diplomacy*, pp. 24–27.

[18] Daniel Druckman, Kathleen Zechmeister, and Daniel Solomon, "Determinants of Bargaining Behavior in a Bilateral Monopoly Situation: Opponent's Concession Rate and Relative Defensibility," p. 522.

[19] For a partial review, see Pruitt, *Negotiation Behavior*, pp. 13–14 and 131–135.

final decisions on whether to hold or to yield on specific points as the agreement is written.[20]

The discussion in the next three sections is based on a similar division into three phases. Each section describes the chief characteristics of a particular phase, links these characteristics to the possible interpretations of concessions and through them to the issue of reciprocation, and adduces the relevant evidence from the major cases. This procedure does not imply that every negotiation is equally susceptible to such decomposition. Nor does it imply that the two bargainers always agree on what stage the negotiation has reached. (What happens when they disagree will be noted in the course of the discussion.) But, for the most part, the transitions from one phase to another are distinct enough, and the similarities between cases great enough, for the scheme to be useful in analyzing the dynamics of concession.

Phase One

In the opening phase of a peace conference, unlike the later phases, the parties lack extensive previous contact with the opponent and thus lack full knowledge of his intentions and of the major conflicts of interest. A central feature of the first phase is therefore *uncertainty*. Neither side is apt to have articulated its position clearly and precisely prior to the start of talks, because of bureaucratic inertia, a preoccupation with the military effort, or the belief that to spell out its objectives would undermine the military effort, as suggested in the previous chapter. Even if the issues at stake had been the subject of pre-war negotiations, the war itself has probably altered each side's position. And either side may still be unsure whether the enemy is genuinely interested in reaching a settlement.

Accordingly, each party's foremost concern during this phase is to increase its knowledge while avoiding errors caused by ignorance. It is a period of probing, of exploring the disputed territory, of finding the outer limits of the opponent's tolerance. Lord Castlereagh's otherwise vague initial instructions to the British commissioners at Ghent made these purposes explicit. The commissioners' immediate task, he wrote, was to "ascertain, as far as possible, the

---

[20] Ann Douglas, *Industrial Peacemaking*, pp. 13–99. Another three-phase conceptual scheme, applied to international negotiations, is in I. William Zartman and Maureen Berman, *The Practical Negotiator*, Chapters 3–5.

views of the American Commissioners without committing your Government." He would furnish further instructions only after they had discovered these views, the powers of the U.S. negotiators, and the spirit in which the Americans were approaching the negotiations.[21]

Uncertainty is a reason for the parties to begin the negotiation with fairly extreme demands. As long as it has little knowledge of what the opposition is willing to lose and where there is room for maneuver, each side tries to maintain a position from which it can later concede only what it must concede.[22] (Usually this means simply retaining, for a while, the more extreme rhetoric that a government uses to drum up enthusiasm for the war effort.) Like two wrestlers circling before locking arms, the bargainers cautiously approach the range of possible agreements, entering it only when they believe that they know its boundaries and that the opponent is also ready to enter. They shed their extreme demands during the course of this first phase, the end of which occurs when each party arrives at a position that it considers a realistic basis for a settlement but that still incorporates its chief hopes and expectations.

The parties are unlikely to interpret concessions made during this first phase as causes of change in either their own incentives or those of the opponent. Movement that is believed to be outside the bargaining range—i.e., the range of possible agreements that both sides would prefer to no agreement at all—does not alter motivations. They do use the other side's concessions as indicators of his incentives, but only to clarify what already exists, not as evidence of change. And it is too early for the opponent's concessions to provide an adequate basis for projecting a trend into the future. Thus none of the first four possible interpretations of a concession is very important in shaping bargaining behavior during this first phase. The other possible interpretations—as a signal (of willingness to drop exaggerated demands and begin the serious pursuit of an agreement), conditionable behavior, or an act which obligates the opponent to return the favor—will more likely govern each party's responses. In general, then, we should expect reciprocation of concessions.

This conclusion, however, depends on whether both sides do in fact begin the negotiation with exaggerated positions that they intend to give up at the appropriate moment (i.e., with what are mis-

[21] Castlereagh to British commissioners, 28 July 1814. Castlereagh *Correspondence*, pp. 67–72.

[22] Cf. Harold W. Davey, *Contemporary Collective Bargaining*, pp. 132–133.

leadingly but commonly called "bargaining positions"). A bargainer who feels he has already shed such demands, or never made any in the first place, sees no need to signal his good intentions and no opportunity or obligation to reciprocate when the opponent finally drops unreasonable demands of his own.

One reason opening negotiating postures vary is that some governments must worry more than others about the effects of exaggerated demands on domestic constituencies or allies. A popularly elected government of a country in which a substantial body of opinion opposes a continuation of the war in support of more extreme demands, as was true of the United States in the Vietnam War by 1968, faces a greater risk of losing essential domestic support by taking a hard line at the opening of talks than does a regime in a country in which public opinion counts for less or happens to flow in a different direction.[23] Similarly, a government relying on the support of a fragile coalition of disparate allies, as the United States was in the Korean War, is more restrained by foreign attitudes in determining its initial position than is one that is less dependent on such an alliance.

The most important source of variation is the character of the pre-negotiation phase of the war. In some respects, the first phase of face-to-face negotiations resembles this pre-negotiation period more closely than it resembles the later stages of bargaining. The process of probing the other's intentions and winnowing the excesses out of a negotiating position often begins before formal negotiations do.[24] When it does, the opening phase of formal negotiations is a continuation, not a beginning. This is one respect in which peace negotiations tend to differ from contract bargaining between a labor union and company management. Although the union may make public some of its general goals before the negotiation begins, formal proposals are usually made only in the conference room. This is particularly true of management; the company generally does not announce any specific offers before it presents them directly to the union

---

[23] The danger of alienating domestic opinion by taking a sham bargaining position in an international negotiation is mentioned in Jack Sawyer and Harold Guetzkow, "Bargaining and Negotiation in International Relations," in Kelman, *International Behavior,* p. 482.

[24] I. William Zartman in "Negotiations: Theory and Reality," p. 74, observes that the realization of each side in an international negotiation that a bargaining range exists and that an agreement is possible may come either before or after the beginning of formal talks.

negotiators. Therefore, probing and exploration do not begin in labor-management bargaining until the first formal proposals are laid on the table. There are fewer exceptions to this rule in labor-management negotiations than in international relations, because the flow of information in the former is more restricted to formal conferences.[25]

The extent to which initial demands in a peace negotiation are exaggerated, therefore, depends on the extent to which the negotiating positions were examined and refined before the conference began. This in turn largely depends upon how long the parties have been prepared to negotiate. The chief reason proposals in labor-management bargaining are more restricted to formal negotiating channels than they are in bargaining over peace agreements is that the opening of a contract negotiation is more certain than the opening of peace talks. Labor and management know that they will sit down according to a prearranged schedule as the expiration date of the existing contract approaches; differences over when and whether to begin negotiations are not as frequent or important as they are in a war. There are no prolonged periods during which one party seeks talks and the other resists them.

When such a period occurs in a war, the belligerent that is seeking talks has an incentive to avoid communicating ambitious war aims to the other side, lest the customer be scared off. It probably uses any opportunities for peace feelers or indirect contacts to communicate a moderate, rather than an extreme, position. The longer it has sought negotiations, the longer it has been communicating and demonstrating moderation. All of this commits the bargainer to a less extreme position once negotiations open. Suddenly to make exaggerated demands at the start of the conference would be inconsistent with previous behavior and would risk scuttling the meeting that had

---

[25] The exception in labor relations that illuminates the rule is Boulwarism, an approach to contract negotiations named after Lemuel R. Boulware, who was a vice-president for labor relations with the General Electric Company during the late 1940s and 1950s. Boulwarism entails the presentation by the company of one complete and, in its view, reasonable offer which it has no intention of changing in the absence of new facts coming to light. There are no deliberately extreme demands, no padding, no "bargaining positions." What is noteworthy is that Boulware's approach—more than the usual company approach to contract negotiations—also emphasized extensive direct communication between the company and individual workers. It was this bypassing of formal bargaining channels that union leaders found most objectionable in Boulware's methods. Boulware's own description of those methods is in Lemuel R. Boulware, *The Truth About Boulwarism,* especially Chap. 13.

been sought for so long. Therefore, a peace conference which opens under these circumstances will be less likely to begin with deliberately padded demands than one that each party had only recently sought. This is particularly true of the side that was first ready to negotiate, though it may also apply to a lesser degree to the other side, since it has had an opportunity to acquaint itself with the opponent's intentions and objectives during the pre-negotiation period. The opening phase of such a negotiation therefore will have few quick concessions, or if there are such concessions, they will come mostly from one side—the side that last accepted negotiations. By contrast, a conference that each party sought only recently, and was not preceded by a lengthy period of probes, feelers, declarations, and initiatives, will begin with exaggerated demands on both sides. Since there is padding to shed, there will be more early concessions, and these concessions will tend to be reciprocated.

Pre-conference behavior accounts for the different patterns of early bargaining in the peace negotiations during, on one hand, the War of 1812, Algerian War, and Vietnam War, and, on the other hand, the Indochina and Korean Wars. In each of the first three, one belligerent had unsuccessfully sought talks for a long time, and the actual peace conference followed a lengthy period of unilateral initiatives and informal probes. In the latter two wars, negotiations resulted from more recent decisions by both sides to seek talks, with relatively little diplomatic activity during the preceding months of war.

The American willingness to negotiate with Britain from the very beginning of the War of 1812 manifested itself in a series of conciliatory moves, particularly on the issue of impressment of seamen, which led the United States to make most of its concessions before the conference at Ghent even began. In his war message to Congress in June 1812, President Madison listed impressment, harrassment of shipping near U.S. ports, illegal blockades, the Orders-in-Council, and British instigation of Indian warfare on the western frontier as the American grievances.[26] In his instructions to the U.S. chargé in London, Secretary Monroe specified that a prior cessation of the maritime abuses, not just a promise to end them, was required for an

---

[26] *American State Papers*, pp. 405–407. Although some past scholars have argued that western expansionism was the actual reason for going to war, the current consensus among historians is that the maritime grievances were in fact the chief causes. A discussion of this issue is in Harry L. Coles, *The War of 1812*, pp. 27–37.

armistice. But he also began softening the U.S. position by suggesting that in return the United States would accommodate Britain's concerns over its naval manpower by agreeing to reciprocal legislation barring the nationals of each country from serving in the other's marine.[27] A month later, he softened the instructions some more: a "clear and distinct understanding" on the maritime issues, rather than a prior cessation of abuses, was sufficient for an armistice.[28] In February 1813, Congress passed (on the recommendation of the administration) a law prohibiting the employment of British seamen in U.S. ships, thus granting unilaterally what the United States had earlier been prepared to offer only as part of a reciprocal arrangement.[29] Two months later, in instructing the American commissioners sent to St. Petersburg for the Russian mediation that never occurred, Monroe wrote that the United States would go even further by agreeing to refuse naturalization to British seamen and to prohibit maritime employment for former British subjects already naturalized. Moreover, a prohibition on impressment was acceptable even if it were limited only to the duration of the European war.[30] In supplementary instructions to U.S. negotiators for the direct talks, written in June 1814, Monroe states that the whole issue of impressment could be postponed to post-war negotiations.[31] Two days later, in his final instruction before the conference began, he wrote that reference to impressment could be omitted entirely.[32]

During these first two years of the war, while the United States was thus whittling its position down to what amounted to the *status quo ante bellum,* Britain neither sought nor prepared for negotiations. The British did not really state their terms until the negotiations at Ghent opened in August 1814. When those terms were presented, they struck the American commissioners as being so excessive that in their private communications they spoke of "when," not "if," the negotiation would break down. (Henry Clay evidently was the only one of the five U.S. negotiators who correctly perceived the initial British position to be part of a probing operation.) In fact, even the British commissioners, who were little

[27] Monroe to Russell, 26 June 1812, *American State Papers,* p. 585.
[28] Monroe to Russell, 27 July 1812, *ibid.,* p. 586.
[29] Adams, *History of the U.S.,* Vol. 6, p. 454.
[30] Monroe to U.S. commissioners, 15 April 1813, *American State Papers,* pp. 695–700.
[31] *Ibid.,* pp. 703–704.
[32] *Ibid.,* pp. 704–705.

more than mouthpieces for the Cabinet in London and whom historians have credited with little imagination, supposed that their government intended the terms to be a basis on which to break off the negotiations quickly.[33] After broaching in the opening meeting the subjects of the fisheries and making peace with the Indians, as well as the desirability of boundary revisions (which, unlike the other two subjects, the Americans said they were willing to discuss), the British made their specific demands in their first formal note on 19 August. Not only were the Indians to be included in the peace, but they were to be assigned a definite territory between the Ohio River and the Great Lakes within which neither party could purchase land. I.e., Americans would not be able to buy land in an area that, according to the peace of 1783, was part of the United States. The fisheries privilege was not to be renewed, but Britain's right to navigate the Mississippi River—which the 1783 treaty had granted as a *quid pro quo* for the fisheries—would be continued. Finally, the territorial demands included giving Britain the exclusive right to fortify the Great Lakes and all of their shores, a revision of the boundary from Lake Superior to the Mississippi, cession of territory in northern Maine, and an assertion of British ownership of disputed islands in Passamaquoddy Bay.[34] In their response, the U.S. commissioners offered an article providing that each party would treat for the Indians in its own territory and try to restrain them from acts of violence against the other party. They rejected all the other British demands and specifically offered a peace on the basis of the *status quo ante bellum,* with each party reserving its rights on other issues.[35]

The initial proposals were therefore highly asymmetrical: the party which had long sought talks (i.e., the United States) had already stripped down its position to a stark compromise, while its opponent was starting with a proposal that it could be confident did not concede anything it did not have to concede. Accordingly, the first phase of the Ghent negotiation, which lasted until the third round of notes in late September, exhibited an asymmetrical pattern of concessions. During this period, the American commission suggested some mutual pledges that might be incorporated into an article that would satisfy the British desire to consider the Indians and

[33] Perkins, *Castlereagh and Adams,* p. 70; and Fred L. Engelman, *The Peace of Christmas Eve,* p. 141.

[34] British to U.S. commissioners, 19 August 1814, *American State Papers,* p. 710.

[35] U.S. to British commissioners, 24 August 1814, *ibid.,* pp. 711–713.

also indicated its willingness to submit the Passamaquoddy Islands dispute to a commission, but otherwise conceded nothing. The British, meanwhile, dropped without reciprocation their most extreme demands, the ones for exclusive military possession of the Great Lakes and the prohibition of land purchases from the Indians.[36]

Like the conference at Ghent, the peace negotiations during the Algerian and Vietnam Wars followed long attempts by one side to get talks started. When its positions are measured against the final Algerian peace agreement, the FLN could not be said ever to have made any exaggerated demands, either before or after the start of formal negotiations. Its 1954 manifesto was a modest document, reflecting the Front's modest resources at the start of the insurrection, which outlined objectives that were to be mostly achieved at Evian. Almost all of the padding to be shed during the initial phase of negotiations was on the French side. If the beginning of the phase is taken to be the beginning of the first direct talks at Melun in June 1960, its end was the opening of the first round of negotiations at Evian the following May, which is when serious discussions of substance concerning a transfer of power in Algeria really began. Most of the probing to discover the enemy's intentions and tolerance occurred not through formal substantive negotiations but rather through Pompidou's informal discussions in Switzerland. The one major concession during this period was De Gaulle's agreement to talk about politics at all: he dropped the demand to put the knives in the cloakroom before discussing Algeria's future. As we saw in the previous chapter, his earlier stance was not part of a probing operation in the manner of the British at Ghent, but instead rested on a hope of settling the conflict without having to deal with the FLN. In any event, a cease-fire with no provision for political change was clearly unacceptable to the FLN. When De Gaulle abandoned that demand, the FLN representatives felt no obligation to reciprocate and in fact did not, except on a few procedural matters that they had raised at Melun.

The first phase of the Vietnam negotiations lasted one year, from the start of the two-sided talks in May 1968 until both sides presented their first comprehensive proposals at the expanded peace conference in May 1969. (Henry Kissinger's first secret mission to Paris came four months later.) As the side which had favored negotiations for three years, the United States entered the talks having

[36] See especially the 3rd British note, dated 19 September 1814, *ibid.*, pp. 717–718.

long since abandoned its hard line of 1964 and earlier, when it was still opposing the concept of a neutral South Vietnam.[37] By the time that talks began, the Johnson administration had already accepted a U.S. military withdrawal, the participation of all South Vietnamese political elements in elections, and reunification of Vietnam through the free decision of the Vietnamese.[38] The Nixon administration's 8-point proposal of May 1969 was in line with its predecessor's position; it was a more precise statement but not a substantive departure. Hanoi, on the other hand, began the Paris talks still adhering to its Four Points of 1965, which demanded the settlement of South Vietnam's internal affairs "in accordance with" the Viet Cong program. As late as November 1968, the Viet Cong chipped in with their equally nebulous "Five Points," which repeated the same demand, made no provision for guarantees, laid no obligations on their own side, and did nothing to dispel the fiction that North Vietnamese forces were not in the south. The Communists' 10-point proposal presented the following May therefore was a substantial departure and the first concrete evidence of their willingness to write a compromise agreement. Rather than a blanket demand for acceptance of one side's program, it was as specific as the Nixon plan, providing for such arrangements as joint or international supervision of elections. And it contained a reference to the "Vietnamese forces in South Vietnam," generally interpreted as a circuitous admission that North Vietnamese forces were in fact in the south.[39] The Communists had finally moved from the realm of fiction and slogans to the arena of serious negotiation. Like the British in 1814 and the French in 1960, they had entered a peace conference which the enemy had long sought, had therefore not yet refined their position as the enemy already had done, and consequently was the party which made concessions during the conference's opening phase while the other side stood pat.

By contrast, both parties in the Korean and Indochina Wars came to favor negotiations only a few months or even weeks before the conference opened (excluding earlier offers to talk that were later

[37] In a press conference on 1 February 1964, President Johnson had rejected the neutralization of South Vietnam unless North Vietnam were also neutralized. *New York Times*, 2 February 1964, p. 62.

[38] See the State Department's 14 Points of January 1966. Text in *Background Information*, pp. 285–286.

[39] Kahin and Lewis, *The United States in Vietnam*, pp. 394–395. Text of the 10-point proposal is in *Background Information*, pp. 628–630.

retracted). There was no prolonged period of informal diplomatic
feelers, thus no occasion for paring demands before the opening of
formal talks, and thus no loss of opportunity by either side to use
extreme demands as part of a probing strategy during the opening
phase of the conference. The Korean talks were different from those
in the other major cases in that the different agenda items were taken
up more or less sequentially, therefore making phases for the entire
conference difficult to identify.[40] At any rate, the initial positions of
both sides on several individual issues were patently padded. For
example, the Communists' initial proposal for a post-conference
Korean political conference would have excluded the Republic of
Korea. For its part, the UNC opened the debate on the line of
demarcation by proposing that it be located somewhat north of the
line of contact, the adjustment in its favor supposedly being a compensation for giving up its air and naval activity in the north. Actually, this was a "bargaining position" that the UNC fully intended to
drop even when proposing it.[41]

The Geneva conference on Indochina, which opened in May 1954,
also began with the two belligerents—each of which had only recently become willing to negotiate—presenting initial demands that
were well outside the range of outcomes acceptable to the opponent.
Each side proposed placing all the military obligations on the enemy
while assuming none itself. The positions were equally extreme with
respect to the character of the agreement and the extent to which it
would settle political issues: the French offered a strictly military
agreement while the Viet Minh demanded recognition of not only
their own independence but also that of the shadowy Communist
movements in Laos and Cambodia.[42] With both sides starting out in
these extreme positions, both sides made concessions during the
conference's opening phase, which lasted until mid-June, roughly
coinciding with the first period during which the foreign ministers of
the principal participants were present. The Communists accepted
the primacy of military arrangements, while the French agreed to

[40] That sequential consideration of issues is the exception rather than the rule says
something about the usefulness of addressing several issues simultaneously, a subject
to be explored in Chapter 6.

[41] Joy, *How Communists Negotiate*, p. 60.

[42] See the proposals presented by French Foreign Minister Georges Bidault on 8
May and Viet Minh Foreign Minister Pham Van Dong on 10 May. Texts in Ministere
des Affaires Etrangères (France), *Conférence de Genève sur l'Indochine*, pp. 395,
397–398.

discuss political provisions. And the two sides recognized that the military obligations would have to be mutual, based on some kind of regroupment of forces. The first phase of the Geneva conference was thus marked by reciprocity of concessions, unlike the corresponding portion of the negotiations which settled the Algerian and Vietnam Wars and the War of 1812.

The first phase of a peace negotiation serves to weed out bogus or unrealistic demands, to educate the parties about each other's intentions and objectives, and hence to clarify and define the outstanding issues. It is important not so much for what is settled as for pointing out what the parties have yet to settle. By the time the foreign ministers left the Indochina conference, for instance, they had a much clearer idea of what questions had to be resolved in order to conclude an agreement than they did when they had first arrived in Geneva a month earlier. Basing the cease-fire on some sort of regroupment of forces implied that the location of a demarcation line or lines, and the timing and procedures for any reunification of the zones, would have to be settled. The preliminary debates had also put into focus differences over arrangements for controlling the cease-fire—specifically, the composition of an international control group and its relationship to joint committees and to the Geneva conference itself.[43] Phase One clears the brush from the field on which, in Phase Two, the belligerents conduct a trial of strength.

Phase Two

The second phase of a peace negotiation begins with the parties' clearly perceiving the issues which divide them, having a fairly good idea of the enemy's genuine objectives, and being reasonably confident that the enemy is serious about negotiating an agreement. They believe that a bargaining range exists and hence that a negotiated peace is possible. But the possibility of a protracted conflict also continues. Under these conditions, concessions take on a substantive importance which they did not have in the opening phase. Rather than being the pre-planned shedding of an exaggerated position, a concession is now more likely to be part of a genuine recalculation of objectives. And as the war drags out and the length of the

---

[43] See Bidault's last speech to the conference on 8 June, in which he reviewed the points at issue. *Ibid.*, pp. 205–212.

negotiation remains uncertain, each side's tolerance of the continuing disagreement costs—and its estimate of the other's tolerance—becomes more important than it did in the shorter Phase One. These considerations imply that concessions will more likely be interpreted as indicators of incentives and as bases on which to project future concessions. The enemy is less likely to read a concession as a signal of intent to negotiate seriously (this was already communicated before or during Phase One) and more likely to read it as a sign of weakening. And as the negotiation becomes protracted, each side has a better basis for extrapolating the opponent's pattern of concessions into the future. The dominant pattern of bargaining during the middle portion of a peace negotiation is therefore one of nonreciprocation; a concession is more likely to be followed by another from the same side than to be matched by one from the opponent.[44]

Because this phase is usually the longest and has the least diplomatic movement, bargaining behavior during it is more susceptible to being shaped by outside events, especially military events. Nevertheless, the pattern of nonreciprocation was generally present in the major cases, apart from the Geneva conference on Indochina, which was exceptional in not having a separate second phase. It was telescoped into the third phase when Pierre Mendès-France, who became Premier and Foreign Minister of France on 17 June 1954, imposed upon himself a 30-day deadline for reaching a peace agreement. (The use of deadlines is discussed in Chapter 5.) In a couple of other instances, Phase Two bargaining was over one single issue of principle that by its very nature could not be considered incrementally, and therefore would not exhibit a reciprocation of concessions. This was true of the issue of repatriation of prisoners in Korea, the last of the items on the agenda at Panmunjom to be resolved. It was also the case during the middle phase of bargaining at Ghent, in which the issue was whether the principle governing the disposition of territory was to be the *status quo ante bellum* or *uti possidetis* (each belligerent being entitled to the territory which it occupied at the end of the war). The United States favored the former; Britain, occupying territory in eastern Maine and expecting success in invasions being launched into northern New York and Louisiana,

---

[44] Cf. this comment on labor-management negotiations: "Once the parties have reached the stage where they are able to discern the real area of difference submerged under their bargaining positions . . . the question of who moves first can sometimes be extremely important in deciding how they come out in the final settlement." Edward Peters, *Strategy and Tactics in Labor Negotiations*, p. 117.

proposed the latter. The concessions which resolved those issues—
the Communists' acceptance of voluntary repatriation in Korea and
Britain's acceptance of the *status quo ante bellum*—resulted chiefly
from events outside the conference room. But the British decision,
at least, also followed a reassessment, based on the experience at
Ghent, of the American negotiating posture. The U.S. commissioners' adamant opposition to *uti possidetis* in the exchanges of notes
throughout October surprised the ministers in London.[45] Britain's
eventual concession on the territorial question therefore exemplified
the sort of convergence of positions following a reestimate of the
opponent's concession rate that is envisioned in Cross's bargaining
model.

When the concession-making was more incremental, and hence
admitted the possibility of reciprocation, it nevertheless tended to
be nonreciprocal. During the nine months following the opening of
the first Evian talks on Algeria in May 1961 (a period which included
three rounds of formal negotiations interspersed with more informal
contacts in Switzerland), President De Gaulle made three major
concessions of principle which were unmatched by anything nearly
as significant emanating from the FLN. One was the acknowledgment that the Sahara was part of Algeria and not, as he had earlier
maintained, a separate territory that would be the subject of future
international agreements between France and all of the states bor-
dering it.[46] A second was his abandonment of the demand that the
European residents of Algeria become citizens of the new state automatically, without requiring any positive act on their part. The third
was his dropping of an insistence on extensive guarantees for these
Europeans and pledges of future cooperation with France, both of
which the FLN opposed as unacceptable infringements upon the
freedom of a future sovereign state.[47] The only diplomatic movement by the FLN during the same period was confined to such
peripheral matters as the retention of the franc as the currency of the
new state. The FLN also reversed an earlier position by accepting
the presence of French troops for a period after the referendum on

[45] Updyke, *The Diplomacy of the War of 1812,* p. 293.

[46] He announced this concession in a press conference on 5 September. Charles De
Gaulle, *Major Addresses,* pp. 144–145.

[47] Both of these concessions came during negotiations at Les Rousses in February
1962. The most complete published account of these negotiations is by one of the
French representatives, Robert Buron, in *Carnets Politiques de la Guerre d'Algérie.*
On these points, see especially pp. 223–229.

independence, but this probably reflected the rebels' own reassessment of what they would need to preserve order when they took power.

What movement there was in the Vietnam negotiations during the three years following the presentation of the opposing proposals in May 1969 came from the American side. The next formal offer to be laid on the table was an 8-point Viet Cong plan in September 1970, which embodied no real change and was aptly described by David Bruce as "old wine in new bottles."[48] President Nixon offered a new 5-point plan the following month which was not necessarily a concession but was at least movement, since it offered the option of a supervised cease-fire in place, without a previous resolution of all of the political issues.[49] The United States pursued this approach further in secret contacts the following May, when if offered to set a deadline for the withdrawal of U.S. troops from South Vietnam, without any corresponding withdrawal by the North Vietnamese, in return for a cease-fire and the release of all POWs. In June the Communists presented a private 9-point proposal, and in July a public 7-point proposal, which specified that a prisoner release could be simultaneous with a U.S. troop withdrawal, but otherwise broke no new ground. A secret U.S. offer in August set a definite deadline for withdrawal of American forces: nine months following an agreement. A further American proposal in October lowered this to six months and also offered a presidential election in South Vietnam within six months of an agreement, supervised by a body representing all political elements in the country and preceded by Thieu's resignation.[50] In May 1972, President Nixon presented a cease-fire proposal similar to that of October 1970 but setting a four-month deadline for U.S. troop withdrawal.[51] In that same month, Henry Kissinger indicated in private conversations with the Soviets that the United States was willing to cease its air attacks against North

[48] *New York Times,* 18 September 1970, p. 1. Robert Shaplen in *The Road from War,* p. 417, quotes from a captured Viet Cong document which described this proposal as part of an effort to atrophy the domestic and international support of the enemy. According to the document, it was "*not* designed to solve the problem of ending the war and bringing about peace in Vietnam." Emphasis added.

[49] *Weekly Compilation of Presidential Documents,* 15 May 1972, pp. 838–842.

[50] President Nixon revealed the secret exchanges of May through October 1971 in an address on 25 January 1972. This address, the U.S. version of its October proposal and Hanoi's subsequently broadcast versions of both side's offers, are reprinted in *Background Information,* pp. 459–461, 643–645.

[51] *Weekly Compilation of Presidential Documents,* 15 May 1972, pp. 838–842.

Vietnam even before all the POWs were returned and would also accept a tripartite electoral commission to run the elections.[52]

During these three years, therefore, the concession-making in the Vietnam negotiations was as asymmetrical as that in the corresponding phase of the Algerian peace negotiations. The Nixon administration had softened several times its position on military disengagement, electoral arrangements within South Vietnam, and the timing of these with respect to each other and a prisoner release, while receiving very little in return. The end of the second phase of the Vietnam negotiations was different, however, because the next concession—and it was major—came from the other side. In secret meetings with Kissinger at the end of September, Le Duc Tho proposed as the political basis for an agreement a National Council of Reconciliation and Concord that would operate on the basis of unanimity; it was not a coalition government and it did not require the prior dumping of Thieu.[53] This revision of the DRV's position owed less to the internal dynamics of the negotiation than to events on the battlefield, making it a good reminder of the limitations of examining the diplomatic arena alone. Those events will be discussed in a subsequent chapter; for the moment, suffice it to note that this exception to the general point concerning nonreciprocation of concessions in Phase Two occurred in the negotiation which lasted the longest (Vietnam) and in the year (1972) during that negotiation when military action was heaviest. Torpid diplomacy and intense combat increase the likelihood that events outside rather than inside the conference room will shape bargaining behavior.

In the Korean truce talks, there was one other subject, besides the repatriation of prisoners, that was the subject of prolonged bargaining: the concrete arrangements for supervising and controlling the cease-fire.[54] As in the Algerian and most of the Vietnam negotia-

[52] Tad Szulc, "How Kissinger Did It: Behind the Vietnam Cease-Fire Agreement," pp. 42–43.

[53] Kalb and Kalb, *Kissinger*, p. 349.

[54] There were five topics on the Korean agenda. In addition to the prisoner and supervision issues, they were the adoption of the agenda, the establishment of the demarcation line, and recommendations to governments concerning a post-armistice political conference. Once the UNC dropped its "bargaining position" on the demarcation line and when it became clear that the final line would be some variant of the line of contact, agreement followed three weeks of the kind of rapid bargaining characteristic of the third phase. (This will be reviewed in the next section.) The parties settled the recommendations for a political conference even more rapidly, an indication of the scant importance which either side placed on this item. The Communists had introduced it as a face-saving substitute for their earlier demand that the withdrawal of foreign forces from Korea be discussed.

tions, concession-making on this item was asymmetrical, but it also sheds light on another question—viz., what happens when the two sides hold differing perceptions of when Phase One ends and Phase Two begins. Refer back for a moment to the peace conference at Ghent. What was identified earlier as the start of Phase Two in that negotiation (about late September 1814, the time of the third round of notes) was more in line with the British perception than the American. Although the British had by then finished their probing operation, and genuinely hoped and intended to settle on the basis of *uti possidetis,* most of the American commissioners thought that the British were still toying with them.[55] This gave the Americans all the more incentive to stand firm; they did not intend to back down from their own genuine objectives when they were not even sure that the enemy was yet serious about negotiating a peace.[56] The U.S. commissioners profited from their misperceptions, which made them more resolute negotiators than they would have been had they correctly assessed the British government's thinking.[57]

Just as the belief that the opponent is still dwelling in Phase One when he has really moved to Phase Two strengthens one's bargaining posture and is likely to improve one's outcome, the opposite misperception has the correspondingly opposite result. Something like this happened in the bargaining at Panmunjom on supervision and control arrangements. The two sides presented opening proposals on this subject on 27 November 1951. The UNC plan provided for a joint supervisory organization having free access to all parts of Korea, and it would have prohibited any increase in forces, supplies, equipment, or facilities. The Communist plan differed in that it required a withdrawal of each side's forces from the islands and coastal waters off the other side's zone (which in practice would

[55] Adams, *History of the U.S.,* Vol. 9, p. 37; Engelman, pp. 234–235; and Updyke, p. 293.

[56] This was probably one reason why they included articles on impressment and blockades in a draft treaty (solicited by the British) which they submitted with their sixth note on 10 November, even though they had long before made it clear that they were willing to be silent on the maritime issues. *American State Papers,* pp. 733–740.

[57] What also seems to be operating in situations like this one is a general resistance to backing down in the face of demands perceived to be excessive or unreasonable. Some experiments which have produced results indicating that toughness begets softness and vice versa—consistent with the generalization about nonreciprocation of concessions in Phase Two—have also shown that this pattern exists only within a range of moderate demands, and that beyond a certain point an increasingly tough bargaining posture does not soften the opponent's position any farther. See, e.g., Gary A. Yukl, "Effects of the Opponent's Initial Offer, Concession Magnitude, and Concession Frequency on Bargaining Behavior."

have affected only UNC forces) and was silent on the augmentation of forces and material and the access to be afforded to the supervisory body. Six days later, the Communists presented three revisions to their proposal: (1) neutral nations, not the belligerents, would compose the supervisory body; (2) no introduction of any new forces, weapons, or ammunition into Korea would be permitted; and (3) the supervisory body would inspect ports of entry as agreed upon in advance. Apparently the decision-makers on the UNC side did not perceive this to be as extreme a position as it was, partly because the second and third changes appeared to respond, as the original Communist proposal had not, to the UNC's concerns about augmentation of forces and inspection, but mostly because the Communist negotiators did not immediately reveal how they would translate their general points into specifics.

Before the negotiation was over, the Communists would reveal how extreme those specific demands were. The Soviet Union was to be designated as a "neutral" nation. The prohibition on the introduction of new forces was to mean that the UNC army would not be able to rotate its troops; when the Communists finally accepted the idea of rotation they proposed such a low monthly figure that the UNC, with its short tours of duty, would still have been unable to maintain anything approaching its then existing strength. The number of ports of entry they were to propose would be so low that it would not only make evasion of the agreement easy but also make it impossible for the UNC, which intended to comply with the agreement, to supply its forces; as with the rotation limit, extensive haggling would be required to arrive at an acceptable compromise figure. The inspection at the ports was also to include detailed perusal of even the most secret equipment, meaning that a "neutral" nation like the Soviet Union could scrutinize U.S. aircraft while the comparable Communist equipment, based in Manchuria, would escape inspection by the West. Not being able to foresee all of this, the UNC began conceding, sometimes unilaterally and sometimes in exchange for the other side's giving up some of its padding. For example, it accepted a withdrawal from the islands and the concept of neutral inspection if rotation of troops were permitted. And it dropped a ban on the construction or improvement of airfields—part of the UNC's prohibition of the augmentation of material but not part of the Communist offer—in an eventual package deal in which the Communists withdrew their nomination of the Soviet Union as a member of the neutral nation's body. Eventually all the padding was discarded, but when the process was over and the result was compared to the initial objectives, the UNC had given up much in return for very little. It had conceded on the issues of the coastal islands, neutral inspection, unlimited access to areas on the ground, aerial reconnaissance, airfield construction, and unlimited troop rotation. The Communists had to accept only a limited and ineffectual inspection arrangement.

The chief UNC negotiator, Admiral Joy, later concluded that his adversaries had interpreted UNC concessions as indicators of UNC incentives—the third possible interpretation of a concession. "Communists," he wrote, "regard any concession made by their opponents as a sign of weakness." Making one is "likely to induce an even more adamant attitude on their part."[58] Given what we know about Phase Two bargaining in general, Joy was probably correct in asserting that UNC concessions reduced, rather than increased, any Communist inclination to concede, either because they were read as signs of weakness or because they were used to project a succession of future UNC concessions. The fact that the UNC was trading meat for fat only accentuated this effect.

Phase Three

The transition from Phase One to Phase Two usually is less distinct than that between Phases Two and Three. The first transition occurs when the bargainers come to view an agreement as possible; the second marks the moment they begin viewing it as probable. At the end of Phase Two, the gap between the two positions has narrowed to where they can now see the conclusion of the negotiation—most likely a successful one, but a conclusion in any case. The slack is gone from the negotiation, the remaining differences are as clear as they will ever be, and the parties see their subsequent decisions as resulting possibly in the breaking off of talks but not in their indefinite prolongation.

Phase Two usually ends with one side making a major concession that ends the waiting game and makes the overall shape of the agreement clear for the first time.[59] In the War of 1812, that moment came when Britain, in responding to the American draft treaty in its sev-

---

[58] Joy, *How Communists Negotiate*, p. 119. See also his remarks on the early concessions on the supervision issue on pp. 124–125.

[59] Zartman apparently is referring to the same thing when he writes of the parties accepting "referents" of a joint decision. Zartman, "Negotiations: Theory and Reality," p. 71.

enth note on 21 November 1814, dropped its demand for *uti possidetis*.[60] The peace treaty would be based on a mutual restoration of territory. In the Korean War, it came in April 1953, at the time of Little Switch, when the Communists accepted the principle of voluntary repatriation. The Chinese and North Korean prisoners would not be forced to recross the line. In the Algerian War, it came during the negotiations at Les Rousses in February 1962, when de Gaulle telephoned his negotiators and expressed to them his impatience, instructed them not to let the negotiations get "stuck in the mud," and authorized them to concede on the principal outstanding issues, particularly the issue of guaranteeing future cooperation.[61] The new Algerian state would achieve independence largely unfettered by commitments to its past master. And in the Vietnam War, the moment came in late September 1972, when Le Duc Tho revealed that Hanoi had finally abandoned its demand for Thieu's ouster and for a coalition government and when he presented, a few days later, a draft agreement incorporating these concessions.[62] The United States and the DRV would make peace while leaving the political future of South Vietnam to subsequent dealings between Thieu and the Communists.

The arrival of the negotiation at this point does not insure that an agreement will follow soon. The agreements at Ghent and Evian were concluded after one more month (as was the Geneva agreement on Indochina, where there was no distinct second phase of negotiation). The Korean and Vietnam agreements, however, each required another three months to complete, periods which saw some of the most intense violence of those two wars. But it is the perceptions of the participants that matter; at the start of Phase Three they believed that an agreement was imminent. Henry Kissinger could assert in late October 1972 that peace was at hand, and whether or not he actually believed it at the moment that he uttered the words to reporters, his frantic diplomatic activity in Paris following the presentation of the DRV's draft agreement a couple of weeks earlier indicated that he believed it then.

The interpretations of concessions which were the most important influences on bargaining behavior in Phase Two become less important in Phase Three. The projection of concession trends and the

---

[60] *American State Papers*, pp. 735–741.

[61] Buron, pp. 223–229; Tricot, *Les Sentiers de la Paix*, p. 286; and Courrière, *Les Feux du Désespoir*, pp. 548–549.

[62] Szulc, "How Kissinger Did It," pp. 51–53; and Kalb and Kalb, pp. 355–356.

estimation of the time it will take the opponent to arrive at a given position become less relevant because the time dimension is compressed. Disagreement costs are now associated not so much with the time it takes to outwait the opponent in the negotiation but rather with the possibility that the negotiation will break down entirely. A breakdown does not mean losing forever the possibility of a negotiated settlement, but it usually does mean a significant delay before negotiations are resumed, and thus a marked increase in the probable costs that will be incurred before the war ends. Concessions during Phase Three are still important as indicators of utilities, but not in the sense of being signs of weakness, since both sides have managed to endure the war for so long and each knows that the other does not expect it to last much longer. Concessions thus are less indicative of general strength or weakness, although they do help to identify the individual issues which are most important to each belligerent.

At the same time, concessions become more important as causes of change in the bargainers' incentives. Differentiating Equation (1), Zeuthen's formula for critical risk, with respect to U_{bb} and U_{ba} yields

$$\frac{\delta C_b}{\delta U_{bb}} = \frac{U_{ba}}{U_{bb}^2} \tag{2}$$

and

$$\frac{\delta C_b}{\delta U_{ba}} = -\frac{1}{U_{bb}} \tag{3}$$

which relate the effects of concessions on B's critical risk to the amount of concession-making which has already taken place. (Reversing the subscripts would of course produce similar results for A.) Equation (2) shows that the more each side has already conceded (i.e., the higher is U_{ba} and the lower is U_{bb}), the more drastically a further concession by B (i.e., a further lowering of U_{bb}) will lower C_b. Equation (3) indicates that the more B has already conceded (the lower is U_{bb}), the more drastically a concession by A (i.e., a raising of U_{ba}) will lower C_b. In short, the closer are the positions of the two sides, the more a concession of any given size will lower the critical risks—i.e., the more it will change each side's incentives. Thus if the negotiators apply Zeuthenian logic at all, its results are most likely to be visible in the late stages of a negotiation. Another way to look at this is that, in line with the comments in the preceding paragraph, bargainers in the final phase of a negotiation will be more cognizant of the connection between their bargaining decisions and the possibility that the negotiation will break down. Zeuthen's model describes this mode of thinking.

Conditions for Reciprocation

As was noted in the opening section of this chapter, however, a concession reduces the critical risk of *both* parties, and therefore whether concessions are reciprocated depends on other factors. If each side begins with an offer that is as distasteful to the other side as continued disagreement, then Zeuthen's model always predicts some reciprocation. At the initial positions in such a case,

$$U_{ab} = U_{ba} = 0$$

since the state of no agreement was assigned a value of zero for each bargainer. By Equation (1) and its counterpart for A, the critical risk of each side at the outset would be 1. Any concession by, say, A would give U_{ba} a small positive value and reduce C_b below unity, while C_a remained unchanged. B would then have a smaller critical risk than his opponent and would be expected to reciprocate his concession. Even though actual bargaining rarely starts with such extreme demands, it at least makes theoretical sense to define the limits of the bargaining range this way in cases in which there are conceivable proposals that one side might make which the other would consider worse than no agreement at all. For example, a company could conceivably propose an hourly wage so low that the workers would rather quit their jobs than accept it, and the union could propose a wage so high that the company would rather go out of business than accept it. The bargaining range includes all wage rates that do not fall into either of those two extreme categories. But the conceivable agreements between warring states do not always extend as far as the utility, for either belligerent, of an indefinite prolongation of warfare. At any rate, once the final phase of the negotiation is reached, proposals this extreme are rare.[63]

It is possible, depending on the utilities of the opening offers and the possible compromises in between, for one party's critical risk

[63] There are additional theoretical reasons to expect a bargainer to rule out some proposals as always unacceptable, even though they have higher utility than what he could assure himself in the absence of an agreement. For a recent discussion, see Ted Mitchell and Roger Heeler, "Toward a Theory of Acceptable Outcomes."

always to be less than the other's. This means that the subsequent application of Zeuthenian logic may lead one party to concede all the way to the opponent's position. Let the utilities of the possible outcomes be portrayed in two dimensions, with A's utilities being the horizontal dimension, B's the vertical, and zero being the utility of no agreement to each. The possible agreements which are Pareto-optimal describe a monotonically decreasing function, $f(u_a) = u_b$, with u_a and u_b being A's and B's utilities, respectively. This function is not necessarily continuous, but for simplicity assume that it is. If we define a function

$$g(u_a) = u_a u_b = u_a f(u_a)$$

then $g'(u_a) < 0$ for the entire domain of u_a is a sufficient condition for A never to be able to make B's critical risk less than his own, no matter how much he concedes. If the bargaining space comprising the possible agreements is not concave, then $g'(u_a) < 0$ for either the entire domain of u_a or all of it except the minimum value of u_a is also a necessary condition. Conversely, $g'(u_a) > 0$ for the entire domain of u_a is the corresponding condition for B never to be able to make A's critical risk less than his own. These propositions are derived in Appendix B.

As an example, consider a set of possible agreements whose Pareto-optimal elements describe the function

$$u_b = f(u_a) = 10 - \frac{u_a^2}{4}, \ 4 < u_a < 6$$

which is shown in Figure 3. (No interpersonal comparison of utility is necessary; the conclusions which follow would still apply after any linear transformation of the function.) In this case,

$$g'(u_a) = 10 - \frac{3u_a^2}{4}$$

which is negative for all u_a in the domain. A's critical risk will always be less than B's, even if B stands pat at the extreme of (4,6) and A concedes so that he is infinitesimally close to that position. Figure 3 depicts a plausible and probably common bargaining situation: one party (B) cares more about the shape of the agreement and/ or is troubled less by the costs of disagreement than the other party (A). That is, the difference between the best and worst possible agreements, relative to the difference between any one agreement and no agreement, is large for B but small for A. In such a situation,

FIGURE 3. A bargaining problem in which Zeuthenian bargainers would not reciprocate concessions.

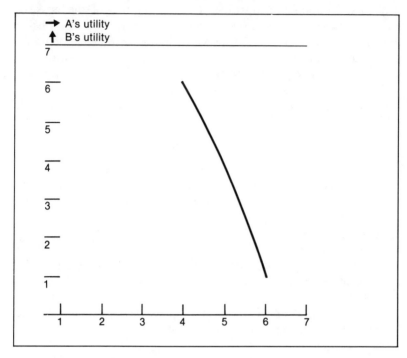

we would expect B to take the tougher negotiating position and A to make most and perhaps all the concessions. That is consistent with Zeuthen's assumptions. A would concede all the way to (4,6); B would not reciprocate.

The kind of asymmetry of motivation depicted in Figure 3 is not required for Zeuthenian behavior to produce unreciprocated concessions. A situation may arise in which two bargainers begin with equal critical risks, but in which a concession by either party makes that party's critical risk less than his opponent's—an inequality that he can never reverse even if he concedes all the way to the opponent's initial demand. In fact, within part of the bargaining range, his concessions only make the discrepancy worse. To see the conditions in which this occurs, assume for the moment that A's critical risk exceeds B's—i.e., that $C_a > C_b$, so that

$$\frac{U_{aa} - U_{ab}}{U_{aa}} > \frac{U_{bb} - U_{ba}}{U_{bb}} \, .$$

Multiplying both sides of the inequality by the positive number $U_{aa}U_{bb}$ and simplifying yields

$$U_{aa}U_{ba} > U_{ab}U_{bb}. \tag{4}$$

So to say that one side has a higher critical risk is equivalent to saying that the product of the utilities to each side of its offer exceeds the corresponding product for the opponent's offer.

This reveals a connection between the Zeuthen model and John Nash's game theoretic solution to the bargaining problem, Nash's solution being defined as the one which maximizes the product of utilities.[64] The equivalence of $C_a > C_b$ to (4) means that Zeuthenian bargaining tends toward the Nash solution as the final agreement.[65] This makes possible a graphic portrayal of the conditions in which Zeuthenian behavior does and does not lead to reciprocation. All the outcomes having the same product of utilities form a hyperbola defined by the function

$$u_b = \frac{k}{u_a}$$

where k is the product and the range and domain of the function are restricted to positive values of u_a and u_b. Varying k produces a set of hyperbolas such as the thin lines in Figure 4. With any pair of offers, the one located on a hyperbola closer to the origin has a lower product of utilities and therefore the party having offered it will be the next to concede. The final settlement will be that outcome which among all possible outcomes is on the hyperbola farthest from the origin. If the bargaining range is not truncated asymmetrically, as in the example in Figure 3, and if both parties begin with offers sufficiently close to the extremes of the bargaining range, then in many situations the final agreement will be somewhere between the two initial offers and will be approached through reciprocated concessions. The possible agreements on a single issue for which the utility to each party is linear with respect to some objective measure would form a straight line, such as that marked I in Figure 4. The

[64] John F. Nash, Jr., "The Bargaining Problem." This connection was first made by Harsanyi in "Approaches to the Bargaining Problem Before and After the Theory of Games."

[65] An assumption underlying this result is that the bargainers have identical perceptions of the costs of disagreement. For a discussion of the implications when they do not, see Vincent P. Crawford, "A Note on the Zeuthen-Harsanyi Theory of Bargaining." Perceptions of disagreement costs are probably often widely divergent at the outset of wars, but more nearly identical by the final phase of the war.

FIGURE 4. **Some conditions for reciprocation or nonreciprocation of concessions by Zeuthenian bargainers.**

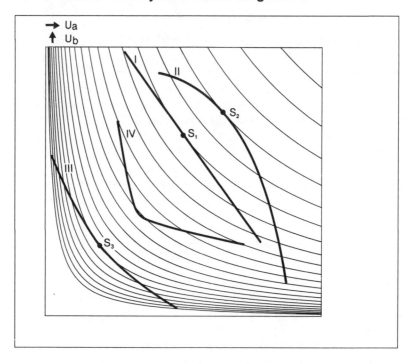

parties would converge upon a settlement at point S_1 (or if the set of
possible outcomes were not in fact continuous, at the outcome
which, like S_1, was on the hyperbola most remote from the origin). If
the possible outcomes formed a convex bargaining space so that
their Pareto-optimal elements were represented by a curve like that
marked II, Zeuthenian bargainers would again converge upon a
compromise settlement, in this case S_2. This could still be true even
if the bargaining space were somewhat concave, provided that the
resulting curve, like curve III, cuts the hyperbolas the same way as
curves I and II. But a bargaining space which is more radically
concave or extends farther from the origin or both, such as one with
a Pareto-optimal set of outcomes like curve IV, produces a different
result. Here the product of utilities is maximized at the extremes. A
concession by either party lowers its critical risk below that of the
other. It stays lower as that same party concedes, without reciprocation, all the way to his opponent's initial demand. The start of bar-

gaining in such a situation is an unstable equilibrium: who concedes first is indeterminate, but the first concession leads to the total capitulation of one side. (Changing the extremes slightly so that they are no longer on the same hyperbola would determine who concedes first but would not change the rest of the sequence.)

The pattern of concessions exhibited by two Zeuthenian bargainers thus depends on the utilities to each bargainer of each possible outcome. In an international negotiation, these utilities are not known directly or precisely, but several conjectures are possible. An overall peace settlement usually consists of settlements on several individual issues. Even after the negotiation reaches Phase Three, there are generally several distinct issues remaining to be settled; this was, in fact, true in all of the major cases. The possible outcomes of the overall negotiation can therefore be viewed as the different possible combinations of settlements of individual issues. Each side's initial position represents a resolution of all the issues in its favor, with the other possible outcomes being settlements that resolve some issues in A's favor and others in B's favor, perhaps compromising on still others. Given this view of the overall bargaining problem in Phase Three, it is impossible for the bargaining space in this problem to generate a set of Pareto-optimal outcomes which, like curve IV in Figure 4, has higher products of utilities at the two extremes than it does anywhere else. If both sides assign the same importance to each individual issue, relative to the other issues, then all of the possible settlements would be on a straight line between the two initial positions; the ratio of the difference in B's utility to the difference in A's utility (i.e., the slope of the line) between any two overall settlements that resolve a specific issue differently would be the same no matter what that issue was. If, as is more generally true, the individual issues do not all have the same relative importance to both parties, the possible outcomes would not all be on this line. At least some of the Pareto-optimal outcomes would be above and to the right of it, indicating outcomes in which an issue tends to be resolved in favor of the party which places it higher on its list of priorities. The overall settlement negotiated in Phase Three will be wholly in favor of one side or the other only if an asymmetry of motivation favors the same side on every issue, which would produce a pattern of Pareto-optimal outcomes having the same overall shape as the curve in Figure 3. This will occasionally occur, although with three, four, or more distinct issues it usually will not. We would therefore expect that in most, though not all, cases, some of the outstanding issues in Phase Three will be resolved in favor of one party and others in favor of the opponent. There will be overall reciprocation which was largely absent in Phase Two.[66]

Phase Three bargaining in the major cases is consistent with this expectation. In one of the five cases— the Algerian War—concessions continued to be largely one-sided, with the FLN getting its way on such issues as whether Algeria would be committed to using part of the Saharan oil revenues to benefit people living in the Sahara (it would not) and whether France would be committed to providing economic and technical aid to Algeria (it would).[67] In the other four cases, the settlement of outstanding issues was much more balanced. The final month of bargaining at Ghent—which will be reviewed in detail shortly—saw the issues fall equally in favor of each side, in contrast to the previous four months of bargaining, during which Britain made nearly all the concessions. The concessions during the final phase of bargaining on each of the agenda items in the Korean truce talks also came from both sides. For example, in bargaining over the handling of prisoners of war (the last item to be settled), the UNC accepted the Communist position that North Korean prisoners who refused repatriation would not be released immediately but would, like the Chinese, be subject to a period of confinement. The Communists acceded to the UNC position that the prisoners should be under the custody of Indian troops within Korea, rather than be shipped outside the country or placed in the hands of all the members of the Neutral Nations Supervisory Commission, which included the Communist states of Poland and Czechoslovakia. Differences over the period of custody and the arrangements under which their former rulers would have access to the prisoners were resolved through compromise.[68] During the hectic period of less than two weeks that brought the Geneva conference on Indochina to a close, concessions also were mutual. France won the right to retain bases in Laos and also got its way in refusing to recognize the rebel movements in either Laos or Cambodia. The Viet Minh won their point on decision-making in the three-nation International Control Commission (it would be by unanimity on ma-

---

[66] I. William Zartman has observed that bargaining becomes more "responsive"— i.e., displays greater reciprocation—during its final stages, once an "image" of negotiations has been established. Zartman, *The 50% Solution*, p. 260.

[67] Buron, pp. 230–253.

[68] Vatcher, *Panmunjom*, pp. 186–193; Rees, *Korea*, pp. 414–417; and Hermes, pp. 425–429.

jor questions, rather than by majority vote as the French preferred) and in refusing any special guarantees for the Catholic bishoprics in Tonkin which would fall in their zone. The location of the demarcation line, the deadline for evacuation of French troops, and the deadline for all-Vietnam elections were all settled through compromise.[69] The final phase of bargaining during the Vietnam War was confused by retractions and the introduction of new issues by both sides following the tentative agreement of October 1972. But by the time the pieces were put together again, it was clear that each side had yielded ground. Hanoi agreed to drop the description of the National Council of Reconciliation and Concord as an "administrative structure" (which could imply a coalition government), agreed to let the neutral supervisory commission have its own logistics, and made a secret commitment for peace in Laos.[70] The United States dropped demands for peace in Cambodia, for removing the election deadline and restricting elections in Vietnam to the presidency, for declaring the demilitarized zone to be inviolate, and for placing restrictions on civilian movement.[71] The size of the supervisory commission was a compromise.

Quantitative Issues

The preceding comments have glossed over the details on how individual issues—many of which themselves have several different possible outcomes—are settled. The pattern of bargaining on each, like the negotiation of the overall settlement, depends on the utilities to the bargainers of the possible outcomes. And like the overall settlement, some conjectures about these utilities are possible even if they are not known with precision.

Some of the issues in Phase Three are quantitative: an outcome consists of a number, with one party wishing it to be higher and the other wanting it lower. Quantitative issues rarely are negotiated before the final phase, because they usually pertain to details that

[69] The most thorough account of this bargaining at Geneva (which, unlike that in the opening phase, took place in informal sessions and therefore is not recorded in the official minutes) is in Devillers and Lacouture, *End of a War*, Chaps. 20–22.

[70] In his press conference of 24 January 1973, Henry Kissinger reviewed the concessions that the United States had won during this period. Text in *Background Information*, pp. 503–516. The secret agreement on Laos is mentioned in Szulc, "How Kissinger Did It," p. 63.

[71] Gareth Porter, *A Peace Denied*, pp. 167–172.

cannot be addressed before general principles are first resolved. Such issues have at least several, and usually many, possible settlements. Hence there is room for mutual concession and opportunities for compromise. Because the difference between one possible outcome and the next is one of degree rather than of principle, no single concession is likely to change abruptly the utility of either party. If utilities are not linear, marginal utility is more apt to be decreasing than increasing, for the same general reasons that it is in most economic situations, which involve such quantitative variables as prices, wages, or rate of production. Thus it is improbable that the pattern of possible outcomes would resemble curve IV in Figure 4. All of this implies that there will be some reciprocation of concessions during bargaining on these issues, and that the settlement will be a compromise between the initial positions of the two sides.

This was in fact true of all the quantitative issues that arose in the major cases. The one such issue at Ghent was the fixing of time limits after which ships captured at sea would have to be returned to their owners. The proposals were phrased in terms of degrees of longitude and latitude which defined different areas of ocean, as well as the number of days after ratification that would serve as the time limit for captures in each area. The settlement was a compromise between the initial proposals, which differed in that they specified shorter time limits for the areas in which the enemy's navy was strongest.[72] At Panmunjom, several quantitative issues were negotiated during the final bargaining on control arrangements and the handling of prisoners, and all of these ended in compromise. They will be mentioned shortly in the course of illustrating some additional points. The settlements of quantitative issues at the Geneva conference were: (1) the establishment of the demarcation line at the 17th Parallel (France had proposed the 18th, while the most extreme Viet Minh demand was the 13th); (2) the time limit of 300 days for the evacuation of French troops from the northern zone (France had initially proposed 380 days, the Viet Minh three months); and the time limit of two years for holding all-Vietnam elections (suggested as a compromise by Soviet Foreign Minister Molotov between the Viet Minh demand for six months and the French position of only grudgingly accepting any deadline at all).[73] In the Paris talks on Vietnam, the setting of the size of the neutral supervisory force at

[72] Protocols of conferences of 1, 10, and 23 December, *American State Papers*, pp. 742, 743, 745.

[73] Devillers and Lacouture, pp. 279–283, 292–294.

1,160 men was a compromise between the U.S. proposal of 5,000 and Hanoi's proposal of 250.[74] Even in the Algerian negotiations, in which the FLN viewpoint prevailed on most other questions, both sides gave up some ground on the quantitative issues. These included the schedule for the withdrawal of French troops, the first 80,000 of which were to be gone one year after the referendum on independence (the FLN initially wanted them to leave immediately after the referendum, while the opening French offer was two years) and the rest in three years (the FLN had proposed one year, France five years). They also included the length of the leases on French military bases in Algeria: for the important naval base at Mers-el-Kebir it would be fifteen years (between the French proposal of twenty-five and the FLN offer of ten), and for the bases in the Sahara five years (France had proposed seven, the FLN four).[75] In general: if the outcomes of an issue can be expressed quantitatively, the settlement of the issue will be a compromise.

If the utilities associated with a quantitative issue are linear, and the parties employ Zeuthenian logic as soon as they begin bargaining on it, then they will arrive at a settlement which splits the difference between their initial positions, or comes as close to doing so as discontinuities allow. This is true regardless of how the marginal utilities of each side compare to the utility of getting any agreement at all. It is also true regardless of the opening offer, provided only that this offer is more favorable to the side that made it than the Nash solution would be. The proposition is derived in Appendix C.

Bargainers are apt to consider utility as linear when they are unsure of the implications of the settlement they reach; the first widget seems as good as the nth widget when one does not really know how useful widgets will turn out to be. An issue in which this was the case arose during the final bargaining at Panmunjom on the handling of prisoners of war. In accepting voluntary repatriation, the Communists insisted that "explainers" be permitted to talk to the prisoners who refused repatriation, to try to persuade them to reverse their decisions. The UNC accepted this on the condition that threats and coercion be forbidden and that the number of explainers be limited, proposing a limit of three explainers per thousand prisoners. The Communist side accepted the principle of limitation but proposed ten explainers per thousand. The two sides then closed the

[74] Kissinger press conference of 24 January 1973, *Background Information,* p. 507; and Kalb and Kalb, p. 411.
[75] Buron, pp. 214–215, 230–231.

gap by trading concessions over the next few days: the UNC raised its offer to five per thousand, the Communists countered with eight, the UNC came back with seven, which the Communists then accepted.[76] Both sides were dealing with an unknown. The attempt by a state to persuade large numbers of its citizens to return home after a war—indeed, the refusal of repatriation by many prisoners of war in the first place—was unusual, and the results of the "explanations" were unpredictable. The Communists wanted in general to minimize the number of nonrepatriates, and the UNC desired to minimize the provocations and harassment to which these prisoners would be subjected, but there was little ground for supposing that the marginal utility of explainers would rise or fall within the range in which the issue was negotiated. So the bargainers exchanged concessions and settled on a number as close to the midpoint between their initial offers as the formula of explainers per thousand would allow. (As it turned out, the "explanations" had little effect; few of the nonrepatriates changed their minds.)

Another quantitative issue involving the disposition of nonrepatriated prisoners in Korea was the duration of the prisoners' captivity before parole. For the same general reasons that determined their preferences regarding the number of explainers, the Communists wanted this captivity to be long and the UNC wished it to be short. The Communists initially proposed six months, the UNC countered with 60 days, and the settlement split the difference with 120 days.[77]

Splitting-the-difference is a common pattern of bargaining in quantitative issues, especially when, as with these two issues in Korea, the implications of the settlement are unclear. It not only is the implied result of Zeuthenian bargaining with linear utility; it also incorporates a common notion of justice, and is a salient solution in an otherwise amorphous bargaining space, which bargainers can use to guide their deliberations when no other guides are available.[78]

[76] This bargaining occurred during the first week of June 1953. Details are in Vatcher, p. 193.

[77] Hermes, pp. 423, 427, 428–429.

[78] On splitting-the-difference as a type of justice, see Zartman and Berman, pp. 103–104. On salient solutions, see Thomas C. Schelling, *The Strategy of Conflict*, Chap. 3. Although salience can sometimes suggest a solution other than a splitting of the difference, in most quantitative issues there are no such obvious alternatives (except insofar as numbers which are round are more salient than numbers which are not). An exception is the establishment of a demarcation line or border, such as the drawing of the line between North and South Vietnam at the Geneva conference, in which the quantitative dimension was degrees of latitude. In such an instance, geo-

When utility is not linear and the parties can associate specific consequences with particular outcomes, they are less likely to split the difference. The Zeuthenian analysis in Appendix C no longer applies with nonlinear utilities. And salience becomes a less important determinant of bargaining behavior when the parties can draw specific inferences from the different possible outcomes. A quantitative issue with these characteristics was the number of ports to be open to inspection as part of the control arrangements in Korea. The bargaining on this issue did not occur near the end of the entire Panmunjom negotiation, as the issues concerning "explanations" to the prisoners did, but it took place at a comparable time during the negotiation over supervision and control arrangements. It arose after the UNC accepted the principle of limited inspection, and it is characteristic of Phase Three bargaining over details. The UNC at first viewed inspection at the ports as a genuine deterrent to evasion of the agreement by the other side, but after the UNC dropped its demand for aerial observation in December 1951, it was clear that inspection of a limited list of ports would not stop the Communists from strengthening their forces in Korea if they were intent on doing so.[79] The issue then became one of the ease with which the UNC could comply with an agreement to ship supplies only through the ports which had been agreed upon (hence its desire to maximize the number of ports) versus the ease with which the Communist side could evade that agreement (its apparent intention, as indicated by its desire to minimize the number of ports). Since each side knew the logistical requirements of supplying a force of a given size, and since the size of the forces remaining in Korea would be governed by considerations going far beyond the number of ports available, the utility of ports open to inspection was unlikely to be linear. The marginal utility of added ports (to the UNC) and of fewer ports (to the Communists) was probably decreasing, since as the agreement became more favorable an additional change in the number would become a matter less of necessity and more of convenience.[80] Figure

graphical features or previous boundaries provide salient solutions. As will be noted in Chapter 4, however, the settlement of the demarcation line in Vietnam was more dependent on another quantitative measure—the amount of territory controlled by each side—than on the salience of the specific boundary.

[79] Joy, *How Communists Negotiate*, p. 88.

[80] Marginal utility was probably more sharply decreasing for the UNC, because the ports to be named, whatever the number, could be expected to be the largest and most useful ones.

FIGURE 5. **Bargaining at the Korean armistice negotiation on the number of ports of entry. (Sources: *New York Times*; Hermes, pp. 160–161; Vatcher, pp. 108–110.)**

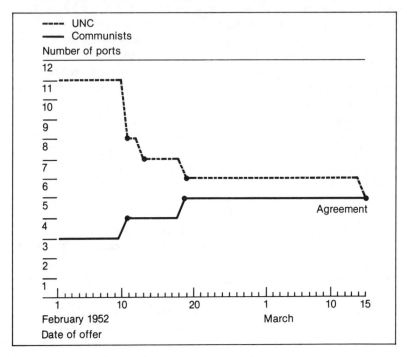

5 depicts the bargaining on this issue, which took place in early 1952. The sequence and timing of concessions produced a general pattern of reciprocity, but one which did not end with a splitting of the difference between the initial positions.[81]

Figure 5 reveals another attribute of the bargaining over ports: the parties converged upon the final settlement asymptotically, with concessions being smaller and/or less frequent as the negotiation proceeded. This is also a common pattern. Figure 6 shows it displayed in the bargaining on another quantitative issue which

[81] Laboratory experimentation has demonstrated how the introduction of nonlinear utilities (achieved artifically, as through a system of bonuses or penalties for reaching or not reaching certain settlements) changes the demands and the final outcome of an otherwise unchanged negotiation of a quantitative issue. See, e.g., John G. Holmes, Warren F. Throop, and Lloyd H. Strickland, "The Effects of Prenegotiation Expectations on the Distributive Bargaining Process."

FIGURE 6. **Bargaining at the Korean armistice negotiation on the monthly rotation limit. (Sources:** *New York Times;* **Hermes, pp. 160–161; Vatcher, pp. 108–110.)**

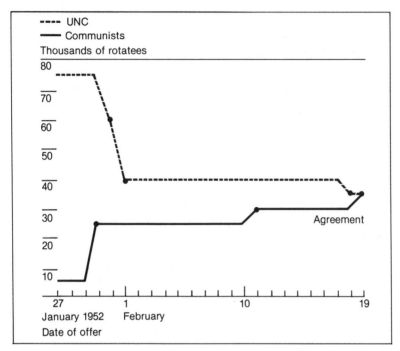

emerged from the earlier stages of negotiation on supervision and control arrangements in Korea: the maximum number of troops to be rotated each month.[82] And that it is not unique to the talks at Panmunjom or to peace negotiations generally is revealed by experimental results obtained in the laboratory.[83] Figure 7 shows the sequence of offers made by a pair of subjects in the earliest published experimental study of negotiation using a format of bilateral monopoly: Sidney Siegel and Lawrence Fouraker's *Bargaining and Group*

[82] As with ports, the utility of permitted rotatees was undoubtedly nonlinear for the UNC, since its rotation requirements were dictated by the policy of one-year tours of duty for American servicemen in Korea, and by decisions taken on other grounds regarding the size of the U.S. force to be retained in Korea. The issue had mainly nuisance value for the Communists—which perhaps explains why, in comparison with the number of ports, the settlement on the rotation limit was more favorable to the UNC.

[83] Pruitt, *Negotiation Behavior,* pp. 31–33.

FIGURE 7. **Bargaining between two experimental subjects (adapted from Siegel and Fouraker, _Bargaining and Group Decision Making,_ p. 77).**

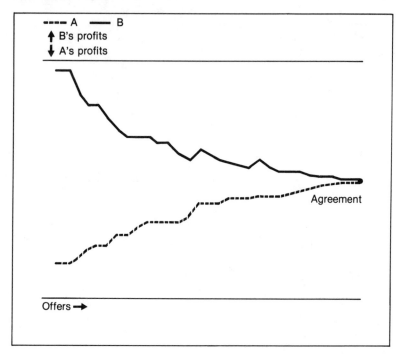

Decision Making.[84] The pattern probably occurs partly because each of these negotiations on a single issue is in at least one respect a microcosm of what occurs when an overall peace negotiation passes through the three phases described in this chapter. The parties begin negotiating an issue uncertain of where the bargaining range lies, and the initially large or rapid concessions are the shedding of deliberately exaggerated demands. But this is only a partial explanation, since the asymptotic pattern of bargaining on an individual issue does not resemble the stalemate in Phase Two and the acceleration of activity in Phase Three that is more characteristic of the larger negotiation.

Zeuthenian reasoning provides another explanation, even though the speed of concession-making plays no role in Zeuthen's own

[84] The subjects alternated offers, which they might or might not change from their previous offers. The horizontal dimension in this case represents not time but offers.

model. If we assume that smaller or less frequent concessions reflect a greater reluctance to concede when concessions become less effective means of reversing an inequality of critical risks, then Zeuthenian logic produces an asymptotic pattern of bargaining if marginal utility is decreasing. To see this, recall that a concession reduces the critical risk of both parties. The effect of a concession by B on his own critical risk is given by Equation (2), while the effect of the same concession by B on A's critical risk is

$$\frac{\partial C_a}{\partial U_{ab}} = -\frac{1}{U_{aa}} \tag{5}$$

obtained by reversing the subscripts in Equation (3). For B's concession to change the difference in critical risks in his favor—i.e., to increase $(C_b - C_a)$—requires the decrease in C_a given by (5) to be greater than the decrease in C_b given by (2). Provided that the increase in U_{ab} associated with B's concession is large enough relative to the decrease in U_{bb}, it will be. But if marginal utility is decreasing for both sides (or decreasing for one side and constant for the other), this will be less likely to be true as B continues to concede; the ratio $\Delta U_{ab}/\Delta U_{bb}$ associated with each additional concession will be closer to zero. B's concessions become less efficient in the sense that he must make increasingly larger sacrifices in order to increase the utility of his offer to A by any given amount. He also moves closer to the point (the Nash solution) where the absolute value of $\Delta U_{ab}/\Delta U_{bb}$ becomes so small that further concession on his part would only decrease $(C_b - C_a)$. Because B does not know A's utilities with certainty, he becomes increasingly unsure of the value of making another concession. If this uncertainty is manifested in less rapid concession making, it produces the kind of pattern depicted in Figures 5, 6, and 7.

Nonquantitative Issues

Nonquantitative issues negotiated in Phase Three have far fewer possible outcomes than do quantitative issues. With some, there are only two possible agreements—one favoring each party—in which case reciprocity in the bargaining on the individual issue obviously is impossible. But even with more than two possible agreements, nonquantitative issues are less likely than quantitative ones to be resolved through compromise, both because there are fewer compromises available and because the ones that are available are apt to offer little satisfaction to either side. Any attempt to find a middle ground is likely to lower the satisfaction of the side offering the compromise while doing little to please its opponent. This means that compromise settlements, even if Pareto-optimal, would have utilities corresponding to the middle portion of curve IV in Figure 4.

This type of outcome set receives little attention in theoretical work on bargaining. Game theorists assume that any concavity in a bargaining space can be eliminated through some randomization procedure which creates a new outcome that is a combination of probabilities that either of the two original outcomes will occur. For their part, economists usually deal with goods that are not only quantifiable but also have decreasing marginal utility for both sides. The lottery of game theory is unlikely ever to be written into international agreements, partly because it would make it difficult to portray a peace agreement as a victory or an embodiment of justice or some other lofty principle.[85] And although the assumption of decreasing marginal utility applies to many issues in armistice negotiations, it may not apply to others, especially nonquantitative issues. Consequently, bargaining on many nonquantitative issues in Phase Three exhibits the behavior we would expect from Zeuthenian bargainers who face an outcome set that looks like curve IV—i.e., a concession by one side is more likely to be followed by another concession from the same side than to be reciprocated.

Because bargaining during Phase Three typically takes place rapidly and in secret or informal sessions, its details are often obscure. One case in which the record is substantially complete—the conference at Ghent—will serve to illustrate the preceding points about the resolution of nonquantitative issues. The final phase of bargaining at Ghent—marked by Britain's dropping of *uti possidetis* in its reply to the American draft treaty—left seven questions to be resolved. One of these, the time limits for restitution of captured ships, was quantitative. As noted, the settlement of this issue was a compromise. It was, in fact, the only issue to be settled in this way; on each of the six other issues, one side or the other won its point entirely.

Three of these were resolved when one party or the other conceded the entire point in a single move. Given the nature of these issues, it is hard to imagine their being settled in any other way. One

---

[85] As we will see in Chapter 6, however, some provisions in armistice agreements have the nature of a lottery insofar as they leave open the possibility that any of several specific future outcomes may result.

of these issues was whether to include the islands in Passamaquoddy Bay among the disputed territories to be referred to boundary commissions; the British finally accepted the U.S. position that they should be so included. The other two issues were resolved in favor of the British: the U.S. commissioners agreed that the boundary commissions should have two members, with reference to a friendly sovereign in case of deadlock, rather than the three members which they had proposed, and they also agreed that the armistice should follow the exchange of ratifications (favored by the British, out of uncertainty over what the Senate might do) rather than signature of the treaty.

In the bargaining on the remaining three nonquantitative issues, one side or the other did make a compromise proposal. But, in all three, the side which offered the compromise subsequently conceded the rest of the way to the opponent's position. One of these issues was how to handle the special privileges of Americans to fish and cure fish in British territory, and of British citizens to navigate the Mississippi River. The American draft was silent on both, implying that the war had not affected either one. The British proposal affirmed the right of navigation on the Mississippi River but was silent on the fishing privileges, suggesting that the war had negated the latter. The British later dropped their original position and offered an article that would have referred both the Mississippi and the fisheries questions to future negotiation. Unlike their earlier proposal, this placed both privileges on the same footing. But the U.S. commissioners still declined to admit an article which implied that the fishing privileges had somehow been called into question because of the war, and the British finally agreed to omit the article altogether.

On the other two issues, it was the United States which first conceded and then gave in entirely. One of these concerned the restitution of captured territory. The British demanded wording that would permit them—as the American draft would not—to remain for the time being on the Passamaquoddy Islands, which they had occupied after the start of the war. The Americans agreed to let them stay, provided a time limit were affixed to settlement of that part of the boundary. The British refused this, after which the U.S. commissioners accepted the British wording in its entirety. The other issue was whether to include an article requiring indemnity for capture or destruction of ships, slaves, or other property; the Americans wanted such an article and the British did not. The U.S. commissioners first offered to limit indemnities to ships seized in port at the outbreak of the war (which in practice would only have meant American ships that had been caught in British ports), and then, in the face of continued British resistance, dropped the demand for indemnities altogether.[86]

The bargaining on these latter three issues demonstrates how attempts to compromise on a question that is more a matter of principle than of degree typically only lowers one side's satisfaction while doing little or nothing to satisfy the opponent. Britain's suggested compromise on the fisheries was unacceptable to the United States because it still admitted the principle that the war could have abrogated the American right. Likewise, Britain rejected the compromise on the Passamaquoddy Islands because to do so would admit that it might not own the islands, and the compromise on indemnities because, however small the actual payments, it would be an admission of British culpability.

Conclusion

The historical evidence reviewed in this chapter has suggested that peace conferences display several recognizable patterns that they share not only with each other but also with other bargaining situations, most of which do not involve warfare or armed force. Abstract bargaining models were useful in analyzing those patterns, but it would be unwarranted to single out any one model as more appropriate than the others. Instead, we saw that their applicability varies with circumstances, and most of all with the phase of the negotiation. Moreover, entire models are sometimes less useful than the assumptions on which they are based. Some of these assumptions can be recombined and reapplied to explain patterns of bargaining behavior not predicted by the original model. For example, we saw that Zeuthen's concept of a comparison of critical risks can lead either to reciprocation or nonreciprocation of concessions, depending on the utilities of the various possible outcomes. And by extending this concept to the rate as well as the sequence of conces-

---

[86] The bargaining on all of these issues is recorded in the American notes of 30 November and 14 December, the British note of 22 December, and the protocols of joint conferences on 1, 10, 12 and 23 December. *American State Papers*, pp. 741–745.

sions, it helped to explain certain patterns characteristic of bargaining over quantitative issues in the final phase.

Although the division of a peace negotiation into three phases is a useful analytical construct, it should be remembered that these phases depict only tendencies, not a uniform and clearly defined blueprint for all peace negotiations. The phases can be compressed, blurred, or otherwise distorted by outside events. Most important, the phases are *perceptions* held by the bargainers themselves, not rules of a game enforced by some omnipotent referee. The perceptions of the two bargainers can differ, and indeed it is when they differ that the greatest negotiating opportunities and hazards are likely to arise.

This chapter's central question—do concessions tend to be reciprocated?—was given different answers for different phases. But is there not something more we can say about bargaining throughout all phases of a negotiation? There is, if we observe a distinction that we have so far glossed over—that between an individual concession and a sequence of concessions. Experimental research has suggested that reciprocation applies more to the former than the latter. That is, negotiations in the laboratory have demonstrated a tendency for a concession by one side to be answered with a concession from the other side, even while showing that an overall negotiating strategy that is soft is likely to be met with one that is tough, and vice versa (toughness and softness usually being defined in terms of the average demand made over a whole sequence of offers).[87] These results are understandable if we assume that several of the interpretations of concessions discussed at the outset of this chapter are operating simultaneously. The fifth interpretation (as conditionable behavior), the sixth (as a signal) and usually the seventh (as an act creating an obligation to reciprocate) refer to individual concessions rather than to sequences, and they also all imply reciprocation. But the fourth interpretation (as a basis for projection of future concessions), which can imply nonreciprocation if previous expectations were not too optimistic, considers concessions only as parts of an overall sequence of offers. Likewise, the third interpretation (as an indicator of incentives) leads to nonreciprocation not because of

---

[87] See the experiments reported in Otomar J. Bartos, *Process and Outcome of Negotiation*, pp. 106 and 153; and the survey of experimental results in Pruitt, *Negotiation Behavior*, p. 35.

what any individual concession does but rather because of what it says about the overall strength or weakness of the opponent.[88]

Bargaining in peace negotiations resembles the experimental results in that most concessions are made shortly before or after concessions by the other side, but without this implying any sort of overall balance in the amount which each side concedes or the extent to which the agreement conforms with each side's original objectives. Usually both sides concede most frequently in the final phase of a negotiation and least frequently in the middle phase; movement by one party does tend to be associated with movement by the other. Yet, this is true not only of negotiations in which the sacrifices made by each side appear to be comparable, but also ones (e.g., Algeria) in which one belligerent clearly bargains away much more than the other.

There are two explanations why a negotiation may exhibit this kind of imbalance even though individual concessions are reciprocated. One is that the initial demands of one side may be more extreme than those of the other. If so, an exchange of concessions can produce a pattern like the bargaining on supervision and control arrangements in Korea, with one side trimming meat and the other fat. The other explanation is that, while concessions are reciprocated, their size is not; major concessions may be answered with minor ones, or vice versa. This has been observed in experimental negotiations which were structured so that the subjects could deduce how the opponent ranked the outcomes but not his exact payoff for each.[89] This resembles conditions in international negotiations, in which the parties have no direct knowledge of each other's utilities. Matching concessions may not be of matching size, there-

---

[88] It is uncertain whether the two Zeuthenian interpretations, as causes of change in each side's incentives, should be considered as applying to individual concessions or to entire sequences of concessions, since they do not focus on the act of conceding per se but do focus on something assumed to change with each concession. In any event, the relative importance of the first and second interpretations depends, as we have seen, on the type of outcome set associated with the issue or issues being negotiated.

[89] Otomar J. Bartos, "Determinants and Consequences of Toughness," in Paul Swingle (ed.), *The Structure of Conflict,* pp. 57–59. See also Donald L. Harnett, Larry L. Cummings, and W. Clay Hamner, "Personality, Bargaining Style and Payoff in Bilateral Monopoly Bargaining Among European Managers," in which a multiple regression is performed on experimental results, indicating that the size of concessions is a more important determinant of a bargainer's payoff than is the frequency of his concessions.

fore, because out of ignorance or misperception the bargainers do not measure any one concession in the same way.[90]

Even with a common measure, reciprocation does not extend to the size of concessions because size is not relevant to those logics—specifically, the fifth, sixth, and seventh interpretations of a concession—which imply reciprocation. During the bargaining at Geneva on the location of the demarcation line in Vietnam, Chou En-lai said to Mendès-France while appealing to him to back down from his demand for the 18th Parallel, "Why not show good will?" In other words, he was asking the French Premier to look upon a concession according to the sixth interpretation, as a signal. After further discussion, the Chinese Premier suggested that each side take a few steps toward the other, although "this does not mean that each must take the same number of steps."[91] By his remarks, Chou made explicit both the notion of reciprocation that is implied in the interpretation of a concession as a signal, and the fact that this extends only to the occurrence, and not to the size, of concessions.

To the earlier statements about bargaining in each phase of a peace negotiation we may thus add the more general statement that individual concessions tend to be reciprocated, but the overall toughness or softness of a negotiation posture does not. With this, we have gone as far as it is possible to go while continuing to disregard military activity. It is to that activity that we now turn.

[90] Even with complete knowledge of the opponent's payoffs, subjects in the laboratory show systematic tendencies to misperceive the opponent's bargaining behavior, such as to perceive his concession rate as less than it actually is. H. Andrew Michener, et al., "Factors Affecting Concession Rate and Threat Usage in Bilateral Conflict," p. 73.

[91] Devillers and Lacouture, p. 281.

CHAPTER FOUR

The Military Instrument

In what ways may armed force be used to support a peace negotiation? In what military and diplomatic circumstances is one usage likely to take precedence over another? And how do these circumstances affect the level of violence employed? This chapter explores these questions and demonstrates how complex military decision-making can be during the negotiation period of a war. In fact, the complexity tends to be even greater than the discussion below suggests, because during this period belligerents may also use their armed forces for purposes other than supporting the negotiation. These other objectives include: preserving and strengthening the military instrument itself; influencing foreign governments other than the current enemy; and preparing for an imminent peace (e.g., last-minute grabs of territory before a stand-still cease-fire). But because this book is not a general treatise on warfare, it sets these other purposes aside and focuses on the use of armed force to influence the enemy's diplomacy.

Because disagreement costs play such a large role in bargaining behavior, and because disagreement costs in warfare are so heavily dependent upon the level and type of military activity, this chapter begins by addressing the manipulation of these costs. It then examines the other ways of using armed force to shape events at the conference table.

Manipulating the Costs of Disagreement

Disagreement costs entered into much of the reasoning in Chapter 3. But diplomatic activity alone affords little opportunity to manipulate these costs, apart from lengthening or shortening the *time* during which the opponent must endure them. Time is particularly important in the Cross model, in which a reduced concession rate leads the opponent to make fresh concessions because it increases his estimate of the time during which he would otherwise incur disagreement costs. Treating concessions as conditionable behavior and rewarding them with counterconcessions also can entail a manipulation of the time of disagreement: the opponent values the counterconcession not only because it shapes the settlement in a desirable way but also because it brings the two sides closer and thus may hasten a settlement.

The military instrument, however, provides warring states with a more powerful, direct, and flexible means of manipulating the costs of disagreement. Using logics introduced in Chapter 3, particularly the Zeuthen and Cross models of bargaining, this section discusses the principles of such manipulation. In doing so, several simplifications are made. The entire discussion involves one such simplification: the exclusion of uses of force designed to influence the enemy's diplomacy in other ways (to be discussed in the subsequent section) and uses of force not intended to affect the negotiation at all (which, as mentioned, fall outside the scope of this book). The section begins with some further simplifying assumptions—that costs consist of a single form of punishment such as casualties, that belligerents consider only the effect of costs on the terms of settlement, and that they pursue objectives with fixed values. These assumptions will later be relaxed, but it should be borne in mind that only a partial picture of warfare is being presented at each point in the discussion. The simplifications are made because of the need for clarity and because, as the evidence will show, the principles elucidated below are consistent with much actual behavior, even when they conflict with other possible determinants of wartime decision-making.

Efficiency

The fundamental idea of cost manipulation is this: disagreement is made more costly for the enemy in order to make him more inclined to concede. That an increase in the opponent's disagreement costs should make him more compliant at the negotiating table is inferable from the most common and informal notions of human behavior. When one situation becomes more disagreeable, the alternatives— imperfect though they may be—will appear more acceptable than before. The same proposition is implied by the principal bargaining models mentioned in Chapter 3. The Zeuthen and Cross models, which are so different in other respects and which can imply different responses to the opponent's bargaining behavior, agree on this. The role of a change in disagreement costs in Zeuthenian reasoning can be seen with a suitable modification of Equation (1), the basic formula for critical risk. If A manages to increase the costs of disagreement to B by the amount D_b, then the utility to B of each possible agreement—which was really the difference between its utility and the utility of no agreement, which was set at zero—is increased by D_b. Equation (1) thus is altered to

$$C_b = \frac{(U_{bb} + D_b) - (U_{ba} + D_b)}{(U_{bb} + D_b)}$$

which simplifies to

$$C_b = \frac{U_{bb} - U_{ba}}{U_{bb} + D_b}$$

Any increase in B's disagreement costs, represented by a positive D_b, decreases B's critical risk. B's bargaining position softens, and in the absence of a larger change in C_a, he becomes more likely than before to make the next concession, or to make a larger concession. His position softens because the differences between possible agreements become less important relative to the importance of getting any agreement at all. In Cross's model, an increase in the costs of disagreement causes a bargainer to concede because the marginal disutility (from disagreement costs) of waiting increases while the marginal utility (from obtaining additional concessions from the opponent) of doing so does not. His optimum demand becomes more modest.[1]

If each side's efforts to impose costs on the opponent were costless to itself, then the role of cost manipulation in a bargaining problem would be simple and straightforward. Each bargainer would impose as much cost on the opponent as it was capable of imposing. But such efforts usually are not costless for the side that makes them. Warfare is no exception: using armed force to inflict pain and destruction on the enemy requires monetary or material expenditure at a minimum, and often the acceptance of pain and destruction in return as well. This can be expected to weaken the manipulator's own bargaining position, presenting the possibility that an effort at

[1] Cross demonstrates mathematically this effect of a change in the costs of disagreement on pp. 153–154 of *The Economics of Bargaining*.

cost manipulation could be counterproductive. It thus raises the question of which out of many possible cost-imposing actions can be expected to be advantageous. For an initial approach to this question, costs will be treated statically, viewing them solely as an influence on the terms of agreement. The implications of a broader, dynamic view of costs will be discussed later.

In the previous chapter it was noted that Zeuthenian bargaining tends toward the Nash solution (where the product of utilities, $U_a U_b$, is maximized) as the final outcome. If the bargainers have equal discount rates and learning abilities, this is also true of Crossian bargaining.[2] The Nash solution thus has the appealing attribute of being the implied outcome, given certain simplifying assumptions, of two determinate but very different models of the bargaining process. Furthermore, experimentation has shown it to have greater predictive power than other solutions to the bargaining problem which theorists have proposed.[3] Although Nash originally derived his solution from axioms pertaining to qualities of the solution itself rather than to the process through which it was reached, and although it is most commonly viewed as prescription rather than description, it thus is nevertheless useful in discussing the actual behavior of bargainers while they are negotiating. This is particularly true of the present subject, the manipulation of disagreement costs. For this purpose, it is convenient to use an alternative form of the Nash solution. Assume that the set of possible outcomes constitutes a continuous bargaining space having a smooth boundary, with the Pareto-optimal elements forming a curve, henceforth referred to as the utility frontier, that is everywhere differentiable.[4] Cross has shown that at the Nash solution, the slope of this curve is $-(u_b/u_a)$.[5] I.e., it is the negative of the slope of a line drawn between the solution and the origin, such as line OS in Figure 8. The significance of this is that any movement of the point of no agreement along this line or an extension of it, such as movement down to O', would leave the ratio (u_b/u_a) unchanged, meaning that the slope of the utility frontier at S is still the negative of the slope of the line be-

---

[2] Cross, pp. 58–59. With equal discount rates, it is true as well of Bishop's model.

[3] Bartos, *Process and Outcome of Negotiation,* pp. 213–214.

[4] Of course, this is not generally true of actual bargaining problems and certainly not of peace negotiations. The assumption merely facilitates the demonstration of a principle which applies, to the extent discontinuities permit, to all cases.

[5] Cross, *The Economics of Bargaining,* p. 20.

FIGURE 8. **Cost manipulation and the Nash solution.**

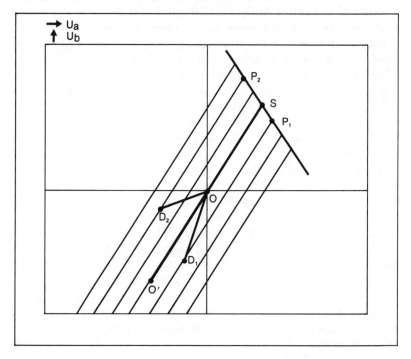

tween S and the new origin, and S is still the solution. Similar lines, which Cross has called "isosettlement lines"[6] can be drawn for every other point on the utility frontier; several are shown in Figure 8. As it is drawn, the utility frontier is a straight line, reflecting linear utilities, and the isosettlement lines consequently are parallel. Non-linear utilities would generate an array of lines that looks different; the implications of this will be considered later.

The isosettlement lines provide a handy means of translating changes in the utility of no agreement into changes in the likely negotiated settlement. An increase in the costs of disagreement to each side represented by movement of the origin to O' implies no

---

[6] The use of isosettlement lines to analyze the effects of changes in the costs of disagreement is taken from Cross, *The Economics of Bargaining,* pp. 123–127. He offers the technique as a static approach to the analysis of disagreement costs that is entirely separate from his dynamic model, except insofar as the latter implies the Nash solution as the eventual outcome.

change in the settlement, but other changes in disagreement costs would. A movement to D_1 would imply a settlement at P_1, making the outcome more favorable to A, while movement to D_2 would imply a settlement at P_2, an outcome more favorable to B. In general, whether or not a cost-imposing action promises to improve the outcome depends on the ratio of the increase in the enemy's costs to the increase in one's own costs, or what may be called the efficiency of the action.

To the extent that a belligerent uses military activity in an effort to manipulate disagreement costs in order to make peace terms more favorable, the efficiency of that activity should therefore govern in part its military decisions. Without knowing the utilities to each belligerent of possible agreements and of disagreement costs, we would not know just how efficient an action would have to be in order for it to appear advantageous to either party. We can say, however, that there is no overlap in the efficiencies of cost-imposing actions advantageous to each side. That is, if $\Delta c_b/\Delta c_a$ is the ratio of B's increased costs to A's increased costs, then there is some value R (in Figure 8, it would be the slope of the isosettlement lines) such that the only cost-imposing actions advantageous to A would entail a value of $\Delta c_b/\Delta c_a$ greater than R and the only actions advantageous to B would entail a value of $\Delta c_b/\Delta c_a$ less than R. Governments at war generally have many different cost-imposing actions available, some more efficient than others. If A and B decide which actions to take according to the above criterion, then A will take all actions for which $\Delta c_b/\Delta c_a > R$ and no others, and B will take all actions for which $\Delta c_b/\Delta c_a < R$ and no others. Even though we do not know R exactly, this means that the value of $\Delta c_b/\Delta c_a$ associated with A's overall military activity should be greater than that associated with B's.

This is by no means an obvious conclusion, if we consider the other uses—besides influencing a negotiated settlement—to which military force can be put. Decisions on military activity designed to seize an objective directly, for example, would rest on the perceived probabilities of success and on absolute, rather than relative, costs. If prevailing military tactics and technology happen to favor the defense over the offense, self-initiated activity undertaken for this purpose might well entail a *less* favorable ratio of costs than enemy-initiated activity. Evidence of the opposite, though not proving that cost ratios and the effect of relative costs on the terms of a peace agreement were important influences on military decisions, would at least be consistent with the assumption that they were and would justify further inquiry into the manipulation of costs.

The assertion about relative efficiencies can be tested in a somewhat crude way by examining patterns of military activity and casualties in the Vietnam War. Vietnam is chosen because the required military data are fairly complete and because the period of fighting-and-negotiating in that war was long enough to permit the use of time series analysis to disentangle the effects of each side's activity.[7] Battle deaths are used here as a measure of disagreement costs, or more specifically the kind of disagreement costs that depends almost entirely on the level of military activity. This is, of course, another simplification, which is one reason that the procedure must be described as crude. Killing enemy soldiers and preserving the lives of one's own are valued for reasons besides influencing the shape of peace agreements, and disagreement costs in warfare go beyond battle deaths to include other casualties, monetary expenditures and much else besides.[8] But, given the attention that battle deaths (and other casualties, which are strongly correlated to them anyway) received at least within the United States, they are—for this war— probably the best single measure of its costs.

Estimates of the cost ratios associated with military activity by each side in this war can be obtained by using multiple regression to relate the numbers of battle deaths within South Vietnam to numbers of armed attacks for each month of fighting-while-negotiating. The period in question runs from May 1968, when the Paris peace talks opened, through January 1973, when the Paris agreements were signed (a total of 57 months). Battle deaths on both sides were caused chiefly by Communist ground attacks, allied ground attacks, and allied air attacks within South Vietnam. Allied ground and air attacks are fairly highly correlated,[9] making it difficult to obtain

---

[7] This is the technique Jeffrey S. Milstein used to examine relationships among a large number of military and nonmilitary variables in *Dynamics of the Vietnam War*. Milstein performed regressions similar to those that follow, although without drawing any implications regarding cost ratios and their role in bargaining and without using any data beyond May 1970.

[8] Another simplification is that U.S. and South Vietnamese casualties are lumped together, although the former obviously had more disutility to American leaders than the latter. They are not treated separately because it would be inappropriate to separate U.S. and South Vietnamese military operations, both of which were part of the single war effort under overall American direction.

[9] The correlation between U.S. combat sorties in South Vietnam (statistics not being available on South Vietnamese air activity) and Allied land operations of battal-

meaningful results from a regression which includes them both. Therefore, only ground attacks (specifically, land operations of battalion size or larger) are used as a measure of allied military activity in South Vietnam. This measure is substantially uncorrelated with Communist armed attacks ($r = -.13$), and thus both can be included as independent variables in regression equations, in which the dependent variables are Communist and allied attacks, with little distortion due to collinearity.

The resulting equations, with standard errors of the regression coefficients given in brackets, are:[10]

Communist deaths = −738
+ (15.01 [2.50] × Communist attacks)
+ (7.21 [3.02] × allied attacks)
Allied deaths = 1740
+ (4.02 [.48] × Communist attacks)
+ (−.40 [.58] × allied attacks)

Communist attacks and allied attacks cannot here be considered exact counterparts (because the Communist attacks are of unspecified size, as allied ones are not, and because the apparent effect of allied ground attacks is partly due to air activity). Therefore, one should hesitate to draw conclusions from a comparison of the individual coefficients within either of these equations. But such problems do not affect the value of a *ratio* of deaths associated with attacks by either side, which is the present concern. The first coefficient in each equation can be used to approximate the Communist-to-allied death ratio associated with Communist attacks:

$$\frac{\text{Communist deaths per attack}}{\text{allied deaths per attack}} = \frac{15.01}{4.02} = 3.73.$$

Similarly with allied attacks:

$$\frac{\text{Communist deaths per attack}}{\text{allied deaths per attack}} = \frac{7.21}{-.40} = -18.03.$$

ion size or larger is .65 for this period. The source of all the monthly data used in this section is Table 1006, Statistics on Southeast Asia (final update), provided by the Office of the Assistant Secretary of Defense (Comptroller), U.S. Department of Defense.

[10] The mean values are: Communist deaths, 10,404; Allied deaths, 2,706; Communist attacks, 326; Allied attacks, 866.

The difference between the two ratios is in the expected direction: Communist military activity was relatively more efficient from the Communist viewpoint, while allied activity was more efficient from the allied viewpoint. In this case, in fact, allied activity was seemingly hyperefficient in the sense that greater activity was associated with fewer allied deaths, although this negative relationship is too small in comparison with the standard error to be significant (which is not the case with any of the other three coefficients).[11]

The precise statistical significance of the comparison of ratios is difficult to determine (even assuming that a time series using one case can be treated as if it were a random sample) because it involves four separate estimates, each with its own probability distribution. But we can gain some feel for it through the following procedure. Suppose we want to determine a maximum estimate for the kill ratio associated with Communist attacks, above which the true ratio has only a .05 probability of falling. We can approximate it with a ratio using the maximum estimate for Communist deaths per attack above which the true value falls with a probability of $\sqrt{.05}$ (i.e., .2236), together with a corresponding minimum estimate for allied deaths per attack. That is, there is no more than a .05 probability that *both* estimates depart this far, in the optimistic direction, from the true values. Given the number of observations, an adjustment of the coefficients by eight-tenths of the standard error places them just within this .2236 range. Thus, a least-favorable estimate of the ratio is:

$$\frac{15.01 + (.8 \times 2.50)}{4.02 - (.8 \times .48)} = \frac{17.02}{3.64} = 4.67$$

A corresponding least-favorable estimate of the kill ratio associated with allied attacks is obtained the same way, but with signs reversed:

$$\frac{7.21 - (.8 \times 3.02)}{-.40 + (.8 \times .58)} = \frac{4.79}{.06} = 83.47$$

[11] A possible deficiency in the data—which were compiled by the U.S. military command—that would affect the values of the two kill ratios would be an overestimation or underestimation of Communist deaths. However, as long as any such error was a systematic bias that distorted the figures for Communist deaths in roughly the same way throughout the period, it would tend to raise or lower ratios in tandem without changing the direction of the difference between them.

So even with pessimistic estimates of the kill ratios, they differ from each other in the predicted manner; each side's attacks were associated with a ratio more favorable to it than were the enemy's attacks. (And the principle that applies to the construction of the individual ratios applies as well to the comparison between them: the probability that both ratios are worse than the least favorable estimates given above is not .05 but more like $(.05)^2 = .0025$.)

Setting aside the question of significance and returning to the best estimates of the kill ratios associated with attacks by each side (i.e., 3.73 for the Communists and -18.03 for the allies), the changes in the point of no agreement corresponding to each can be depicted as in Figure 9. The lengths of OC and OA reflect the mean number of monthly attacks (i.e., the coefficients in the regression equations are multiplied by 326 for Communist attacks and 866 for allied attacks to determine the coordinates of C and A). Figure 9 thus provides a rough picture of cost imposition in a typical month during the negotiation period of the Vietnam War. If we equate battle deaths with

FIGURE 9. **Cost manipulation in the Vietnam War.**

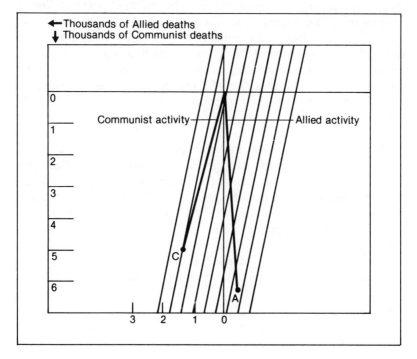

units of disutility (the meaning of such an assumption will be addressed below), then it may be viewed as a real-life equivalent to the hypothetical cost manipulations in Figure 8. We do not know the exact shape of the bargaining space, but a possible set of isosettlement lines for which attacks producing the given kill ratios would be advantageous to the side making them are shown.

Motivations

One outstanding characteristic of Figure 9 is the steep slope of the isosettlement lines implied by the slopes of OA and OC. If the belligerents did in fact observe the criterion of efficiency, the minimum slope of the actual isosettlement lines could be only slightly less than the slope of the hypothetical lines shown. This in turn implies that the utility frontier—although none is drawn and the actual one was no doubt nonlinear—was correspondingly steep. To mention the slope of this curve raises the topic of how belligerents value different outcomes. It also leads to an observation about cost manipulation and about the strength of motivations which has been made, though only in an incomplete way, by earlier observers. Clausewitz linked motivation to the ending of wars when he wrote that a belligerent will yield well before it is overthrown if its "motives and passions are slight."[12] Alexander George has written in a similar vein about coercive diplomacy in pointing to a favorable "asymmetry of motivation" as one of the conditions for the successful use, or threat of use, of military force to elicit a decision from another government.[13]

Taken at face value, these observations—especially the one by George—entail a comparison of the utilities of the two parties to a conflict. As such, they run into the same problem that any other effort at interpersonal (or intergroup) comparison of utilities runs into: the absence of a common scale or standard makes the comparison meaningless. What *is* meaningful, and what probably underlies the statements cited, is a comparison of the way in which each side values possible agreements with the way in which the same side values disagreement costs. It may be convenient to make an ad hoc comparison of the utility of disagreement costs, as was done in Figure 9 by equating battle deaths with units of disutility, and then to

[12] *On War*, Vol. 1, p. 30.
[13] Alexander L. George, "Comparisons and Lessons," in George, Hall, and Simons, *The Limits of Coercive Diplomacy*, pp. 218–219.

speak of different levels of motivation concerning the terms of agreement. It is convenient to do so here because the very questions which are of interest involve objective measures of the level of violence. I.e., we are interested in the conditions in which a belligerent stages more rather than fewer attacks, endures more rather than fewer casualties, etc. But it must be remembered that one could just as easily, and just as arbitrarily, consider the difference in utility to each side between two possible agreements to be equal and then speak of different levels of motivation concerning disagreement costs.[14] To be complete, a statement about motivation and cost manipulation must make the comparison between valuation of agreements and valuation of costs explicit. The conclusion that follows from the steep slope of the implied utility frontier in Figure 9 is that the Communists must have cared more about the shape of the agreement *relative to their concern with disagreement costs* than did the Americans.

Similarly, a more complete version of George's observation would be that success in the use of military force to elicit a decision from an adversary depends upon having a greater concern over the terms of an agreement, relative to one's concern over the costs of military action. This is a statement about responses to the use or threat of use of military force, but the underlying idea is also the basis for a statement about opportunities for advantageous manipulation of costs. The belligerent which cares more about the terms of settlement, relative to its concern with disagreement costs, can profitably take less efficient actions than can its opponent; it has a wider range of opportunities for cost manipulation. It would, to the extent that these considerations influence decision-making, tend to employ more fully its capacity for violence.

[14] Graphically, being less motivated to minimize disagreement costs would mean that the scale along which they are measured is more compressed than the corresponding scale for the other bargainer. Suppose that a representation of the U.S.-North Vietnamese bargaining problem, similar to Figure 9, were constructed, except that the difference in utility to each side between any two possible agreements was defined to be equal. The slope of the utility frontier would then be -1, the slope of the isosettlement lines would be 1, and military activity having the slope of OC would no longer be advantageous to Hanoi. But if the North Vietnamese really were less concerned about their casualties, relative to their concern with the terms of agreement, than the Americans were, the scale of Communist casualties along the vertical dimension would be more compressed than the scale of Allied casualties along the horizontal dimension, meaning that the slope of OC would be less than it is in Figure 9.

The remarks about efficiency and motivation can be made less abstract by referring to more direct evidence of leaders' thinking during the Vietnam War.

The deliberations of the Politburo in Hanoi during this period may still be a closed book, but we at least know from North Vietnamese writings on the war against the French how much emphasis the North Vietnamese placed upon the attrition of the opponent's troops. The destruction of enemy manpower was the "essential thing," wrote General Giap, and it was essential not just to frustrate French military efforts but to wear down all Frenchmen and to make them more weary of the war.[15]

American decision-making also took heed of the role of casualties as disagreement costs, but with only a belated recognition of how relative costs and motivations determine the effectiveness of military actions. General Westmoreland's search-and-destroy strategy could register impressive enemy body counts without softening Hanoi's diplomatic position if U.S. casualties were also sufficiently high and if the North Vietnamese cared more about how the war was settled. Secretary of Defense McNamara did recognize these elements of the situation in a memorandum which he wrote to the President in October 1966, although it would be more than a year before his chief recommendations would become U.S. policy. McNamara began by arguing that the war had become more a contest in the imposition and enduring of disagreement costs than an effort to seize or retain objectives. "I see no reasonable way to bring the war to an end soon," he wrote. "Enemy morale has not broken—he apparently has adjusted to our stopping his drive for military victory and has adopted a strategy of keeping us busy and waiting us out (a strategy of attriting our national will)." The Secretary then noted the adversary's remarkable toleration of disagreement costs, particularly casualties. Enemy battle deaths had increased and the "infiltration routes would seem to be one-way trails to death for the North Vietnamese. Yet there is no sign of an impending break in enemy morale. . . ." McNamara based his recommendations on the idea that the aggressive American military strategy used until then could not achieve the high level of efficiency which, given the apparent discrepancy in motivations which Hanoi's surprising persistence had revealed, would be necessary to elicit

[15] Giap, *People's War, People's Army*, p. 161. See also George K. Tanham, *Communist Revolutionary Warfare*, pp. 14–15.

concessions from the Communists. It would be more effective to tailor strategy to minimize U.S. costs. Among other things, this would mean stabilizing both U.S. force levels in South Vietnam and the level of bombing of North Vietnam. "The solution," McNamara concluded, "lies in girding, openly, for a longer war and in taking actions immediately which will in 12 to 18 months give *clear evidence that the continuing costs and risks to the American people are acceptably limited,* that the formula for success has been found, and that the end of the war is merely a matter of time."[16]

Thinking similar to McNamara's underlay the various measures taken during the last year of the Johnson administration and throughout the Nixon administration to reduce American casualties. These efforts included a general halt to the escalation (Johnson's decisions in early 1968 to curtail the bombing of North Vietnam and not to send large reinforcements into the south), a turn away from search-and-destroy (associated with the replacement of Westmoreland by Creighton Abrams in April 1968), a shift of the combat burden to soldiers whose deaths would be less costly to Americans (Vietnamization), and even offensive action (the May 1970 incursion into Cambodia, the chief rationale of which was the protection of the U.S. troops still in Vietnam). Vietnamization had several facets, including a demonstration to Hanoi of Saigon's ability to stand on its own feet and perhaps even a long-term alternative to a negotiated settlement, should Hanoi remain unconvinced. But a major goal undoubtedly was the reduction of U.S. casualties, which were so much more salient to Americans than were South Vietnamese casualties. The troop withdrawals were accompanied by fresh orders to military commanders to make such a reduction their primary objective.[17] Once Vietnamization got underway, the reduction in American casualties was almost rapid enough to conform to McNamara's recommended timetable. June 1969 (when the first troop withdrawal was announced) was the last month in which U.S. battle deaths exceeded 1,000; June 1970 was the last one in which they exceeded 400; and June 1971 the last in which they exceeded 100.

It would be too cynical to think that the efforts to reduce the

---

[16] Text in *Pentagon Papers,* Vol. 4, pp. 348–354. Emphasis added.

[17] Kalb and Abel, *Roots of Involvment,* p. 281. The virtually zero relationship between Allied attacks and Allied casualties that emerged from the regression analysis suggests that conservation of even South Vietnamese troops was a major consideration in operational decisions taken during this period by General Abrams' command.

deaths of GIs were not motivated in part by a concern for the lives themselves, and too unrealistic to assert that they were not also motivated by a desire to reap the domestic political benefits which would accrue regardless of what happened in negotiations with Hanoi. But the effect that a change in casualty rates could have on the U.S.-North Vietnamese bargaining problem was surely one of the most important considerations.[18] Hanoi would realize that reducing the loss of American lives would make disagreement more tolerable to U.S. decision-makers—both directly through their own sensibilities and indirectly by defusing domestic criticism of the war.

Relative costs perhaps played a somewhat greater part in military decision-making in the Vietnam War than they have in other wars that have been settled through negotiation, because with no front line which the American public could use as an indicator of progress, the human and monetary costs were more salient. But any such difference should not be overstated. Consider American military decisions in the Korean War, in which there *was* a front line. General Mark Clark, who directed the UN war effort during its last year, summarized the basis for those decisions this way:

> Since it was not our government's policy to seek a military decision, the next best thing was *to make the stalemate more expensive for the Communists than for us,* to hit them where it hurt, to worry them, to convince them by force that the price tag on an armistice was going up, not down.[19]

Besides basing his strategy on considerations of relative costs, Clark showed a sensitivity to the kind of discrepancy in motivations that the data on the Vietnam War revealed. Making disagreement more expensive to the enemy than to ourselves was not simply a matter of making Communist casualties more numerous than allied ones. Manpower was the Communists' "long suit," he explained. I.e., it was more expendable to the Communists, and human losses were less costly to them (relative to their concern with settlement terms). Therefore he would not trade a UN life for a Communist life. "In fact I wouldn't," Clark wrote, "if I could help it, trade one American or allied life for ten or more dead Communists with nothing to show for it but a few additional acres of Korean real estate."[20]

---

[18] The attitudes of leading figures in the Nixon administration toward Vietnamization are discussed in Kalb and Kalb, *Kissinger,* p. 128. See also Landau, *Kissinger: The Uses of Power,* p. 217.

[19] Clark, *From the Danube to the Yalu,* p. 69. Emphasis added.

[20] *Ibid.*

Clark's 1 : 10+ ratio sounds off-the-cuff and probably was, but it would be comparable to the considerable difference in relative motivations in the Vietnam War that was implied by the cost imposition depicted in Figure 9. Different in many other ways, the Korean and Vietnam Wars were similar insofar as each pitted a free society against an authoritarian regime that evidently cared more about its territorial ambitions than about the suffering of its subjects. This is one reason the U.S. authorities concluded in each case that, during the period of negotiations, they would have to husband their manpower much more carefully than the other side and to take only the most efficient possible military actions.

This later phase of the Korean War demonstrates how wartime military decisions taken in order to manipulate disagreement costs can differ markedly from ones taken according to other criteria. Clark's cautious posture did not stem from any lack of confidence in the UNC's ability to push the Communists northward, should it have been willing to pay the price. In fact, in October 1952 (when the truce talks went into indefinite recess following the Communists' refusal to accept any of the UNC's proposals on prisoner repatriation) he had offered to Washington a plan for a major offensive up the peninsula that would have required a large expansion of UNC forces, the employment of Nationalist Chinese troops, and air and naval action against mainland China.[21] His plan quickly died because the Truman administration had already decided in favor of a negotiated settlement based on a demarcation line somewhere in the vicinity of the 38th Parallel, which is evidently what Clark meant in referring to the government's policy not to seek a "military decision." Whereas a military plan intended to revise the war map implied escalation and aggressive action, a plan designed to manipulate disagreement costs implied the opposite, because the rugged terrain and the Communists' improvement of their defensive positions since the stalemate began would have made the costs of a renewed offensive unacceptable. Accepting the criterion of relative costs, Clark himself turned down various proposals for offensive action made by the Eighth Army Commander, General James Van Fleet, on the grounds that the best way "to make the stalemate more expensive for the Communists than for us" was to sit back and let the enemy try to hammer away at the UNC's (similarly improved) defenses.[22]

[21] Hermes, *Truce Tent and Fighting Front*, p, 366.
[22] See *ibid.*, p. 293.

Responses to the Enemy's Military Activity

Having taken an initial look at how cost manipulation is related to the efficiency of military actions themselves and to the value that belligerents place upon outcomes and war costs, we now consider how all this might be affected by the enemy's military activity. When one side manipulates costs, does this expand, contract, or leave unchanged the other side's opportunities for manipulation?

If utilities are linear, as in the bargaining problem in Figure 8, it should leave them unchanged. Suppose bargainer A were contemplating the cost-imposing action represented by movement from O to D_1. Starting from O, it would be advantageous for him to take it. Even if B had already taken an action moving the point of no agreement from O to D_2, it still would be advantageous. In fact, no matter what sort of cost manipulation B had previously undertaken, it would be a profitable move; with parallel isosettlement lines, A's minimum necessary efficiency remains unchanged. But the lines are parallel only if utilities are linear, which is unlikely to be true in most actual cases. In real bargaining problems the bargaining space could assume any of an infinite number of shapes, but to prevent the analysis from becoming intractable we will relax the assumption of linear utilities just enough to consider the implications and meaning of overall convexity or concavity.

Figures 10 and 11 show two different utility frontiers, together with the associated isosettlement lines, which are similar to the one in Figure 8 except that the utilities of agreements are no longer linear. The lines in Figure 10 are the product of a convex bargaining space; those in Figure 11 imply a concave space. Suppose that, in the bargaining problem in Figure 10, B takes an action which moves the point of no agreement from O to O'. O' is on an isosettlement line with a slightly lesser slope than the one on which O is situated, meaning that B's standards for selecting subsequent cost-imposing actions have become more stringent, while A's have become less so. There are some possible increases in costs which formerly would have been advantageous to B but which now would be to A's advantage. In general: with a convex bargaining space, a change in disagreement costs which is to one side's advantage restricts that side's subsequent opportunities for favorable cost-imposing action and expands the opponent's. Similar reasoning regarding a move of the point of no agreement in Figure 11 from O to O' leads to the opposite conclusion when the bargaining space is concave: the bargainer who

FIGURE 10. **Cost manipulation with a convex bargaining space.**

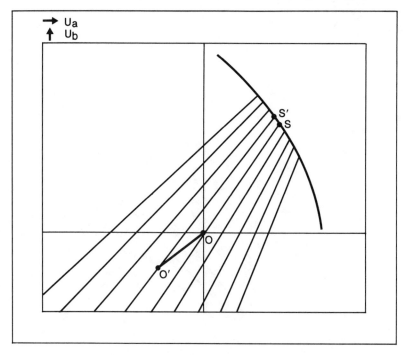

benefits from the move now has even greater opportunities for further cost imposition, while his opponent's opportunities are restricted.[23]

When a bargainer's opportunities for advantageously manipulating disagreement costs expand due to a change of this type, he will generally respond by raising the level of violence—i.e., he will escalate. The actions which already were efficient enough to benefit his position are still worth taking, and in addition there are other actions which are now efficient enough to take as well. Therefore, if we can make an informed guess about the overall shape of the bargaining space in a particular peace negotiation, we can predict how the belligerents should respond militarily to changes in relative disagreement costs—specifically, whether they will increase or decrease

---

[23] These generalizations do not imply that the contest in cost manipulation has an equilibrium. The discussion in this chapter is intended to show how the manipulation of war costs can be rational and comprehensible even if rationality in this context is not necessarily well defined in a game theoretical sense.

FIGURE 11. Cost manipulation with a concave bargaining space.

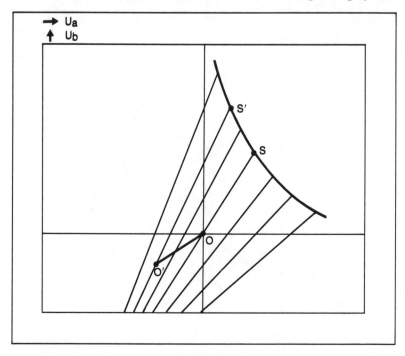

their activity. The Vietnam War can again provide material for the exercise, simply because the data on attacks and casualties are available and extend over a long enough period to permit a test. The stakes in Vietnam centered on the fundamental question of who should rule South Vietnam, and that is the sort of issue on which compromises tend to be difficult and offer little satisfaction to either side. Solutions which leave open the possibility that the enemy eventually will take power are not highly valued because they pose a risk not only to one's political goals but even to one's life.[24] Although during the period of American involvement it was an international war, and although this phase ended with a negotiated settlement as most modern international wars do, the issues resembled those in most civil wars. What this all means is that the Vietnam bargaining space was generally concave. Therefore, if the belligerents were basing their military decisions at least partly on considerations of relative disagreement costs, each should have responded to

[24] See Gelb, "Vietnam: The System Worked," pp. 150–151.

favorable changes in relative costs with escalation and to unfavorable changes with de-escalation.

This can be tested by noting the direction of the relationships, if any, between relative costs, as the independent variable, and the level of military activity by each side, as dependent variables. The measure of relative costs will be the Communist-to-allied ratio of battle deaths, and that of military activity will be the same figures for ground attacks that were used before. Because it takes time for decision-makers to evaluate and respond to an altered strategic situation, the dependent variable should be lagged. Here a four-month lag is used, which seems appropriate for decisions which often would involve not only re-evaluations but also redeployments of forces. (Shortening or lengthening the lag by a month or two would change the size of the resulting correlations somewhat but not their directions.) The correlations for the 57-month negotiation period[25] between the number of Communist attacks in any month and the Communist-to-allied death ratio four months previous is $-.26(p <$ $.10)$; the corresponding correlation for allied attacks is $.62(p < .001)$. Both are in the predicted direction: a higher ratio was associated with a subsequent lower level of Communist activity and a higher level of allied activity.

It may be appropriate to introduce a control to allow for the fact that periods of high or low military activity by either side tended to spread over several adjoining months, meaning that the number of attacks by each belligerent in any one month were positively related to the number of attacks by the same side four months earlier. (This is particularly true of the Allied side, for which the correlation between attacks in month t and attacks in month $t - 4$ was .65. The corresponding figure for the Communists was .29.) A partial correlation coefficient that measures the association between attacks by one side at t and the death ratio at $t - 4$ while controlling for attacks by the same side at $t - 4$ would exclude any reverse effect that those same attacks had upon the death ratio, thus being a better indicator of how the later level of activity was a response to changes in this ratio. This partial correlation coefficient for Communist attacks is $-.31(p < .05)$, and for allied attacks $.35(p < .02)$. In other words, the control has a small accentuating effect on the coefficient for Communist attacks and reduces the coefficient for allied attacks,

---

[25] The first month for the independent variable is May 1968 and for the lagged dependent variable September 1968, so the number of observations is 53.

although it remains positive. The result is thus two moderately sized coefficients of correlation which have the signs one would predict with bargainers that are manipulating disagreement costs in the context of a bargaining problem in which, like Vietnam, the possible compromises offer little satisfaction to either side.

The principle at hand may be rephrased, in a way that enhances the meaning of the stark lines in the diagrams, as follows. In a conflict with a convex bargaining space, there are compromise settlements which, because they give each side most of what it wants, are attractive in every sense of the word. The attraction of these solutions extends to the manipulation of costs. A belligerent attempting to impose costs in order to push the settlement toward its favored end of the utility frontier finds it increasingly difficult to do so. The criterion of efficiency becomes more stringent for it and less stringent for its opponent. The existence of acceptable compromises is a force for stability that is lacking in Vietnam-type conflicts with a concave bargaining space. In the latter, the extreme solutions give one side all of what it wants while being little worse to the opponent than a compromise. These solutions exert an attraction of their own, and as one belligerent succeeds in employing violence to relocate the point of no agreement, it becomes free to use less efficient actions. If there is any sort of stability observed in the contest in cost manipulation in this type of conflict, it is due not to considerations of efficiency but rather to limitations to each side's capacity to use violence, or to reasons having to do with absolute rather than relative costs. It is the latter topic to which we now turn.

Time and the Level of Violence

To this point, cost-imposing actions have been analyzed only insofar as they may influence the terms of settlement. This simplication must now be dropped. Costs qua costs, not just as shapers of agreements, influence military decisions; i.e., governments seek to minimize their casualties and material losses not just because this will improve their bargaining position, but because they value these lives and resources for their own sake. (Of course, if they were not so valued, their loss would not be expected to have any effect on bargaining positions.)

Our change of perspective involves moving from a purely static examination of the relationship between costly actions and likely settlements to a dynamic view that considers the *time* required to reach agreement or otherwise end the war. Relative costs, the focus of attention so far, do not depend on time, as absolute costs do. A game theorist such as Nash would view what we have referred to as manipulations of disagreement costs as timeless—and costless—mental exercises which reveal the threats available to each bargainer and thereby provide a common basis for bargaining.[26] Threats which are never carried out (a subject to be addressed later in this chapter) may very well affect peace negotiations, but cost manipulation in warfare also involves real military activity with losses of real lives and resources. How long that activity lasts—and it can be a matter of days or of years—determines the magnitude of the losses. This expanded perspective is the basis for the observations on cost manipulation in the remainder of this section. First we examine the role that expectations about the length of the war play in military decisions. Subsequently, we return to the question of the shape of the bargaining space and relate this to the overall level of violence in a war. After that, we note how the sequential nature of wartime decision-making can lead the belligerents to a level of violence well above what either one would have considered acceptable at the outset.

It is not immediately obvious exactly how a concern for absolute costs and the length of time during which they are incurred would alter a military decision based solely on relative costs and their effect on the terms of agreement. On one hand, the desire to minimize the rate at which one incurs costs would dampen any inclination to escalate in an effort to improve the terms of the agreement. Even if a given military action were efficient enough to improve the settlement, a government must consider whether this improvement would be worth the resulting increase in its own costs. If the decision-makers anticipated that disagreement would persist—and the higher level of costs would have to be endured—for an appreciable length of time before a settlement was reached, they might decide that escalation was not worth while. But, on the other hand, a belligerent would also consider the effect that escalation could have on the period of disagreement itself. It might escalate in order to soften the opponent's bargaining position, not as a way of getting a better agreement, but as a way of getting an agreement sooner. Such a shortening of the period of disagreement could lower its total disagreement costs for the war, even though the escalation would in-

---

[26] John Nash, "Two-Person Cooperative Games."

crease the rate at which it incurred costs. In fact, if the expected reduction in costs were great enough, it might take a relatively inefficient action that would soften its own diplomatic position as well and make the terms of the eventual agreement *less* favorable than they otherwise would have been. The settlement would be more valuable only insofar as it would come sooner.[27]

Given these conflicting tendencies, it is difficult to specify precisely the conditions under which a decision-maker who weighs these considerations will elect to employ more rather than less violence. However, there are several situations in which we can expect a sensitivity to absolute costs and to the dimension of time to steer military decision-making in directions that it might not otherwise take.

An increase in the rate at which costs are incurred, or an upward revision in the expected duration of the war, is the sort of change which is apt to induce a belligerent to resort to escalation in an effort to hasten a settlement. Such a decision may be made regardless of whether negotiations are already in progress. In the Mexican-American war, for example, it was growing domestic discontent over prolongation of the conflict, and the political costs which this implied, that led President Polk in late 1846 to reject plans merely to occupy the territory already conquered in northern Mexico, and to opt instead for a march on Mexico City.[28] A similar situation faced Prussia in its war against France in 1870. Bismarck, concerned that additional expenditures of manpower would create political difficulties in Prussia and strain the alliance with the other German states, called in December for the immediate bombardment of Paris, in the hope that this would quickly end the war.[29] Both of these decisions were attempts to compress time and to force an outcome. They also, incidentally, suggest how violent actions intended to shorten a war can differ in type and locale from actions intended to influence the shape of an agreement. A capital city frequently is seen as a national jugular vein which offers the quickest way to get the opposition to

[27] See Cross, *The Economics of Bargaining*, pp. 151–157, where he draws some of these possibilities out of his dynamic model. Given his assumptions, every increase in disagreement costs softens a bargainer's demand, after which he expects to stand pat at his new position. Therefore, every time—not just some of the time—a Crossian bargainer escalates in order to speed agreement, he does so despite his expectation that the terms of the agreement will be less favorable.

[28] Otis Singletary, *The Mexican War*, pp. 110–111.

[29] Michael Howard, *The Franco-Prussian War*, p. 389.

capitulate, to negotiate, or to conclude a negotiation. The costs and risks involved, even if not justified on other grounds, seem justified in order to hasten the end of the war.

Polk and Bismarck made their decisions against backdrops of military success that made it realistic to think that their wars could be quickly concluded. The higher rate at which costs would be incurred was acceptable because the risk that the war would drag on, despite the augmented military effort, was small. This leads to a more general point concerning the relation between the time dimension and any decision on escalation to improve the settlement. Because the desirability of such manipulation depends in part on the increase that the manipulator expects it to have on his own absolute costs, and because the magnitude of those costs depends on how much longer the war will last, it follows that an expectation that peace is near will make cost-imposing activity appear more attractive. As a result, we should expect violence to increase toward the end of a negotiation, after a narrowing of the gap between the two diplomatic positions has made a settlement appear imminent.[30] As with long-distance runners on the last lap, the realization that the pain will soon be over induces the belligerents to use their strength to the fullest to make the outcome of the contest more favorable.

This expectation is consistent with patterns of military activity in the three of the major cases—Korea, Algeria, and Vietnam—in which the negotiating period was long enough to reach a conclusion on whether violence increased or decreased as the end of that period approached.[31] During most of the two years of negotiation in Korea,

[30] Cross (*The Economics of Bargaining*, p. 158) derives a similar result mathematically from his bargaining model, but the reasoning is markedly different. As noted earlier, under his assumptions the only purpose of escalation can be to hasten a settlement, not to improve the terms. This does not seem plausible in conditions in which an agreement appears imminent anyway. His result regarding escalation near the end of a negotiation depends on another implication of his model—viz., that the concession rates of a pair of similar Crossian bargainers tend to decrease as the negotiation progresses. This would not be consistent with the evidence presented in the Chapter 3 showing that the final phase of a peace conference usually exhibits fairly rapid concession-making; the inconsistency is not surprising in light of the reasons given in the same chapter why Crossian reasoning is important in the second phase of a negotiation but tends to be supplanted by other logics in the final phase.

[31] The Geneva conference on Indochina was too short to disentangle military responses to the imminent conclusion of the negotiation from responses to its start. Although the conference at Ghent was two months longer, the trans-Atlantic communications lag made it effectively as brief. Some observations will be made below on how the level of violence tends to change as negotiations begin.

and particularly during 1952, the front was quiet compared to the action of the first year of the war. Combat then intensified during 1953, particularly during the final two months when the Communists launched the largest assaults of the entire negotiation period. In Algeria, the FLN was more active during the last three months of the war, while the final rounds of negotiations took place at Les Rousses and Evian, than they had been for the previous three years. Armed attacks and terrorist incidents during this final period took place at an annual rate of 19,000 per year, the highest since 1958.[32] The last full year of the Vietnam War—1972—was by some measures the most violent of the entire war, and by most measures more violent than the previous two. Casualties on both sides were the highest since 1969, and Communist attacks were far more numerous than in any other year (6,584, versus the next highest total of 3,921 in 1968, the year of the Tet offensive). The higher level of violence continued even after the offensive stalled and Hanoi again became serious about negotiating a settlement, presenting its draft proposal which led to the tentative agreement in October. Whereas Communist armed attacks during the year prior to the start of the offensive in April had averaged less than 200 per month, they did not again dip below 500 until January 1973, the month that the agreement was signed, when they numbered 423. On the allied side, the spring of 1972 also marked the dropping of most restrictions on U.S. air activity over North Vietnam and the beginning of bombing more intense than any which had taken place for the previous three and a half years. The most intense of all were the assaults of B-52s known as the Christmas bombing, taking place little more than a month before agreement was reached.[33]

---

[32] Figures in Tripier, *Autopsie de la Guerre d'Algérie*, p. 664.

[33] Some of the acts of escalation just mentioned had purposes other than manipulating the costs of the principal adversary. The final Chinese assaults in Korea were directed against portions of the line held by South Korean forces and took place after virtually all details of the truce had been settled with the UNC; they obviously were intended to punish Syngman Rhee and to warn him against obstruction of the agreement and about future misbehavior. One of the purposes of the Christmas bombing probably was to placate President Thieu, whose balking at the provisional terms negotiated in October had become a major stumbling block to attaining an agreement. This suggests, not that the point being made is invalid, but rather that it can be expanded beyond the subject of this chapter: escalation for *any* purpose, not just to manipulate the enemy's costs and thereby improve the terms of the agreement, is more attractive when peace seems imminent.

Possible Outcomes and the Level of Violence

Having examined the role of absolute costs in military decision-making, we can now return to the discussion of the different sorts of agreements which may be available (i.e., differently shaped bargaining spaces) and address a question not yet touched—viz., how the possible agreements affect the total amount of violence used. We have already noted how a government that is considering a manipulation of disagreement costs intended to improve the terms of the settlement must weigh the value of improved terms against whatever increase in its own absolute costs the manipulation would involve, and how varying the expected period of disagreement, and hence the absolute costs, would therefore affect its decision. But assuming the absolute costs to be unchanged, varying the amount of improvement in the terms of the settlement clearly would affect the decision as well. We know that the amount of improvement depends partly on relative costs, but it also depends on the shape of the bargaining space.

Consider movement of the disagreement point from O to O' in Figures 10 and 11, viewing it as a possible manipulation of costs being contemplated by B. If the scales in the two diagrams are the same, then the change entails the same absolute and relative costs. Yet the improvement, from B's viewpoint, in the terms of the implied settlement (which in each case is now located as S' rather than at S) is greater in Figure 11, where the bargaining space is concave, than in Figure 10, where it is convex. (With linear utilities and a similar overall slope of the utility frontier, as in Figure 8, the amount of improvement for B would be somewhere between the two.) The convergence of the isosettlement lines in Figure 11 reveals that, in general, concavity of the bargaining space accentuates the effect that any given increase in disagreement costs can be expected to have on the settlement. The principle can be expressed more informally in a way that complements the earlier remarks about changes in the standard of efficiency: when an attractive compromise is available (convex space), changes in the costs of disagreement must be more drastic to push the bargainers away from it, while bargaining problems which lack such a compromise (concave space) also lack this kind of stability. In the latter, with no particular settlement exerting a strong attraction by virtue of its value to both parties, the outcome will be more dependent on the contest in cost manipulation. An implication is that, with a concave space, some acts of manipulation will appear advantageous which otherwise would not, because for the same absolute cost they produce a greater impact on the agreement. As a result, there is likely to be a greater overall level of costs imposed.

The corresponding conclusion regarding warfare is that when, as in Vietnam, the available compromises offer relatively little satisfaction to either side, the level of violence will be higher than in otherwise similar conflicts. With so many other differences, it is impossible to find "otherwise similar" wars to make such a comparison directly, but the conclusion is suggested when we observe how the level of violence in modern wars has changed as negotiations began. The principle probably helps to explain the difference in the direction of the change in Korea, on the one hand, and in Vietnam and similar wars, on the other. Military activity in Korea during the final two years of the war, after truce talks had begun, was distinctly lower than in the first year. We have already pointed to the tactical facts of life and the strength of the defense as one retardant on cost-imposition during this period, but an additional reason was the obvious availability of repartition as the basis for a compromise settlement. The question at stake in the Korean truce talks was not who would rule in Korea, but rather the details and implementation of a compromise that would leave different parts of the country in different hands. Behind General Clark's unwillingness to spend one UNC life for ten Communist ones was the realization that the return for any such expenditure in the form of improvements in the agreement would be meager. In Vietnam, where the issue *was* who would rule the country, the beginning of negotiations did not see a similar de-escalation. To the contrary: by many measures, violence was on average greater during the negotiation period (May 1968 through January 1973) than during the previous portion of the war (January 1966, when complete figures on military activity begin, through April 1968). Communist armed attacks increased from an average of 191 per month to 326 per month. Allied land operations rose from 454 per month to 866 per month. Despite Vietnamization and a reduction in the American share of the ground war, U.S. combat air sorties in South Vietnam increased slightly, from 182 per month to 202 per month. The only sector of combat which was less active during the latter period was the air war over North Vietnam, with the curtailment of U.S. bombing being part of the arrangement under which negotiations began.

In Algeria, as in Vietnam, the issue was who would rule the country, and compromise settlements with an attraction comparable to that of repartition in Korea were lacking. The opening of negotiations between France and the FLN in mid-1960 was accompanied by a resurgence of FLN military and terrorist activity, which had been steadily declining for the preceding four years. That activity had dropped to 13,000 violent incidents in 1960 (less than half the total in 1956), but increased slightly to 13,900 in 1961 and to the previously mentioned annual rate of 19,000 for the first three months of 1962. The violence in Algeria never regained the level that it had reached earlier in the rebellion, but the evidence suggests that this was because of the French army's earlier success in reducing the rebel forces. The FLN's army within Algeria was, during the last two years of the war, only a fraction of what it had been when its strength was at its peak in 1958, and the resurgence of activity during the negotiation period took place despite a continued decline in the number of rebel troops.[34]

The conflict of interest between the French and the Viet Minh in Indochina was not wholly of the Korean type or of the Vietnam-Algeria type. As with Korea, the eventual settlement was based on partition. Unlike Korea, however, partition did not mean reinstitution of the *status quo ante bellum;* it emerged as a basis for settlement only after the conference was underway, and for at least one side—the Viet Minh—it was acceptable not as a compromise of indefinite duration but only as a way-station along the road to control of all of Vietnam. Who should rule that country was very much the central issue in the conflict, just as it was in the later war involving the United States. And as with the later war, the opening of the peace conference coincided with an increase in military activity. The general expectation in 1954, probably more so than in 1968, was that the opening of the conference meant that an armistice was imminent, and the upsurge in violence probably also reflected a principle posited earlier—viz., that an expectation that peace is near increases the incentive to manipulate costs in an effort to improve the settlement. Whatever the exact mixture of motives, the most spectacular act of escalation was Giap's gigantic effort to besiege the French garrison at Dienbienphu, which fell on the very day that the Geneva conference opened. French losses, including prisoners, at Dienbienphu numbered 12,000, and the Viet Minh losses have been

---

[34] Figures in Tripier, p. 664.

estimated at twice that.[35] The timing of the operation and the diplomacy which preceded the Geneva conference suggest that the former was based on the latter, and that this immensely costly action was intended to deliver a sudden and devastating blow to French confidence at the moment when it would have the greatest impact on the terms of settlement.[36] The Communist escalation did not stop with Dienbienphu; with the conference in progress, Giap increased the pressure throughout northern Indochina and rapidly moved his siege troops eastward to the Red River delta to threaten Hanoi with encirclement.[37] The Dienbienphu campaign paralleled the Tet offensive that would be staged fourteen years later, both being audacious acts of escalation intended to steer a peace negotiation in the desired direction. The principal difference between the two was that in the first the Viet Minh strategists were reacting to diplomatic processes which had already begun, whereas in the second they saw themselves as more in control of events, hoping that their action would elicit the kind of response they did in fact receive when President Johnson made his March 1968 address.[38]

Sequential Decision-Making and the Level of Violence

Military decisions themselves, not just the costs which result from them, have a time dimension. A war is the product not of two grand decisions at the outset that determine the intensity and duration of violence, but rather of a series of choices. As the war continues, the belligerents must repeatedly decide whether to continue the struggle, and if so whether to raise, lower, or maintain the level of vio-

---

[35] Tanham, p. 979.

[36] Robert J. O'Neill, *General Giap: Politician and Strategist*, pp. 138–139; and Buttinger, *Vietnam at War*, p. 814. Jules Roy in *The Battle of Dienbienphu*, pp. 144–145, argues that the diplomatic activity did not influence the Viet Minh's decision to invest Dienbienphu, the decision having been taken in late November 1953. But he evidently overlooks the fact that by then the major powers had already agreed to a conference at Berlin, where one of the topics to be discussed would be a further conference to settle Asian issues. Ho Chi Minh's offer of direct talks made at about this time also suggests that the Viet Minh had just come to realize that a peace negotiation was not long off.

[37] Devillers and Lacouture, *End of a War*, pp. 173–175.

[38] McGarvey, *Visions of Victory*, p. 55. See also George Ball's comparison of Tet with the Dienbienphu campaign, reported in the *New York Times*, 6 May 1968, p. 15.

lence. Being the outcome of a large number of individual decisions made under different conditions, the overall war effort may not correspond to anyone's optimum amount of violence. For several reasons, it often exceeds the optimum.

One reason is that in weighing the expected benefits and costs of continuing or increasing the violence, the war effort to date may enter into the benefit side of the equation but not the cost side. The relevant costs are strictly marginal costs; what matters is not the violence which has already occurred but the added future violence being contemplated. However, the probability of obtaining the desired benefits (i.e., concessions from the enemy) might be seen to depend on the course of the entire war. It is plausible to view (although this view is not necessarily accurate in each instance) the process of softening or weakening the enemy as one in which the effects of violence are at least partly cumulative. From this perspective, past effort is an investment, and the perceived probability of obtaining a return on that investment after just a little more effort may be relatively high.

A further consideration is that there frequently is greater discontinuity in diplomatic options than in military options. The future violence being contemplated may be only a small increment to the violence that has already occurred. Yet, the objective might be a key concession of major importance. In other words, expected benefits may be high compared to expected costs, not only because of a high perceived probability that the enemy will concede, but because of the high value of the concession.

The important point is that an individual decision to continue and/ or to escalate the war may be justified for these reasons *even if the war has already escalated well out of proportion to the value of the objectives at stake.* Past costs cannot be erased; only future ones are subject to manipulation.

Several features of this process of escalation growing out of sequential decision-making are duplicated in an experimental procedure called the "both pay auction." Two subjects bid for an object, and although only the high bidder receives it, each must pay the house his highest bid. Past bids, like past military actions, are thus irretrievable costs. And while "escalation" with a higher bid may increase costs by only a small amount, the goal at stake is indivisible and the potential benefit (receiving the desired object rather than not receiving it) is therefore relatively large. The usual result is that both subjects wind up paying significantly more than the value of the object.[39]

This phenomenon of escalation through sequential decision-making is reinforced by a widespread tendency for peoples at war to treat past costs as an investment, regardless of whether the effects of violence on the enemy are truly cumulative. When Lincoln declared that the dead at Gettysburg "shall not have died in vain" and that their passing should inspire their living compatriots to complete their unfinished work, he gave expression to a feeling that has been felt and expressed during many other wars. The mechanism which probably is operating is a reduction in cognitive dissonance;[40] mounting costs engender an upward revaluation of one's objectives, thereby reducing the discomfort of knowing that one has incurred costs without sufficient reason. This revaluation in turn makes further costly efforts even more justifiable.[41]

Even assuming that the valuation of objectives remains fixed, however, we have seen sufficient reason to expect a series of separate decisions to carry a belligerent to a level of violence that would not be justified if it were the result of a single decision. As in the French and American wars in Vietnam, a government may continue to employ cost manipulation, perhaps successfully, even after most of its supporters as well as its critics would agree that the total costs already incurred had not been worth the candle.

Deprivation

Disagreement costs have so far been discussed as if they were limited to the material and human losses inherent in combat. This is of course a simplification, because disagreement during warfare is also costly insofar as it deprives a state of benefits to be gained from peace, or at least peace under certain terms. It was an appropriate simplification because, of the two types of costs, the first is more

---

[39] In one set of experiments, a dollar bill was auctioned off; the mean winning bid was $1.30 and the mean losing bid was $1.11. Richard Tropper, "The Consequences of Investment in the Process of Conflict."

[40] Leon Festinger, *A Theory of Cognitive Dissonance.*

[41] As will be noted in a later chapter, it also tends to stiffen a belligerent's diplomatic position.

Another psychological mechanism that may be operating is a rise in decision-makers' anxiety as their values become increasingly threatened by escalation of the war. This reduces their cognitive abilities. See Richard Smoke, *War: Controlling Escalation,* pp. 286–289.

generally manipulable through military action; the level of pain and destruction is directly dependent upon the size and number of armed actions. The second type, which is more in the nature of opportunity costs, is not always so directly tied to military events; many of the benefits of peace which warring nations do not enjoy—such as economic intercourse with each other—would be denied them whether the level of violence were high or low. Nevertheless, armed action is often used to manipulate this second type of disagreement cost. It is therefore appropriate to note how this approach to cost manipulation resembles or differs from the other, and under what circumstances it is most often used.

Capturing the objective one seeks obviously is one way to use armed force to manipulate costs of deprivation advantageously. But a belligerent that is capable of doing this at an acceptably small expense can forget about negotiations; this is direct achievement, not a distinct approach to the use of military force to influence an agreement. What *is* a distinct approach is to deprive the enemy of something that *he* values. This entails either the capture of objects, the possession of which was not one of the original issues in the war but which could be traded for other concessions (i.e., the acquisition of bargaining chips), or the denial of the enemy's war aims.

A strategy based on bargaining chips obviously requires suitable targets—be they cities, prisoners of war, or any other tangible objects—which the enemy values and which are vulnerable to capture. Beyond this, it is most apt to be used when the actual war aims are not themselves suitable objectives for military action. For the United States in the War of 1812, Canada was an apparently excellent bargaining chip. Besides being clearly of value to the British, the lightly garrisoned Canadian provinces seemed at the start of the war to be an easy target for U.S. forces (although this would prove to be a seriously overoptimistic appraisal even before British reinforcements arrived from Europe in 1814). Furthermore, the American war aim—elimination of the maritime abuses—was an intangible objective that was not liable to capture, or indeed obtainable through any sort of direct military action, except perhaps to some extent through protective activity at sea.

Another desirable (though not essential) attribute of a bargaining chip is that it have at least some intrinsic value for the side capturing it. This serves as a partial hedge against failure to reach agreement; but, more important, it makes the possibility of indefinite retention by the captor in the absence of any trade more plausible in the eyes of the enemy. An American annexation of Canada in 1812 was plausible enough, and desirable to enough Americans, for the prospect of an indefinite retention of Canada by the United States (had its armies been more successful) to be useful in bargaining. In fact, following the receipt of some good news from the Niagara front, Secretary Monroe once suggested to the U.S. peace commissioners that they raise the subject of a cession of Canada.[42] That was as far as the idea of annexation went within the U.S. government; Monroe himself had earlier explicitly described Canada as trading material only,[43] and the U.S. commissioners evidently never seriously considered it as a negotiating objective. But the acceptability of annexation within the United States enabled the administration (before military setbacks on the frontier dashed its hopes of an easy conquest) to play upon this sentiment in attempting to induce the enemy to come to terms. In his early instructions to the U.S. chargé in London, Monroe wrote that the British should be advised that unless they reached a quick armistice, a successful invasion of Canada would so affect American public opinion that it would be "difficult to relinquish territory which had been conquered."[44]

When political objectives are themselves suitable as military objectives (as when the central issue is control of a piece of territory), the imposition of deprivation costs more often takes the form of preventing the enemy from attaining his war aims—i.e., a strategy of denial. Appropriate bargaining chips may not be available, and, even when they are, there are advantages to making the military objective the same as a political one. In particular, it usually makes it easier for one's soldiers and citizens to understand and accept the war effort.

Belligerents frequently have the capability to deny even when they lack the capability to attain their own objectives directly. Unless a belligerent is totally exterminated, it can still keep its enemy from enjoying his objectives in peace and quiet. Failure in conventional battle leaves the possibility of guerrilla or terrorist activity, and the crushing of all armed resistance leaves the possibility of nonviolent noncooperation.[45] Even if expelled from a disputed terri-

---

[42] Monroe to U.S. commissioners, 23 June 1813. *American State Papers*, pp. 700–701.

[43] Monroe to John Taylor, 13 June 1812. James Monroe, *Writings*, p. 207.

[44] Monroe to Russell, 26 June 1812. *Ibid.*, pp. 212–213.

[45] For a review of thought on nonviolent resistance, see Anders Boserup and Andrew Mack, *War Without Weapons*.

tory, a belligerent can still continue to make life difficult for the enemy, such as by positioning an armed force near his borders, where he must maintain expensive defenses, and by agitating world opinion against his cause. The FLN's government and army in exile used both these techniques against the French and undoubtedly would have continued to use them in the absence of an agreement even if rebel activity within Algeria had been snuffed out entirely.

But even if war aims are construed so that they include, say, control over an entire territory but not peace and quiet as well, belligerents often are militarily capable of denying the enemy his objectives but incapable of achieving their own. Many wars exhibit a kind of equilibrium in which, for logistical and other reasons, the closer either side comes to achieving all of its goals, the more difficulty it has in making further progress. The farther south the front line in Korea moved, the more of an advantage the UNC had, because its own supply lines were then shorter while the enemy's were longer. Conversely, northward movement gave the Communists the logistical advantage. UNC commanders came to recognize this, and their Communist counterparts probably did as well.[46] In the Indochina and Vietnam Wars there were similar equilibria, not only between different regions where each side had its greatest strength but also between town and countryside. There was also a temporal balance between daytime and nighttime in individual villages; each side could deny effective control to the other for part of each day.[47]

The denial of objectives to the enemy can thus be an important part of the military strategy of a belligerent seeking to negotiate a peace. This is especially likely when the enemy is suspected of harboring the belief that he is militarily strong enough not to have to compromise. This was the French perspective in the summer and autumn of 1953, when the prevailing opinion in Paris had come to accept the need for a negotiated peace but the Viet Minh continued to show no inclination to talk. The government told General Navarre that his objective was "to make the enemy realize that it [is] impossible for him to win a military decision."[48] It was also the perspective in Washington when the United States was fighting the same foe

[46] See Ridgway, *Soldier*, pp. 219–220.

[47] Obviously, there are elements that can upset such an equilibrium, especially a shattering of morale on one side when the military balance tips far in one direction and there appears to be little hope of change (e.g., Germany in 1918, or South Vietnam in 1975).

[48] Quoted in Devillers and Lacouture, p. 43.

in the later Vietnam War. Despite the attention which the bombing of the north received during his administration, President Johnson contended that he always believed that it was less important than the military outcome in the south. To deny the Communists control over South Vietnam, not to punish them for attempting to control it, would be most decisive.[49]

It is important to realize that the strategy of denial discussed here is a form of cost manipulation intended to support a peace negotiation; it is not direct achievement, the capability for which need not exist. General Navarre's elaboration of his government's policy in Indochina in 1953 expresses the idea clearly: "The goal was . . . to demonstrate to the Viet Minh that, if we were not able to win the war, they did not have any better chance to defeat us militarily, and it was necessary to compromise."[50] Because this thinking also underlay the U.S. military effort in South Vietnam, one of the most infamous quotations to emerge from the Vietnam War—"It became necessary to destroy the town to save it"[51]—had a strategic, not just a tragicomic, meaning. Destroying towns may make sense if the object is to save them *from* the enemy, rather than *for* oneself or anyone else.

The costs to the enemy of combat may be an important part of a strategy of denial, but this is nevertheless different from attempts to influence the terms of agreement through punishment alone. Clausewitz postulated two ways in which an adversary could be induced to give up an armed struggle despite his ability to continue it: making his success improbable and making it excessively costly.[52] Manipulating the probability or costs of success is a strategy of denial if "success" means the attainment of war aims. An effort at denial may concentrate on probability, on cost, or on some combination of the two; the choice would depend upon the capabilities of the denier, the opportunities open to him, and his estimate of what would

[49] Johnson, *The Vantage Point,* p. 240. This line of thinking is also revealed in a 1965 memorandum in which Assistant Secretary of Defense John McNaughton attempts to define victory in that war: "With respect to the word "win," this I think means that we succeed in demonstrating to the VC that they cannot win; this, of course, is victory for us only if it is, with a high degree of probability, a way station toward a favorable settlement in South Vietnam." *Pentagon Papers,* Vol. 4, pp. 292–293.

[50] Navarre, *Agonie de l'Indochine,* p. 72.

[51] The statement was attributed to an unidentified U.S. Army major, referring to the fighting at Ben Tre during the 1968 Tet offensive. Don Oberdorfer, *Tet!* p. 184.

[52] *On War,* Vol. 1, p. 29.

most readily influence the decisions of the adversary.[53] Clausewitz, however, evidently means more than this when he writes of the costs of success. From his examples (e.g., invading and devastating the enemy's territory) it appears that he is including not only manipulation of the costs of achieving objectives but the manipulation of disagreement costs generally.[54] In fact, Clausewitz never does distinguish between the two in On War, a reflection of the more duel-like nature of wars of his time and before, in which disagreement tended to exist only as long as the outcome of opposing efforts to achieve certain objectives militarily was in doubt. But the distinction does exist, and at least in modern wars is often an important one. In particular, a belligerent that enjoys possession of a disputed territory has greater opportunity to employ a strategy of denial and less reason to resort to simple punishment than does its adversary.

The strategies of both sides during the latter part of the Algerian War, when the French had control over almost all of the contested territory, are illustrative. The French army's extensive static defenses, including the *quadrillage* in the countryside and the barriers along the borders, served to discourage any attempts by the FLN to re-establish substantial base areas in Algeria, by promising to make such attempts not only unsuccessful but costly. Meanwhile, French offensive activity designed to seek out and harass or kill rebels was reduced and then virtually ended altogether with the start of the first Evian talks in April 1961, when President De Gaulle proclaimed a unilateral "truce" under which French soldiers would not fire unless fired upon.[55] The costs to be imposed upon the rebels would be solely the costs of deprivation. In contrast, the FLN, which did not have the same opportunity to use deprivation, denounced the "truce" and continued to rely on simple punishment as a means of

---

[53] Military measures intended to lower the probability that the enemy will achieve his objectives may be entirely different from ones designed to raise the cost of achieving them, even though both would implement a strategy of denial and not of punishment. A simplified tactical analogy will illustrate the point. A defender who seeks to maintain his position against a lightly armed enemy force has a choice of building a high wall or laying a minefield. To lower the probability of success the wall would be the better choice, because it is unlikely that the attacking force could scale it even though it would suffer few casualties in the attempt. But to raise the cost of success the minefield would be the more effective measure, since the enemy would suffer more casualties in attempting to cross it even though the bulk of his force would probably succeed in doing so.

[54] On War, Vol. 1, pp. 32–33.

[55] Courrière, Les Feux du Désespoir, pp. 257–258.

manipulating its adversary's costs. Both sides thus continued to kill each other's soldiers, but one did so to make the enemy's military efforts costly (and less successful), while the other did so to make disagreement itself costly.

Despite its distinctive features, the denial of objectives is still a form of cost manipulation, and as such is subject to the principles advanced earlier in this chapter. Take the criterion of efficiency, for instance. Relative costs are as important in denial as they are in punishment; the most advantageous actions not only impose costs of deprivation on the enemy but also make it possible to lower one's own disagreement costs in the process. President De Gaulle's efforts to find a way of reducing French costs while continuing to deny the FLN its objective of total control over Algeria led him to suggest that in the absence of an agreement France could partition the country, with the Europeans and pro-French Moslems regrouped into a strip of territory along the coast.[56] That would have continued to deny the FLN its goal of control over a unified Algeria, but it turned out to be a useless threat because, as De Gaulle and his advisers came to realize, it would not really have reduced French costs appreciably. Not only would the economic dislocation associated with regroupment have been enormous, but a substantial French military presence in Algeria would still have been required.[57] A more effective strategy is to shift the burden of denial to a friendly indigenous force, permitting the government doing the negotiating to reduce substantially its own direct costs. In each of the modern major cases, the Western power attempted to do just that. In Indochina, the French government looked to Vietnamization—the term, as well as the strategy, was used in this war as well as the later one—as a way of continuing "to make the enemy realize that it is impossible for him to win a military decision," while at the same time reducing French costs. However, the shakiness of the Bao Dai regime and its strained relations with Paris prevented the development of a non-Communist Vietnamese army strong enough to assume most of the Expeditionary Corps's burden. During the war against the FLN there was talk of Algerianization, but the "third force" in Algeria was even weaker than its counterpart in Vietnam. No one seems to have used the term "Koreanization," but a shift of the military burden to South Korean forces became a major facet of U.S. strat-

[56] Charles de Gaulle, *Memoirs of Hope*, pp. 114–115.

[57] Terrenoire, *De Gaulle et l'Algérie*, pp. 238–239; and Tricot, *Les Sentiers de la Paix*, pp. 201–202.

egy as the Korean War stalemate set in during the spring of 1951.[58] The most far-reaching of these efforts—and for a while, the most successful—was the Nixon administration's program of Vietnamization, which has already been mentioned as an instance of cost manipulation. The point to note here is that the continued denial of Communist control of South Vietnam was as important a part of the strategy as was the reduction in U.S. casualties. At the beginning of the program, President Nixon explicitly tied American troop withdrawals to, *inter alia,* progress in the training of South Vietnamese forces.[59] The costs of deprivation to Hanoi were as much a part of the bargaining problem as the other disagreement costs; ARVN would be relied upon to continue to deprive the enemy of its objective, while the United States eased the pain to itself of disagreement. Hanoi responded militarily with its spring offensive in 1972, which evidently was designed to discredit Vietnamization by showing that ARVN was not capable of standing on its own feet and serving indefinitely as a barrier to a Communist takeover.[60] If this interpretation is correct, the offensive was not a rejection of negotiation but rather an effort to influence the terms of settlement by demonstrating that Hanoi could not be denied its goals forever if the United States continued to withdraw.

Mutual De-Escalation

The violence directed by each belligerent against the other is not only a background to bargaining, but also a subject of bargaining in its own right. A less violent war can be a partial agreement, a bargain which might be struck (either explicitly or tacitly) before the parties reach a complete agreement and end the war. A look back at the static relationship between disagreement costs and the probable terms of settlement depicted in Figure 8 suggests the attractiveness of such partial agreements. Any upward movement from the existing point of no agreement that stays on the same isosettlement line (such as a movement from O' to O) would reduce both parties' cost while implying the same terms of settlement.[61] Mutual de-escalation cor-

---

[58] Collins, *War in Peacetime,* pp. 303–305.

[59] *New York Times,* 9 June 1969, p. 16.

[60] See Porter, *A Peace Denied,* p. 104; remarks by John P. Roche in Morton A. Kaplan, et al., *Vietnam Settlement: Why 1973, Not 1969?,* pp. 157–158; and a report in the *New York Times,* 24 January 1973, p. 19.

[61] Cross, *The Economics of Bargaining,* pp. 142–144.

responding to such movement would be "fair" in the sense that it would not alter the relative advantage of one side over the other.

In practice, however, there are several reasons why belligerents often fail to strike such partial bargains. Discontinuities in military options may make it difficult to de-escalate without seeming to give one side or the other an advantage. The real-life counterparts of the lines in the diagrams will be anything but clear, and consequently the two sides often will have different perceptions of what constitutes a "fair" de-escalation. Finally, the Nash solution—although it is the implied outcome in more than one bargaining model and has been useful in illuminating the major principles of cost manipulation—is still only a simplified and imperfect depiction of how disagreement costs translate into a settlement. By the very nature of a bargaining problem, there is always some uncertainty regarding where within the bargaining range the settlement will be made. Given this uncertainty, an important consequence of mutual de-escalation is a constriction of the bargaining range (assuming that the range was large enough to begin with); some outcomes which both belligerents would previously have considered preferable to continued disagreement are now—because disagreement is less costly—unacceptable to one side or the other. This means that mutual de-escalation is a partial agreement not only in the sense of bringing about a less violent war but also in the sense that it reduces the number of possibilities for complete agreement. Bargaining over de-escalation becomes in part a surrogate for bargaining over the terms of a peace settlement. And using armed action to punish the enemy for not reducing his own military activity can serve the same purpose as using it to punish him for not conceding at the conference table. Bearing in mind these aspects of de-escalation helps one to understand the difficulties encountered in efforts to reach a partial agreement on lowering the violence—e.g., the FLN's hostile response to De Gaulle's termination of offensive action in Algeria, and Johnson's failure to induce Hanoi to de-escalate on the ground in return for a bombing halt. Disagreement over the terms of de-escalation is a child of disagreement over the terms of the peace; the former can be as difficult to resolve as the latter.

Other Military Actions Intended to Influence Agreement

The manipulation of disagreement costs is not the only way in which military activity is used to influence the terms or timing of a peace agreement. This section examines the others, beginning with a topic closely related to cost manipulation, then turning to the manipulation of perceptions on one's own intentions and finally to the role of territorial control.

Threatening Escalation

The costs of war may not actually have to be imposed in order to influence diplomacy. The prospect that they will be imposed in the future, given certain contingencies, may be enough to induce a belligerent to concede. The enemy can exploit this possibility by threatening escalation should concessions not be forthcoming. To threaten to escalate is to attempt to attain the benefits of cost manipulation without suffering actual losses of life or resources in the process. In fact, the threatener does not even need to reach a definite decision regarding the circumstances in which he would escalate. This is illustrated by the best-known threat of escalation in any of the major cases: President Eisenhower's hints that he would expand the Korean War in early 1953 should the Communists not come to terms. He made no specific commitments in this regard, but he permitted the belief to emerge that his administration would not be bound by the limitations of geography and weaponry that were observed by the Truman administration. Upon returning from his pre-inauguration trip to Korea he made a statement about impressing the enemy through deeds "executed under circumstances of our own choosing," and shortly afterward met with the then-retired Douglas MacArthur, who was known to favor bolder measures to hasten the end of the war.[62] But evidently Eisenhower never did reach a decision to escalate in the event the stalemate continued.[63]

In many respects, threats made during wartime to encourage concessions at a peace negotiation resemble threats made during international crises. Since the latter subject has been well studied, the

---

[62] Dwight D. Eisenhower, *Mandate for Change*, p. 181; and Rees, *Korea: The Limited War*, pp. 404–405. The plan which MacArthur presented to Eisenhower included explicit threats to the Soviets that should no acceptable agreement be reached, the United States would clear North Korea of enemy troops (possibly by using atomic weapons and the sowing of radioactive wastes to cut off supply routes) and would probably have to neutralize Communist China's capacity to wage modern war. He did not specify whether such actions actually should have been carried out if the effort to coerce the Soviets failed. Douglas MacArthur, *Reminiscences* (New York: McGraw-Hill, 1964), p. 411.

[63] Eisenhower mentions no such decision in his memoirs, and according to Robert Donovan none was taken. Robert J. Donovan, *Eisenhower: The Inside Story*, p. 119.

same ground will not be covered here.[64] What will be done instead is to point out how wartime threats do differ from crisis threats, and how they influence military strategy.

With a war already in progress, a government has a greater range of military options to support a threat, whether as a means to communicate it, or to increase its credibility by demonstrating a willingness to employ a particular kind of armed force, or to set into motion processes which would make further escalation more likely if the war continued. This is not to say that such opportunities are absent in peacetime crises; even without any firing, the movement of armed forces can be used to communicate a threat or to increase the risk that violence will break out if the adversary does not back down. Besides, some of the military actions which support threats in wartime (including Eisenhower's in 1953) may not themselves be acts of war. The principal military actions taken by the Eisenhower administration to back up the threat of escalation in the Korean War were crisis-like force demonstrations such as the movement of nuclear missiles to Okinawa, a partial alert of the Strategic Air Command, and the President's announcement in his initial State of the Union address that the Seventh Fleet in the Taiwan Strait would no longer shield mainland China from a possible Nationalist invasion.[65] Nevertheless, when a war is underway, the belligerents have already crossed one of the largest and most distinct thresholds on any scale of military actions: the outbreak of hostilities. They have available not only actions below that threshold, but at least some above it as well. The menu of possible methods of employing armed forces to support a threat is larger.

Military actions above the threshold of overt hostilities can be used as a sample of greater violence that would come if the enemy does not make the desired concessions. That is, the action that is threatened and the action used to support the threat are the same, except that the former is larger, more intense, or more prolonged than the latter. In such a case, the smaller action serves to communicate the threat (showing by example what kind of violence would be

[64] In addition to the literature on crises cited in the Introduction, see also Charles Lockhart, *The Efficacy of Threats in International Interaction Strategies.*

[65] Eisenhower, p. 123; Donovan, pp. 28–30; and Rees, pp. 370–371. Even the announcement regarding the Seventh Fleet's role did not involve real changes in its activity, because the Navy had, since the beginning of the war, been tolerating Nationalist raids and may even have assisted Chiang in maintaining contact with his guerrillas on the mainland.

employed if the threat were carried out), to give the enemy a taste of the consequences, and to demonstrate the ability and willingness to employ that type of violence. Because the distinction here between making a threat and executing it is only one of degree, a military action or sequence of actions can be a combination of the two. Rolling Thunder, the Johnson administration's bombardment of North Vietnam (although it preceded the start of negotiations and was intended to achieve results on the battlefield and not just at the conference table), exemplified such a combination. The bombing program was a series of increasingly severe attacks; each stage both fulfilled what earlier attacks had threatened and communicated a threat of more to come.[66]

As with any other purpose of military action during a war, its use to support a threat may conflict with alternative uses. Although in one sense a threat of escalation is just another way to manipulate costs—the costs involved being future rather than present ones—a strategy based on threats may be to some extent incompatible with a strategy based on the imposition of actual costs. Manipulation of present costs might require the commission of the same acts of violence that a focus on future costs would leave hanging as a threat over the enemy's head. Hitler limited damage to English cities during the early months of his air war against Britain in World War II, partly because he hoped that by leaving them intact, the implicit threat of their destruction would encourage the enemy to come to terms.[67] The same thinking influenced American decision-makers during the early part of Rolling Thunder. One of the reasons for their restraint was the fear that intensified bombing would cause so much destruction that there would be nothing left to threaten during later negotiations.[68]

Demonstrating Determination

Increasing the enemy's costs, or threatening to do so, alters his incentives by changing the value to him of continued disagreement. But the disutility of disagreement is of course only one element in his decision whether to concede. Another is his estimate of the opponent's intentions, and this estimate, like disagreement costs,

[66] *Pentagon Papers,* Vol. 4, p. 18.
[67] George Quester, "Bargaining and Bombing during World War II in Europe."
[68] William E. Simons, "The Vietnam Intervention, 1964–65," in George, Hall and Simons, p. 193.

can be manipulated through armed action. B examines A's military activity for evidence of A's motivations, objectives, and morale. Knowing that B will scrutinize his activity in this way, A has reason to shape his military strategy so as to produce perceptions of his incentives which will encourage B to concede.

The distinctions involved here parallel some of the distinctions between interpretations of concessions that were presented in Chapter 3. The manipulation of costs is the military counterpart to the first and second interpretations of concessions—the Zeuthenian views that focus on causes of change in incentives. A concession changes incentives by altering the utility of proposed agreements; a military action does so by altering the utility of disagreement. More precisely, imposing costs on the enemy corresponds to the first interpretation of a concession (a cause of change in the enemy's incentives), while acting to minimize one's own costs corresponds to the second (a cause of change in the actor's own incentives). Similarly, tailoring military strategy to influence the enemy's perceptions of one's own frame of mind corresponds to the third interpretation of a concession (an indicator of incentives).

Designing military strategy to shape these perceptions advantageously has several aspects. But the most important one is the use of military activity to make one's own side appear strong, confident, highly motivated, and unlikely to concede—in short, to demonstrate determination.

Demonstrating determination may lead to a military strategy that differs markedly from one devised with other objectives in mind, because it can require actions which entail high costs to one's own side, either absolutely or relative to the enemy's costs. If a belligerent willingly incurs high costs, this suggests to the opponent that it cares deeply about the terms of agreement, relative to its concern about costs, and consequently that it will drive a hard bargain at the conference table. The opponent might then revise his estimate of the other side's motivations, lowering his aspirations and softening his diplomatic posture (and perhaps de-escalating) because he now sees fewer military actions as being efficient enough to be worth taking.

Some major armed actions which would be too costly or too inefficient to be advantageous as acts of cost manipulation may be worthwhile as demonstrations of determination. Their other detrimental effects may be outweighed by the benefits, diplomatic and military, that ensue if the opponent substantially revises his estimate of motivations. Herein lay much of the value to the Vietnamese Communists of their offensives at Dienbienphu in 1954 and, even more so, during Tet in 1968. The Tet offensive, besides inflicting direct human and material costs on the allied side, increasing political costs to the government in Washington, and demonstrating the fragility of the security which the American military effort had supposedly achieved in South Vietnam, also vividly demonstated the fanaticism with which the Communists intended to pursue their objectives despite immense losses to their own side. It drove home a point which McNamara's 1966 memorandum had made: that the leaders in Hanoi were too highly motivated to back down, even in the face of the terrible human costs to their countrymen who trod southward along the infiltration routes.

The importance of demonstrating determination varies with circumstances. It is most important when reasons exist for the enemy to think that one's determination is weakening. As observed in Chapter 2, an offer to open negotiations is commonly feared to convey an impression of weakness; hence, another reason for escalation at the start of a peace conference (in addition to one already suggested—that the time during which costs will have to be endured now appears shorter) is to demonstrate through armed action that one's diplomatic initiatives do not indicate a weakening of will. This was probably a motivation of the leaders of the Viet Minh/DRV, not only in besieging Dienbienphu and staging the Tet offensive, but also in launching another major offensive in February 1969, shortly after the opening of the four-sided Paris peace talks.

Diplomatic actions are not the only ones which can suggest weakness. Changes in military strategy, especially if they involve deescalation or a retrograde movement, may be feared to have such an effect. This can be sufficient reason not to make the change in the first place; it was President Johnson's reason for deciding not to curtail the bombing of North Vietnam any sooner than he did.[69] Alternatively, the change may be made, but compensatory moves are taken in order to demonstrate renewed determination. In May 1954, during the opening phase of the Geneva conference, French military leaders decided to ease the task of defending the Red River delta by drawing in and thus shortening the perimeter. Although this would strengthen French defenses against future Viet Minh attacks in the area, any retrograde movement could be seen as a retreat and as an indication of weakness. Fearing that this would make the

[69] Johnson, pp. 368, 408, 600–601.

bargaining at Geneva more difficult, the French government elected to accompany the contraction of the delta defenses with a call-up of reserves and with the shipment of additional regular army troops to Indochina.[70] However, bearing in mind a point made earlier in this chapter about the role of time in decisions to manipulate disagreement costs—viz., that a government may resort to escalation not to improve the terms of settlement but rather to hasten the end of the war and thereby put an end to disagreement costs which have become too high—we see that decision-makers have to consider the possibility that escalation such as that which the French undertook may demonstrate, not determination, but the opposite. U.S. Under Secretary of State Nicholas Katzenbach noted this in a memorandum on the conduct of the Vietnam War in June 1967. He argued that to greatly increase U.S. troop strength in Vietnam "might well be viewed by Hanoi as another sign of U.S. impatience and unwillingness to persist."[71]

Demonstrating a Willingness to Settle

To encourage the enemy to come to terms, one needs to appear tough but not too tough. Actions which demonstrate determination help to persuade the enemy that he will have to make concessions if an agreement is to be reached. But actions which demonstrate an unwillingness to settle, or to settle only on the most onerous terms, may discourage the enemy from pursing a negotiated agreement. With the price too high, the customer is scared off, gone to find another way to attain his objectives or to fight on until his opponent becomes more conciliatory. Shaping military strategy to avoid this effect is the other side of demonstrating determination, and, like it, corresponds to the interpretation of concessions as indicators of incentives. It also corresponds in part to the sixth interpretation of a concession: as a signal. The barriers to communication between belligerents are formidable enough for military as well as diplomatic acts to be useful as signaling devices. De-escalation, like a concession, can be a good-will gesture, a message that "I am willing to settle."

A concern for not scaring the customer away is a reason for keeping the level of violence lower than would otherwise be the

---

[70] Robert F. Randle, *Geneva 1954*, pp. 247–249.
[71] *Pentagon Papers*, Vol. 4, p. 507.

case. Sometimes it acts as a general restraint on military activity. For example, among the Johnson administration's reasons for making Rolling Thunder a gradual and limited campaign was that all-out bombing would have suggested that American ambitions in Southeast Asia were much greater than they actually were.[72] But the concern is most evident when critical diplomacy is taking place. In Korea, the United States postponed some B-29 missions against sensitive targets in North Korea that had been scheduled for April 1953 lest they lead the Communists to scuttle Little Switch, the exchange of sick and wounded prisoners. Later, after the exchange was complete and the talks at Panmunjom had resumed but it had become clear that the Communists would not settle quickly, American bombers resumed their previous level of operations and attacked the dams and power plants which had earlier been reprieved.[73] A similar concern led to the abandonment of proposals for the intervention of American air power to save the French garrison at Dienbienphu in the spring of 1954. Secretary of State Dulles insisted that any such intervention be part of an allied "united action," preferably with a multilateral treaty and an anti-Communist declaration. The French balked; they wanted the intervention without the political baggage, believing that new treaties and declarations would stiffen the attitude of the Chinese and increase the chances of failure at Geneva. Even if this difference of views had not scuttled the proposals for intervention, Britain would have done so. The British, would-be participants in any "united action," believed that with or without the political arrangements, an allied intervention would have signaled extreme intentions and thereby wrecked the conference.[74]

Manipulating the War Map

Earlier in this chapter, we saw how the capture of territory can influence the terms of agreement by imposing deprivation costs on the enemy. To the extent that war continues to fill its traditional role as a duel, the capture of territory can also be used to influence agreement in another way: by registering success and strength which, it is hoped, will translate into favorable peace terms. I.e., the

---

[72] *Ibid.*, p. 18.

[73] Hermes, pp. 460–461.

[74] Ely, *L'Indochine dans la Tourmente*, pp. 88–89; Anthony Eden, *Memoirs: Full Circle*, pp. 118–119; Buttinger, pp. 820–821; and Devillers and Lacouture, pp.96–98.

war map functions as a kind of scoreboard for keeping track of military outcomes.

There are two conditions which encourage this use of armed action. One is that the war map be capable of change. If it is not, it is as useless as a gauge with a stuck needle; it may be a valid indicator of what it purports to measure, but it is not worth watching. During the negotiation period of the Algerian War, for instance, the war map was not worth watching because the FLN had no real control over territory or hope of attaining any. By contrast, the volatile military situation during the final months of the Indochina War made it an important consideration, at least in French military planning. Despite heavy pressure on the Expeditionary Corps following the fall of Dienbienphu, General Navarre resolved to postpone major withdrawals until the autumn of 1954, if by then the conference had failed and the war was continuing.[75]

A second condition is that the disposition of territory be one of the issues to be negotiated. For two reasons, the resolution of a territorial issue is more likely to depend on the war map than is the settlement of most other issues. One reason is that the disposition of territory is essentially a quantitative issue—a matter of degree rather than a discrete choice. Signposts or salient solutions are therefore useful in identifying a likely agreement. And being a relatively important issue and one in which utilities are likely to be nonlinear, something more is required than a simple splitting of the difference between the initial demands. The second reason is the apparent propriety of using a territorial result to settle a territorial issue. It somehow seems more fitting to base the political outcome on a military one when the same commodity is at stake in both. The transition from military duel to peace agreement then appears more natural and more just.

A demand for *uti possidetis,* such as Britain made at Ghent, is the most direct possible expression of linkage between the war map and a territorial settlement. It is worth noting that the British government's dropping of this demand was not an abandonment of the idea of linkage but rather a realization that, under it, Britain would not be entitled to a cession of land anyway. Probably the single most important input to this decision was the advice of the Duke of Wellington, whose prestige at the time was enormous and whose opinion on military matters in particular carried great weight in London. Dis-

---

[75] Navarre, pp. 271–275.

missing the British presence in eastern Maine as too small to be worth considering, he based a recommendation to drop *uti possidetis* squarely on the notion of military possession as entitlement to legal possession. "In regard to your present negotiations," he wrote to the Prime Minister, "I confess that I think you have *no right* from the state of the war to demand any concession of territory from America." By demanding *uti possidetis* Britain could get no territory, he continued, and "the state of your military operations, however creditable, *does not entitle* you to demand any. . . ."[76]

Despite the decline of the duel-like qualities of warfare that was discussed in Chapter 1, the war map continues to influence territorial settlements in modern wars, even where there exist other guides, such as historical facts or geographical features which provide salient solutions. It was already noted that the Korean armistice agreement established a boundary at the military front line and not at the 38th Parallel, which had the attraction of historical precedent. In fact, the parties made the transition from military outcome to territorial settlement semi-automatic by defining their agreement on the demarcation line in terms of the military front, with the actual drawing of a line on a map to wait until the entire armistice agreement was ready for signature.[77] The same effect is produced when the parties never draw lines on maps but apportion territory solely and explicitly in terms of areas of military control, as in the standstill cease-fire in Vietnam.

The influence of the war map is even more noteworthy when the parties use it as a guide in specifying a boundary even though that boundary does not duplicate the military front. In such a case, any settlement based on the war map can offer the attraction only of *corresponding* to the military outcome, not of being identical with it. This was the situation at the Geneva conference in 1954. The joint decision against a stand-still cease-fire or "leopard spot" arrangement and in favor of partition necessitated the establishment of a boundary between the northern and southern zones that would coincide with no front line. In Chapter 3 it was observed that the location

[76] Wellington to Liverpool, 9 November 1814. *Wellington's Supplementary Despatches*, pp. 424–426. Emphasis added.

[77] The agreement on the demarcation line reached in November 1951 provided that if the armistice were concluded within the next thirty days, the line would not be the military front at the start of the cease-fire but rather the front line as it had existed at the start of the thirty-day period. Since the armistice was not concluded this soon, this clause became inoperative.

of this boundary was a quantitative issue in which offers were expressed in terms of degrees of latitude, but one in which the parties could associate specific consequences with different outcomes and therefore did not resort to a simple splitting of the difference between initial demands. Some of the proposed boundaries were salient for geographical or historical reasons. The 18th Parallel, for which the French held out during most of the bargaining, ran along a range of limestone mountains that was not only prominent but would have been a barrier to subsequent invasion.[78] The 16th, where the Viet Minh negotiators arrived after dropping demands for a more southerly line (and which Soviet Foreign Minister Molotov seemed to have in mind as an eventual settlement), had historical significance similar to that of the 38th Parallel in Korea: it was the line established at the end of World War II to separate the zones in which the Chinese (in the north) and the British (in the south) would receive the surrender of Japanese troops in Indochina. The actual settlement, the 17th Parallel, did not have comparable salience, either geographical or historical, but it probably corresponded more closely than did any of the other lines to the extent of each side's territorial control at the end of the war. The resulting regroupment, in which French forces evacuated Hanoi and the Red River delta while the Viet Minh left the areas they occupied in the south (mostly in the central highlands and along the coast south of Danang), appeared from the war map to be an equitable trade.[79] In the settlement of this issue, the military outcome proved to be more important than geography, history, or the dynamics of the negotiation itself.

Although a manipulation of the war map resembles the use of armed force to impose deprivation costs, it differs from it in two respects.

One is that the criteria for selecting military objectives are different. In denying an objective to the enemy or acquiring a bargaining chip, a target is important if the enemy values it highly. In manipulating the war map in its capacity as a scoreboard for the military duel, what matters is not so much the value to either side of possessing a given piece of real estate but rather the clarity, drama, and shock effect of its loss or capture. The capture of certain spots on the map is apt to stand out, regardless of how intrinsically important

[78] Navarre had first drawn attention to this line in recommendations to his government in April. Ely, *L'Indochine dans la Tourmente,* pp. 110–113.

[79] A map showing the approximate areas controlled by each side at the time of the conference is on page iii of Devillers and Lacouture, *End of a War.*

those spots may be. After Dienbienphu, the French government placed high priority on avoiding another spectacular defeat while the Geneva conference was in session. This meant preventing any part of the Expeditionary Corps from falling into a similar trap,[80] but it also implied avoiding the loss of especially prominent places on the map. Hanoi, the capital and principal city of Tonkin, was such a place, even though it was otherwise far more of a liability than an asset to the French, and it would not have been of much benefit to the Viet Minh either as long as the war continued. General Paul Ely, who took command in Indochina in early June, carried out some of the withdrawals in the Red River delta which Navarre had resisted, but he elected to stand fast at Hanoi, despite the fact that the contraction of the perimeter was turning it into a dangerously exposed salient.

The other difference is that the capability for long-term retention of an objective is not as important as it is in the imposition of deprivation costs. The territorial scoreboard registers past outcomes; it is not a projection of future ones. By the time of the Geneva conference, the French Expeditionary Corps's position in the Red River delta had become too precarious for France to threaten credibly to remain there—and hence to deprive the Viet Minh of it—indefinitely. Yet, the French command was determined to maintain its toehold while the conference was in session (which it succeeded in doing), in the expectation that this maintenance of the war map would be reflected in the territorial settlement—which, as noted above, it was.

Asserting Claims

Armed action to influence a peace agreement may take another form which is similar to manipulation of the war map but in which actual capture or retention of territory, even temporarily, is not critical. This is to stage attacks in certain areas as a way of asserting territorial claims. Asserting a claim is akin to threatening escalation or demonstrating determination in that it involves the use of armed force to convey a message to the enemy. An attack becomes a showing of the flag, the military equivalent to a property deed. It was to assert its claim to the Sahara that the FLN made a special effort during its rebellion to launch attacks in that region, even

[80] See the government's directive to Navarre dated 18 May 1954, quoted in Ely, *L'Indochine dans la Tourmente*, pp. 129–130.

though the rebels were not particularly strong in the area. The Sahara was not the best place to hurt the French, and the FLN had no hope of actually capturing territory there.[81]

Conclusion

This chapter has demonstrated how wartime military activity can reasonably and profitably be interpreted as bargaining behavior, and how the battlefield serves as an extension of the conference table. The various interpretations of concessions that were introduced in Chapter 3 imply military as well as diplomatic strategies. The use of armed force to support a peace negotiation is largely a matter of altering the enemy's incentives by manipulating costs, although cost manipulation was seen to be far more complicated than merely inflicting as much pain as possible on the adversary. To identify an advantageous cost manipulation strategy requires attention to relative as well as absolute costs, the nature of the issues at stake, the expected duration of the war, and the opportunities for using deprivation as well as punishment. Moreover, military decisions also may involve the other bargaining objectives, in addition to alteration of incentives, that were discussed in Chapter 3, such as the sending of signals and the manipulation of perceptions of one's own incentives. In short, the complexity of wartime military decisions in large part mirrors the complexity of wartime diplomacy.

Because several different logics are involved, the military side of bargaining behavior, like the diplomatic side, often poses dilemmas. An action that would be expected to strengthen a belligerent's bargaining position in one respect could weaken it in another (e.g., escalation makes the war costlier for the enemy, but might also be read as a sign of impatience). Wielding the military instrument advantageously thus does not mean simply maximizing this or minimizing that, but rather determining which parts of the enemy's decision calculus are most readily changed, and then carefully choosing the course of action best suited to change them.

The empirical material in this chapter was used chiefly to illustrate principles of bargaining, but it also indicates the considerable extent to which real belligerents have acted in accordance with those prin-

---

[81] Tripier, pp. 519–521; and Joan Gillespie, *Algeria: Rebellion and Revolution*, pp. 148–149.

ciples. The evidence that wartime decision-makers have functioned as rational bargainers has included: statements by the decision-makers themselves; the timing of major military operations, such as Dienbienphu and Tet, to coincide with critical diplomatic events; and data from the Vietnam War that suggest that the belligerents were mindful of the efficiency of their combat operations and their effect on each side's bargaining position. In several instances we have seen how military strategy would have differed substantially had the strategists not been thinking primarily as bargainers—e.g., in the last portion of the Korean War, when the United States eschewed some opportunities for further military gains and instead gave overriding priority to relative costs as an influence on the bargaining problem.

The foregoing leaves open the question of when, how, and to what extent the enemy actually responds diplomatically to military events. We have noted how territorial settlements frequently reflect the war map at the end of the war. Beyond this, however, diplomatic responses depend on several further considerations, to which we turn in the next chapter.

CHAPTER FIVE

The Diplomatic Response
to Military Activity

Combat does not influence diplomacy directly; it does so through the intervening variables of a belligerent's perceptions, interpretations, and expectations. Peace negotiations thus seldom take the form of simple, straightforward responses to military events. To note this is not to invalidate the reasoning in the previous chapter regarding cost manipulation and other uses of the military instrument, nor is it to suggest that military efforts to affect peace settlements are in general ineffective. But it does mean that the diplomatic response to military activity is fully comprehensible only when considered in the context of all the considerations, discussed in Chapters 3 and 4, that make a wartime bargaining problem inherently complex.

The present chapter explores several further complications, each of which is a reason why diplomatic responses may vary from one case to another, and why some of those responses may appear incongruent with the military events that preceded them. The first reason is that negotiation decisions are based less on past military activity than on expected future activity. This has implications, addressed in the first section below, regarding the impact of critical battles, the importance of separate but simultaneous conflicts, and the effectiveness of threats and ultimata. The second reason is that violence, destruction, and other wartime losses are costlier to some decision-makers than to others. Third, armed actions are subject to a variety of interpretations, and to possible misinterpretation. Finally, participation in a war often gives rise to certain new motivations, which may not have been among a belligerent's original war aims but which can affect its diplomatic decisions once the conflict is underway.

The Anticipation of Military Outcomes

Trends and Prospects on the Battlefield

In Chapter 2 we saw that belligerents base their decisions regarding the timing of peace negotiations on their expectations about future military developments in a continued war. Similar thinking can be expected to underlie diplomatic decisions once talks have begun. Each such decision—each choice of whether to concede or not to concede—requires an estimate of the costs of disagreement. More precisely, it requires an estimate of the costs of *future* disagreement, of the disagreement that will exist or not, that will be longer or shorter, depending on what diplomatic action the belligerent takes and how the enemy responds to it. This in turn requires an estimate of future military events in a continued war, events which will affect the extent of the costs.[1] Clausewitz emphasized the importance of expectations in inducing the enemy to submit to one's will. The disadvantageous position in which we place the enemy through force of arms should not appear to be transitory, he wrote, lest the enemy hold out in the hope of a change for the better. If there is to be any prospective change in his position, it should be a change for the worse.[2]

If negotiating decisions are based less on military activity which has already taken place than on activity expected to take place in the future, it follows that, for several reasons, diplomacy will not be a direct, after-the-fact response to military activity.

Diplomatic behavior can be a response to an *anticipated* military event, which would make the response observable before the event itself. This is most often true of a government's responses to its own military initiatives, since it of course is aware of the plans and preparations for such initiatives even if the enemy is not. The diplomatic behavior in question may be a specific demand or proposal, such as Britain's original demand at Ghent for *uti possidetis,* which was made because of what British troops were expected to capture, not what they had already captured. Alternatively, it may be inaction or

---

[1] This is especially true with costs of punishment, such as casualties and the destruction of property, which depend entirely on the intensity and duration of future military operations. It is less the case with costs of deprivation, which may be the lasting result of a past armed action. But even estimates of deprivation costs usually require predictions of future military developments, which could lead to the capture or recapture of territory or other objectives.

[2] *On War,* Vol. 1, p. 5. See also Smoke, *War: Controlling Escalation,* pp. 268–270.

an adjustment of timing, as exemplified by Hanoi's dawdling in early 1972 over the resumption of secret talks with the United States, which had been in recess since the previous autumn. President Nixon propossed a new round of secret meetings in January; after a delay of several weeks, the North Vietnamese accepted the offer, as well as the date in mid-March suggested by the Americans. Two weeks before the scheduled meeting, Hanoi requested a postponement of the meeting until 15 April. Henry Kissinger already had a previous commitment for that date, and suggested 24 April instead. On 31 March, after another delay of ten days, Hanoi finally accepted. On that same day, the North Vietnamese revealed the reason, which Nixon and Kissinger had not been able to divine, for the delaying tactics: they launched their spring offensive. As Kissinger himself later observed, the North Vietnamese had carefully used the delays to make the negotiation support their military objectives. "It was," he said, "very smart, tough bargaining on their part."[3]

Diplomacy which anticipates military activity, however, need not be confined to the side planning the activity. With sufficient information and/or suspicion, the opponent will also respond to it in advance, whether by action or inaction. For example, President Johnson justified his refusal to reply to the lull in Communist activity in Vietnam during the summer of 1968 by referring to intelligence reports suggesting that a new enemy offensive was in preparation.[4]

Another implication of the role of expected future events, as distinct from past actual ones, is that changes in a belligerent's diplomatic posture are more likely to reflect changes in expectations, rather than changes in the events themselves. To put it differently, armed actions—even large-scale ones—will not evoke a diplomatic response if the enemy was expecting them to occur. The diplomatic decisions already taken would have been based on these expectations, and confirming the expectations would not occasion any change. The Johnson administration's bombing of North Vietnam, although it involved a gradual escalation that appeared to implement Clausewitz's recommendation to make things progressively worse for the enemy, brought no change in North Vietnamese diplomacy during the three years of Rolling Thunder because the escalation itself became a regular pattern that formed the basis for Hanoi's expectations. Each increase in the violence confirmed those expec-

[3] Kalb and Kalb, *Kissinger,* pp. 284–285; and Szulc, "How Kissinger Did It," pp. 34–35.

[4] Transcript of press conference, *New York Times,* 1 August 1968, p. 16.

tations; it did not change them. The Canadian diplomat Chester Ronning, after his unofficial visit to North Vietnam in June 1966, reported that the North Vietnamese already were "confident" that the United States would lay waste much of their country, and that Hanoi was prepared for the destruction.[5]

The North Vietnamese attitude demonstrates how even escalation may fail to reshape expectations. Nevertheless, if military activity alters expectations at all, it is most likely to do so when that activity *changes*. A reversal of momentum, or a departure from a previous line of march, is what is most apt to cause a revision of estimates and hence a revision of diplomatic positions. In fact, prior military outcomes, by providing the context in which subsequent changes in military trends are perceived, may encourage a response that is the opposite of what they would elicit by themselves. That is, setbacks appear more striking when placed against a background of past successes, and vice versa. Russian perceptions of Japan's performance during the Russo-Japanese War are instructive in this regard. Baron Roman Rosen, who was the Russian Ambassador to the United States during the war and who served as the second-ranking member of his country's delegation at the Portsmouth peace conference, remarked to President Roosevelt before the start of the conference that the recent course of the war boded well for Russia. Japan had made no significant gains since her victory at Mukden four months earlier; in view of the ability and enterprise which the Japanese commanders had already exhibited, said Rosen, this could only mean that they were now unable to advance farther.[6] A paradoxical implication of Rosen's remark—and the Russian military and political leaders generally shared his optimism and the reason for it—was that if the Japanese had not shown so much ability and enterprise in battle earlier, their enemy would not now believe that they had become so weak.

We already saw in Chapter 2 that the opening of peace negotiations usually must await a common perception of the trend of military events. Because such a common perception is most likely to emerge when trends have become stable, major or rapid reversals are rare once a negotiation has begun. Even so, the future military trend which both belligerents foresee may differ from the one which

[5] *U.S.-Vietnam Relations*, Vol. VI.C.1, p. 187. See also Robert Jervis, *The Logic of Images in International Relations*, pp. 221–222; and Wallace J. Thies, *When Governments Collide*, pp. 280–281.

[6] White, *The Diplomacy of the Russo-Japanese War*, p. 238.

has just prevailed in the past. That is, a reversal which has occurred
or is obviously about to occur may be part of the common perception which makes it possible for talks to commence. One likely
cause of such a reversal in military trends is the exhaustion of one
side's resources. A nation inferior in population and wealth may
score early military successes by skillfully using what it has, but
nevertheless face a bleak future if it reaches the limit of its resources
while its opponent still has strength yet to be mobilized.[7]

The Russo-Japanese War was the outstanding example of this,
producing a peace settlement which, except for some issues involving territory where the armies had fought, appeared to be drastically
at variance with the military outcome. Russia, a "nation hopelessly
beaten in every battle of the war," as the *New York Times* reported,
had "dictated her terms to the victors" at Portsmouth. Observers in
America, according to the *Times,* considered the result of the conference to be "as astonishing a thing as ever was seen in diplomatic
history."[8] The brilliant victories by the better-prepared Japanese
were there for all to see; what was less obvious was that by the
opening of the conference Japan had reached the end of its tether
and in a continued war would be outmanned, outgunned, and out-
financed by the larger Russian Empire. Troops from European Russia were moving eastward along the Trans-Siberian railway at a rate
that the Japanese could not hope to match, and, while both sides
were becoming deeply indebted, Japan's finances were in worse
shape than Russia's.[9] Japanese leaders foresaw all of this even before the war began, and by the time the diplomats met at Portsmouth
their Russian counterparts did too. An impending reversal of the
string of Japanese military victories was part of the shared perception which underlay the peace agreement. If the result was more
astonishing to outside observers than most peace settlements are, it
was because the Japanese leaders were more prescient than most
concerning their own country's military limitations, and because
they executed their military-diplomatic plan so well. The Japanese
commanders, through their "ability and enterprise," extracted
every advantage they could from the resources available to them,
and the scheme to enlist Roosevelt's aid at the proper moment in
order to negotiate a peace before the tide was turned also went like

[7] See Klaus Knorr, *Military Power and Potential,* pp. 21–22.
[8] Quoted in Warner and Warner, *The Tide at Sunrise,* p. 535.
[9] Okamoto, *The Japanese Oligarchy and the Russo-Japanese War,* pp. 106–109.
153.

clockwork. The Japanese leaders did not suffer, as other leaders have (e.g., the French in Indochina until mid-1953, the Communists in Korea until mid-1951), from delusions of "victory" until it was clear to all that victory had dropped from their grasp. This fact, and the skill with which they overcame the usual barriers to the opening of negotiations, meant that the peace conference was held before a final reversal of military fortunes actually took place, rather than after, as is more often the case. The one crucial task which the Japanese could not accomplish was to conceal from the Russian decision-makers how dire their own situation really was. In their attempts to do so, they managed only to deceive the astonished observers in third nations and, what was worse, their own people. The Tokyo crowd which shouted "banzai" while seeing the diplomats off to Portsmouth to consummate the glorious victory later rioted when the bitterly disappointing terms of settlement were announced.[10]

Critical Military Events

An awareness of the role of trends and prospects helps to explain why diplomatic responses often appear incongruent with the military events preceding them. The other side of the same coin is that when there is congruence—when a tougher diplomatic position follows a military success or a softer one follows a failure—expectations for the future are serving once again as an intervening variable. Certain individual battles evoke diplomatic responses because they cause those expectations to be revised.

Some observers have noted that sudden armed actions, especially if they are large, are most likely to destroy an enemy's determination to continue a war.[11] Individual failures in attempting to use armed force to induce the enemy to back down, such as Rolling Thunder in Vietnam, have been attributed to the gradual nature of the actions used;[12] individual successes, such as the final breaking of German will in World War I, have been attributed to suddenness.[13] The effects of large and/or sudden armed actions may be partly attributed to a shock effect, whereby organizations or individual

---

[10] *Ibid.*, pp. 146–148, 207–214.

[11] E.g., Calahan, *What Makes a War End?* pp, 230–231; and Iklé, *Every War Must End*, pp. 55–56.

[12] A. P. Sights, Jr., "Graduated Pressure in Theory and Practice," pp. 41–45.

[13] B. H. Liddell Hart, *Strategy*, pp. 218–219.

leaders who would otherwise let inertia determine their policies are jolted into realizing that changes are in order.[14] But there is another explanation that is consistent with the earlier analysis in this chapter: such actions provide a government with the type and quantity of evidence which is most likely to lead it to revise its estimates of military trends and prospects. A battle can be what Robert Jervis has called an index—an action which not only projects an image but also provides inherent evidence that the image is correct because it is linked in some way to the actor's capabilities or intentions. As an index, a given military event can have a disproportionate effect on expectations if it serves as a test of capabilities.[15] I.e., it is important not so much for what was won or lost, but rather for what it demonstrates the armies are capable of winning or losing in the future. Large-scale actions tend to carry greater weight as indices because they involve larger samples of the opposing forces and hence serve as better tests. Sudden actions appear to have a disproportionate effect because the testing, the revision of expectations, and consequently the diplomatic responses are more compressed in time and therefore more noticeable than would be true with more gradual actions. What is important, however, is not size or suddenness per se but rather the extent to which a battle is a fair test of future combat in a continued war.

A test is most conclusive when one belligerent makes a determined effort with its best forces under the most favorable circumstances—militarily, it puts its best foot forward—and still suffers a setback. If it could not succeed when conditions were most propitious, it is unlikely to succeed at all. The battle of Plattsburg in September 1814, in which the Americans turned back the main British invasion from Canada, had the greatest immediate impact on the peace settlement of any battle in the War of 1812, even though it was less bloody than some others.[16] The outcome encouraged British concessions because the battle had been the trial of strength which London had been awaiting—the chance to put into the field large numbers of seasoned regulars released from their duties in Europe.

[14] Graham Allison, writing in the context of his organizational process model of foreign policy decision-making, has argued that only highly visible costs will have a direct impact on leaders without the information having been filtered and distorted in organizational channels, and that a major disaster is usually required to provoke dramatic change in an organization's behavior. Allison, *Essence of Decision,* pp. 85, 262.

[15] Jervis, pp. 18, 30.

[16] Coles, *The War of 1812,* p. 171.

The setback was the most vivid possible demonstration of the point which the Duke of Wellington would later make to his government—that without naval superiority on the lakes, even an augmented army in Canada could not be expected to change the complexion of the war. The French defeat at Dienbienphu had similar significance in the Indochina War: the French commanders had chosen the spot as a good location for a showdown and had garrisoned it chiefly with elite paratroopers and Foreign Legionnaires. They welcomed a battle there as a means of inflicting high casualities on the Viet Minh.[17] On a larger scale, the Communist offensive in Korea in May 1951 and Hanoi's spring 1972 offensive in Vietnam, because they both were maximum efforts that demonstrated the limits of the attacker's capabilities, were useful indices of future combat which led to revisions of expectations and a willingness either to negotiate or to make fresh concessions.

Dienbienphu, incidentally, demonstrates another reason that a diplomatic response may be the very opposite of what would be expected if one did not consider the role of anticipated outcomes. As was noted earlier, it was not so much the fall of the garrison that weakened the French diplomatic position but rather the prior realization that the fall was inevitable if the war continued. Once the end at Dienbienphu finally came, the French diplomatic posture actually stiffened slightly, not only because France wanted to avoid showing weakness but also because what had been the chief incentive for a quick cease-fire during the preceding weeks—the salvation of the garrison—had vanished.[18] In general, the anticipation of a dreaded military event is a burden which weakens one's bargaining position, because it increases incentives to concede on other issues in order to avoid it. Occurrence of the event, however dreadful, lifts the burden.

Outside Military Events

Another reason for congruence between military outcomes and subsequent diplomacy, even when the diplomacy actually reflects expectations of the future, is that past military activity augments or diminishes the resources available to each side for future action. A

---

[17] Jervis (p. 31) cites Dienbienphu as an example of a battle serving as an index of future military outcomes.

[18] Ely, *L'Indochine dans la Tourmente*, pp. 106–108; and Devillers and Lacouture, *End of a War*, p. 151.

military setback which entails a substantial loss of men or material implies a lesser capability for further combat, and this may be sufficient to revise expectations for a continued war. Of course, the effect of a military event on remaining resources may not correspond to other measures of tactical success or failure—hence the notion of a Pyrrhic victory. In any case, the point to note is that military capabilities are an intervening variable; anything which causes them to increase or diminish is a reason to revise expectations and possibly to revise one's diplomatic posture as well. Although military activity itself is a major cause of changes in those capabilities, it need not be activity in the same war in which a peace settlement is in the balance. Action in a simultaneous but separate conflict can, through either attrition or diversion, engender such change; military outcomes in one war influence the settlement in the other.

This becomes most obvious when one nation is a participant in both wars, especially if, as in the War of 1812, the peace negotiation in question concerns the smaller of the two. The diplomacy of the Anglo-American conflict probably depended more on events in Europe than upon the battles fought in North America. We already saw how the Americans accepted direct negotiations after receiving news of Napoleon's defeat at Leipzig, with all that it implied concerning the imminent release of British troops from Europe. The earlier U.S. acceptance of the Russian offer of mediation had also been encouraged by bad news from the European front, in this case the fate suffered by the French army in Russia.[19] By the same token, Britain's later decision to abandon the demand for *uti possidetis* reflected not only its defeat at Plattsburg but also the threat of a new European war's arising either from a revolution in France or from a falling out among the allies at the Congress of Vienna.[20]

Military events in an outside war can evoke such responses even if no belligerent is participating in two wars at once, provided there is some possibility of diverting resources from one to the other. In this regard, the settlement of the Korean War in July 1953 encouraged the French to negotiate a peace in Indochina, because they believed that China would henceforth be able to provide increased aid to the Viet Minh.

[19] Perkins, *Castlereagh and Adams*, p. 20.

[20] These were among the reasons that the government gave for its decision in instructions to the British commissioners. Engelman, *The Peace of Christmas Eve*, pp. 253–254.

Future Wars

Military events can alter expectations of the outcome of combat not only in a continuation of the present war, but also in any future war, particularly one involving the same belligerents. Such a change in expectations affects the ability of a government to threaten a renewal of hostilities, as well as its prospects for success should fighting actually resume. This influences diplomatic postures in a peace negotiation because the consequences of any breakdown of the settlement are in effect part of the package being negotiated. Each government considers the military posture that it will have after an armistice, just as it weighs any other attribute of a possible peace agreement, even if this is not a subject of explicit bargaining at the conference table. As with the other attributes, the better that posture is, the more attractive the total package becomes and the more willing a government is to sign an armistice even if other terms of the agreement are less satisfactory. In particular, a bolstering of post-war military strength, or an upward revision in the estimate of that strength, makes a belligerent more tolerant of proposed terms which: (1) are vague or uncertain of execution, or the execution of which depends upon the good faith of the adversary, hence making them likely grounds for the future use of force to redress grievances; or (2) tend to improve the *enemy's* post-war military posture. The result is another reason for apparent incongruence between military outcomes and diplomatic responses: emerging from combat in better fighting condition, insofar as this affects expectations for a future war, makes a belligerent more—not less—willing to offer concessions and to conclude an armistice.

Such considerations induced the British to make peace with France in 1801 on otherwise unfavorable terms which required them to relinquish almost all of the French, Spanish, and Dutch colonies that they had captured in the French Revolutionary wars. Although the fighting had strained its resources in many other ways, Britain emerged with a navy that was greatly superior to that of France. The British government defended the agreement against its domestic critics by arguing that nothing essential could be lost as long as this naval supremacy was maintained. Britain would be in an advantageous position should hostilities resume, as they in fact soon did.[21] In the Vietnam War, President Nixon made his October 1970 offer of a cease-fire in place—which he had earlier considered too hazardous

[21] Geoffrey Bruun, *Europe and the French Imperium, 1799–1814*, pp. 53–54.

to the Thieu regime—after being favorably impressed by ARVN's capabilities during the Cambodian operation earlier in the year.[22] Nguyen Van Thieu's own acquiescence in the peace agreement of January 1973, which he had stubbornly opposed three months earlier, stemmed from an improvement in his post-war military prospects. The terms had not changed much in the interim; what had really changed was Thieu's military posture relative to that of the Communists, thanks to an accelerated airlift of military supplies from the United States and the December bombing of North Vietnam. (Placating Thieu may have been one of the purposes of the bombing.)[23] Once he was better situated for renewed combat, the aspects of the agreement at which he had balked, especially the continued presence of Hanoi's troops within South Vietnam, became more tolerable to him.

Ultimata and Deadlines

Expectations of future outcomes also determine the success or failure of attempts to induce the enemy to concede by threatening escalation. It was noted in Chapter 4 that the threatening of future costs can be a highly efficient method of extracting concessions, and that the tactic is not fundamentally different from threats made in crises that fall short of the war. But a further question may be raised about the opportunities for using this tactic during wartime which does not apply to the same degree to peacetime efforts at coercive diplomacy. We have seen that military trends in a war are apt to have stabilized by the time peace negotiations begin, with the parties having previously demonstrated the limits of their willingness and ability to extend the war. This being the case, how can either belligerent credibly threaten to escalate that war? There must be some other basis, besides the threat itself, for anticipating an alteration in its war policies. The best such basis is a change of government or regime, as had occurred in the United States shortly before President Eisenhower hinted in early 1953 that he would escalate the Korean War. If the Communists were in fact responsive to this threat, it was because the Eisenhower Administration, being so new, had not yet demonstrated the limits of its willingness to accept the costs and risks of a continued war.

The point becomes clearest when a belligerent imposes a deadline, as Pierre Mendès-France did upon becoming Premier of France

[22] Kalb and Kalb, pp. 173–174.
[23] Szulc, "How Kissinger Did It," pp. 62–63.

on 17 June 1954, declaring in his investiture speech that if an Indochina peace agreement were not concluded by 20 July, his government would resign.[24] A deadline puts into sharp relief the question of what will change in the event of noncompliance: How will the war become different if it continues beyond the specified time? Mendès-France's deadline is instructive because—although many observers felt at the time that he was foolishly tying his own hands by making his fall from power the result of a continued stalemate—the ploy was, by most standards, successful. The deadline was met (with a little help from someone who stopped the clocks in the conference hall for a few hours on the night of 20 July)[25] after the kind of frantic bargaining which often occurs in a labor contract negotiation as a strike deadline approaches. And the agreement was considered favorable enough for it to win easy approval in the National Assembly.

The episode invites comparison with the UNC's unsuccessful insistence in November 1951 on a thirty-day time limit for reaching an agreement in Korea, as a condition of accepting the Communists' interpretation of the demarcation line. The time limit was virtually the same as the one used during the Indochina War, and, like Mendès-France's move, the stated objective was the conclusion of an agreement rather than any particular terms. The chief reason that one deadline succeeded where the other failed was the change of government and policy that Mendès-France's resignation would have entailed. He was probably the most doveish of all the French premiers who held office during the Indochina War; the Communists no doubt realized that if he failed he would be replaced by someone less tractable, and many French would come to see no alternative to a continuation of the war. Mendès-France himself pointed to this when he said in his investiture speech that, while pursuing an agreement, he would take the necessary measures to permit a successor government to carry on the fight. Specifically, he declared that his last act before resigning would be to request that reinforcements be sent to Indochina, and he proceeded to have French troops in Germany vaccinated and equipped in preparation for this.[26] In contrast, the expiration of the "Little Armistice" in Korea implied no change of personnel or policies in Washington. The Truman administration had already demonstrated its unwillingness to sustain a major and

[24] The text of Mendès-France's statement is in Cameron, *Viet-nam Crisis, A Documentary History*, pp. 275–277.

[25] Devillers and Lacouture, pp. 297–298.

[26] Pierre Mendès-France, *Choisir*, pp. 53–54.

costly new drive into North Korea to support its diplomatic demands. There was no reason to suppose that it now would become bolder, especially in the face of improved Communist defenses.

An impending election, because it raises the possibility of a change of government, might serve as a deadline. The other belligerent may fear that its opponent will become more intractable after the election, either because a more hawkish leadership will assume power or because the current leadership will be freed from domestic political constraints against continuing or escalating the war. The North Vietnamese evidently viewed the 1972 U.S. presidential election in this light, even though President Nixon enjoyed a huge lead in the opinion polls and showed no special anxiety about reaching an early agreement. The leaders in Hanoi—not the most perspicacious observers of American politics—probably believed nevertheless that Nixon keenly wanted a settlement to show to the voters before they cast their ballots, and that the weeks immediately preceding the election were thus the DRV's last good chance to get favorable terms. This helps to explain Hanoi's fervid efforts in October to accelerate the negotiations.[27]

Because the effectiveness of ultimata and deadlines depends so much on the possibility of major political change, there are apt to be few opportunities to employ them successfully as tactics in peace negotiations. Mendès-France's ploy in 1954 was seemingly a brilliant act of diplomatic imagination, but it was actually more a desperate response to military and political pressures that left him little room for maneuver. Although naturally he did not fully voice his concern at the time, he was so alarmed by the situation on the battlefield that he decided a quick truce was imperative.[28] Besides, he might not have won confirmation as premier in the first place if he had not made such a dramatic gesture.[29]

Costs of Violence

The analysis in Chapter 4 glossed over the details of how the capture or destruction of objects of value translates into utility or

---

[27] I. William Zartman, "Reality, Image, and Detail: The Paris Negotiations, 1969–73," in Zartman, *The 50% Solution*, pp. 372–398 at p. 386.

[28] Mendès-France, pp. 53–54; Pierre Rouanet, *Mendès-France au Pouvoir*, pp. 63–64; and Devillers and Lacouture, pp. 245–246.

[29] Randle, *Geneva 1954*, p. 287.

disutility to governments at war. Variation in the value placed on the lives of soldiers was mentioned, but the possibility of slippage between violence inflicted and costs sustained goes beyond that to include almost any object that may be destroyed or captured in war. Much of the variation in diplomatic responses to violence may be attributed to differences in the valuation that governments place on such objects.

There are two elements in this. One concerns the way an entire nation at war values certain kinds of objects. There is probably no single type of object valued so highly by every nation that its impending or actual loss would inevitably be of decisive importance in shaping the peace settlement.[30] Consider capital cities, which as noted earlier are often viewed as particularly vulnerable spots where a successful attack would bring a quick end to a war. The impact of the loss of capitals varies, partly for reasons discussed in the previous section; the battle for a capital may or may not be useful as an index, and its loss may or may not make it substantially more difficult to support armies in the field. But a major source of variation is simply that a capital means different things to different peoples. If it is the heart and soul of a nation, its capture or destruction may lead to quick capitulation, as the fall of Paris has for France on more than one occasion. If it is an object of general indifference, the effect will be much smaller. For example, the burning of Washington in 1814, with the spectacle of the President and other members of his government fleeing to the hills, caused remarkably little dismay among citizens of the United States, a young federal republic in which many felt no more affection for the U.S. capital than for a foreign one.[31]

The other element is variation in how the utilities of citizens and soldiers relate to the utilities of their leaders. The former may suffer most in warfare, but it is the latter who direct diplomacy. The citizens' costs may be linked to their leaders' conduct in either of two ways, both of which vary markedly from one nation to another. The first is for the leaders to accept the costs as their own, because of empathy, or because they share the costs first-hand, or because they recognize that the suffering and discontent will harm their own positions, politically or otherwise. Any or all of these linkages may be absent. Leaders may be more ruthless than empathic (which is one

[30] Cf. Lewis A. Coser, "The Termination of Conflict," p. 350.

[31] Vagts, *Defense and Diplomacy*, p. 464. On the effects of the burning of Washington, see Coles, *The War of 1812*, pp. 181–182.

possible meaning of the earlier statements about a belligerent's placing a low value on the lives of its soldiers),[32] be insulated from the
suffering, and find that the hardships to the population are supporting their position rather than undermining it.[33]

The other means of linkage is for the population to force the hands
of the leaders. This was essentially the mechanism envisaged by
Giulio Douhet and the other early champions of the aerial bombardment of civilians, who believed that such attacks would shatter the
morale of the populace and cause it to rise up and demand an early
end to the war.[34] Subsequent experience has demonstrated not only
the general limitations of the Douhet thesis but also some of the
specific conditions in which its validity is particularly low. Chief
among these conditions is the absence of any alternative leadership
which can serve as a rallying point for a discontented population.
Study of the World War II bombing of cities in Nazi Germany
showed that with no one to turn to but the totalitarian regime, the
German people did not convert their depressed morale into action
which would change German military and diplomatic policy.[35] Jeffrey Milstein's statistical findings, using time series data from the
first part of the Vietnam War, suggest that the absence of adequate
linkage with the leadership contributed to the inefficacy of the bombardment of another country with a totalitarian regime—North Vietnam. The level of bombing was positively associated with the number of defections of Communist soldiers, an indication that the aerial
assaults did erode the morale of individuals even though they had no
apparent impact on the diplomatic posture of the regime. Such costs
of the war as U.S. casualties similarly affected individuals in the
United States (as indicated by the association of these costs with a
lower level of support for the administration in the public opinion
polls), but with a political system in which the government is more
accountable to popular sentiment, the impact on policy was
greater.[36]

[32] The other possible meaning is that the soldiers themselves are motivated enough
to die gladly for their cause.

[33] Cf. Lockhart, *Bargaining in International Conflicts*, pp. 70–71.

[34] Giulio Douhet, *The Command of the Air*, especially pp. 57–59, 126. See also
Edward Warner, "Douhet, Mitchell, Serversky: Theories of Air Warfare," in
Edward Mead Earle (ed.), *Makers of Modern Strategy*, p. 498.

[35] Bernard Brodie, *Strategy in the Missile Age*, pp. 131–134.

[36] Jeffrey S. Milstein and William C. Mitchell, "Dynamics of the Vietnam Conflict:
A Quantitative Analysis and Predictive Computer Simulation," in Walter Isard (ed.),
Vietnam: Some Basic Issues and Alternatives, pp. 180–181; and Milstein, *Dynamics*

Interpretations of Armed Actions

Even if we disregard slippage between violence inflicted and costs sustained, the multiplicity of possible purposes of armed actions in warfare—both the ones described in Chapter 4 and any which are not oriented toward influencing the timing or terms of the peace agreement—is itself a source of variation in diplomatic responses. This is true of the actor's diplomacy as well as the adversary's.

The actor's own responses may vary in this way because, as we have seen, outwardly similar military actions can have distinctly different purposes. Increasing the punishment inflicted on the enemy, for example, may be intended to improve the terms of the peace agreement or only to hasten agreement. In the first instance, the actor's diplomatic posture, if it changes at all, can be expected to toughen; in the second, it may very well soften.

The adversary's responses are variable not only because there are many possible aims of a military action but also because the adversary might misinterpret the action, failing to discern its true aim. A government at war faces several handicaps in trying to divine the intentions behind the enemy's military activity. First, the receiving end of a violent attack is hardly the best place for carefully analyzing someone else's behavior; for governments as well as for individuals, this is a stressful situation, and high stress tends to reduce perceptual and cognitive capabilities.[37] Second, errors in execution can convey a false impression of the enemy's targeting policy. For example, the early Luftwaffe raids on London during the Battle of Britain were intended to destroy industrial targets, but the inaccuracy of the attacks led the British to interpret them as indiscriminate terror bombing.[38] Third, there are different methods of measuring military activity, and so the level of violence may be debatable even when execution is perfect. This was true of the disagreement be-

---

of the Vietnam War, pp. 54–55. A discussion of the problems faced by the U.S. government in trying to coerce the North Vietnamese leadership through bombing during the pre-negotiation phase of the Vietnam War is in Thies, *When Governments Collide*.

[37] Dean G. Pruitt, "Definition of the Situation as a Determinant of International Action," in Kelman (ed.), *International Behavior*, pp. 395–396; Holsti, *Crisis Escalation War*, pp. 12–13; J. David Singer, "Inter-Nation Influence: A Formal Model," pp. 428–430; and Sawyer and Guetzkow, "Bargaining and Negotiation in International Relations," p. 499.

[38] Quester, "Bargaining and Bombing during World War II in Europe," pp. 429–430.

tween Hanoi and Washington, which took place while Marigold was breaking down in late 1966, over what kind of signals the United States had been sending, intentionally or inadvertently, through its bombing of North Vietnam. There were several dimensions on which to measure escalation or de-escalation of the air war—quantity of ordnance, location of targets, types of targets—and it was unlikely that both sides were using the same system of measurement.[39]

Even if all these difficulties were surmounted and the belligerents, in full possession of their interpretative faculties, held a common view of the battle, the existence of different possible purposes of any one action makes the target nation's responses unpredictable, just as it does the actor's own responses. The difference is that the target nation's interpretations may still be incorrect, meaning that its responses are not only variable but also potentially inappropriate. The example cited earlier—that escalation may be used to seek either better terms or a quicker agreement—can be occasion for misinterpretation.[40] So can de-escalation, which may be the result of an exhaustion of resources, an effort to conserve resources for a prolonged conflict, or a signal of willingness to settle. Each of these interpretations had a part in perceptions within the U.S. administration of the lull in Communist activity in Vietnam which occurred in the late summer of 1969, around the time of Henry Kissinger's first secret negotiating session in Paris. Some viewed the lull as a sign of weakness; others, including Kissinger, thought it might be a first step toward mutual withdrawal. The absence of further de-escalation through the autumn caused him to conclude instead that Hanoi had decided to conserve its strength for fighting that would follow additional unilateral U.S. troop withdrawals. The change in interpretation led to a change in American diplomatic tactics, and specifically to President Nixon's televised address in November, in which he revealed secret meetings between Ambassador Lodge and Xuan Thuy, an exchange of letters with Ho Chi Minh, and various indirect contacts.[41]

---

[39] See *U.S.-Vietnam Relations,* Vol. VI.C.2, pp. 20, 85–86.

[40] For example, the Canadian ICC representative Blair Seaborn saw indications during a visit to Hanoi in March 1965 that the DRV leardership interpreted the early bombing of North Vietnam as an act of impatience, an effort by the United States to extricate itself from the war quickly (*U.S.-Vietnam Relations,* Vol. VI.C.1, p. 6). This interpretation underestimated the extent to which American motivations at the time concerned the terms, not just the timing, of peace.

[41] Landau, *Kissinger: The Uses of Power,* pp. 227–228.

Interpretations of Diplomatic Responses

The multiplicity of ways to view a concession, like the multiplicity of purposes of military activity, also helps to account for variation in diplomatic responses to armed action. It does so in two respects.

First, most of the interpretations of concessions enumerated in Chapter 3 may be described alternatively as *purposes* of concessions, and a leader's response depends on what purpose he has uppermost in mind as he reaches a diplomatic decision. The alternative logics underlying the interpretations discussed in that chapter may imply opposite—though, in their own ways, appropriate—responses to the same military event. For instance, a Crossian bargainer would respond to de-escalation by the opponent by toughening his diplomatic position (perhaps even retracting previous concessions) because the rate at which he incurs disagreement costs has lowered. On the other hand, a bargainer more concerned with rewarding the enemy for his restraint or signaling his own good will would make fresh concessions.

Second, a belligerent must cope with the possibility that the opponent will make inaccurate or unwanted interpretations of his diplomatic behavior. Military activity creates a context which encourages some interpretations of concessions and discourages others. Consequently, governments often tailor their diplomacy to avoid concessions when they are apt to be interpreted unfavorably. This is primarily a matter of avoiding a show of weakness, by refraining from concessions after suffering military setbacks. To sustain a tactical military defeat generally implies a softening of one's diplomatic posture, because one's overall bargaining position has weakened. But precisely because concessions in this context are susceptible to being interpreted as indicators of weakness, a belligerent may resist making ones that it might have been willing to grant in other circumstances. The avoidance of an impression of weakness was, for example, part of the reasoning of General Navarre and the French High Commissioner in Indochina in recommending to their government, once Dienbienphu fell, to take a hard line at Geneva.[42]

The Arousal of New Motivations

So far, the interests of warring states in any one conflict have been considered as fixed, with diplomacy and combat being a matter of

[42] Ely, *L'Indochine dans la Tourmente*, p. 106–108.

promoting or damaging those interests. But in fact the objectives at stake may well change in the course of a war. One possibility is for events to diminish the importance of certain issues. The negotiators at Ghent, for instance, found it easier to agree on the article concerning peace with the Indians after receiving word that most of the tribes had already been pacified anyway. And the maritime issues like impressment faded after the peace in Europe led Britain to abandon the practices which the United States had found offensive.

More common is an expansion of objectives. Interests which earlier in the war were only what Charles Fairbanks has called "latent war aims"—ones which are not part of either belligerent's conscious motivations for fighting although they would be objects of concern if called into question—became actual war aims.[43] The expansion of objectives is often a straightforward result of an expansion of combat. We saw in Chapter 4 how the violence can be carried to a level far above what would be justified by the original objectives. Such escalation, once it occurs, in turn justifies the pursuit of larger objectives. The more costly that disagreement becomes, the greater the number of possible settlements which a belligerent would prefer to continued disagreement; increasing the violence extends the bargaining range. Geographic expansion of a war also tends to extend the range of interests at stake, not just by increasing costs of punishment or deprivation but also by extending the war map, which guides the bargaining on territorial matters. And the previously noted tendency to view past costs as investments whether or not this view is accurate encourages belligerents to harden their diplomatic posture when they escalate; a larger investment demands a larger "return" in the form of more favorable peace terms.

All of this is directly derivable from the analysis in earlier chapters. The present concern, however, is a pair of interests which, though they seldom are motivations for going to war in the first place, frequently shape diplomatic responses once a war is underway. They are new motivations which military activity can arouse even when the war does not expand beyond the size that either belligerent had anticipated. They do not correspond to any uses of force described in Chapter 4, and they are often the chief reasons for force's being counterproductive. One is the maintenance of a repu-

---

[43] Charles H. Fairbanks, "War-Limiting," in Klaus Knorr (ed.), *Historical Dimensions of National Security Problems,* p. 183.

tation for not yielding under pressure; the other is the maintenance of an image of military strength.

Upholding a Bargaining Reputation

One of the most widely observed attributes of bargaining behavior at any level is an unwillingness to appear to be backing down under pressure. Many experimental studies, using a variety of procedures, have produced evidence of this, whether the pressure took the form of threats alone or actual punishment.[44] The laboratory subject evidently resists in such circumstances because submission would be a blow to self-esteem. Similar explanations have been made for resistance to pressure in international relations. An eighteenth-century observer of diplomacy, Francois de Callières, wrote:

> Menaces always do harm to negotiation, and they frequently push one party to extremities to which they would not have resorted without provocation. It is well known that injured vanity frequently drives men into courses which a sober estimate of their own interests would lead them to avoid.[45]

A modern government's unwillingness to be seen backing down in a negotiation may stem at least in part from this type of personal response when a leader merges his image of himself with that of his state.[46] But it also has a slightly different explanation, which does not require assumptions about the vanity of individual statesmen. A government is continually in the business of nurturing its image, not just to preserve organizational self-esteem but also to improve the setting for future interactions with other governments. Entirely apart from the substantive issues in any current negotiation, it has an interest in preserving a reputation for not yielding to force.[47] It puts that reputation on the line willy-nilly whenever it makes war and negotiates a peace. Even if nurturing its bargaining reputation were not one of a belligerent's reasons for waging war in the first

[44] See, e.g., Morton Deutsch and Robert M. Krauss, "Studies of Interpersonal Bargaining"; Morton Deutsch, et al., "Strategies of Inducing Cooperation: An Experimental Study"; and Barry R. Schlenker, et al., "Complaince to Threats as a Function of the Wording of the Threat and the Exploitativeness of the Threatener."

[45] Francois de Callières, *On the Manner of Negotiating with Princes*, p. 125.

[46] Sawyer and Guetzkow, "Bargaining and Negotiation in International Relations," p. 484.

[47] Cf. Singer, "Inter-nation Influence: A Formal Model," p. 430; and Glenn H. Snyder and Paul Diesing, *Conflict Among Nations*, pp. 187–188.

place, it becomes an objective once the war is underway. It is a new motivation and an independent reason for not conceding in response to the armed actions of the other side.

This motivation is most likely to influence the diplomacy of a state which has many outside commitments, or can expect to be a party to future conflicts in which the stakes are at least as important to it as those in the current war. In practice, this means great powers or states which aspire to become great powers. Above all, it means a great power waging war against a smaller state, in which case any impression of yielding to force would be especially damaging to its prestige. For the larger belligerent in such a war, upholding its bargaining reputation may become a matter not just of resisting concessions but also of insuring that the opponent is seen to make major concessions of his own. This will be especially true if military events have created a context in which its prestige is likely to be called into question, as was true of Soviet prestige after the Red Army's initial setbacks in the war against Finland in 1939-1940. The expansion of Soviet aims during the course of that conflict was partly due to what Molotov called the "logic of war," by which he meant the effect of discontinuity in military options; the Soviets found that they could not secure their more modest initial objectives without a major effort to smash Finnish forces, which in turn brought other objectives within their grasp. But it also resulted from a need to demonstrate beyond any doubt, through the terms of the peace treaty, that the Soviet Union was not going to let a small neighbor bend its will.[48]

Because maintaining a bargaining reputation is a matter of impressions conveyed to the wider world, the extent to which it governs the response to an armed action depends not only on the nature of the action itself but also on the way it is portrayed and whether it is made known to outside observers at all. It is the appearance, more than the reality, of backing down under pressure that is to be avoided. This can be a reason for describing one's own attacks in a low-key manner, inflicting punishment without issuing a public challenge. It was for this reason that Washington instructed Ridgway and Clark during the Korean War to give only routine publicity to even the most major air strikes against targets in North Korea.[49] The same consideration led the French to reject Dulles's proposal for a treaty and declaration to accompany any allied intervention in Indochina; they feared that the Chinese, against whom such a political

---

[48] Max Jakobson, *The Diplomacy of the Winter War*, pp. 167–168.

[49] Hermes, *Truce Tent and Fighting Front*, pp. 33–34, 277.

arrangement would appear directed, would become obdurate at Geneva lest they lose face.[50] Similarly, it was to spare the enemy a loss of face that President Nixon made no public statement on the reasons for the B-52 raids against North Vietnam in December 1972. The Christmas bombing "got the message through to Hanoi," he later explained, "while still allowing them to back off their intransigeant position without having to acknowledge that they were doing so because of military pressure from us."[51] Such precautions, however, are of only limited help in decoupling the enemy's diplomatic responses from his prestige. Wars are rarely fought in secrecy, and outsiders will usually perceive coercion as coercion, regardless of how the coercer tries to portray it.

Upholding a Military Reputation

Besides the appearance of yielding under duress, another impression which participants in conflict at all levels try to avoid is that of being a "loser," of having failed in the contest which preceded the decisions on whether to yield. Maintaining a bargaining reputation is a matter of will; this is one of capability. The first involves not crying "uncle" when in a painful position; the second involves not getting into a painful position in the first place. The latter, like the former, can be a very personal response in that defeat is a blow to self-esteem. But for a government with broader concerns, avoiding the image of a military loser can be important for other reasons. In particular, it is necessary for demonstrating the ability to protect interests at stake in other, possibly more important, conflicts. This applies especially to the same states for which upholding a bargaining reputation is important: great powers, especially when at war with small ones. For example, demonstrating the strength of the Red Army, as well as that of Stalin's determination, became important to the Soviets after the initial setbacks in the Russo-Finnish War.

Avoiding a loser's image may also be necessary to ward off internal discontent. The discontent could exist chiefly within the military—the element whose self-esteem is most damaged by battlefield defeats—as was true on the French side during the Algerian War. Or it could be spread more generally among the civilian population, to whom military outcomes often are a clearer measure of success and failure than are clauses in a peace treaty.

[50] Ely, *L'Indochine dans la Tourmente,* pp. 88–89.
[51] Richard M. Nixon, *RN: The Memoirs of Richard Nixon,* p. 736.

Whatever the precise mixture of motives, governments some-times seek tactical victories at least partially to uphold their military reputations, not just to attain more favorable peace terms. This touches a side of wartime strategy not discussed in Chapter 4. The subject is raised here because diplomatic behavior in the peace nego-tiation—although not providing the motivation for this mode of mili-tary decision-making—is nevertheless affected by it. Moreover, it is affected in a seemingly incongruous manner, with a tougher diplo-matic line following military defeats and a softer one following vic-tories.

To project an image of military success, it may be necessary to redeem past defeats with future victories. In attempting to do so, a government may find it useful, for either of two reasons, to make extreme diplomatic demands. First, it is a way of assuring that the enemy will not come to terms promptly and thereby spoil the oppor-tunity to win some battles before peace is concluded. Baron Rosen, the second-ranking member of the Russian delegation at the Ports-mouth peace conference, saw this as a reason for making extreme demands of Japan in the summer of 1905. As he later wrote, he did not want peace to follow "a series of defeats without our army being given a chance to redeem the glory of our arms by a victory . . ."— a circumstance which, he feared, would hasten revolution in Rus-sia.[52] (He was overruled, however, by the chief of his delegation, Count Witte, who believed that a prolongation of the war would do more to encourage revolution than would an absence of military victories.) Second, an ambitious but simply stated and easily under-stood diplomatic objective may help to inspire one's population to support a more vigorous war effort. The Allies' "unconditional sur-render" formula in World War II served this purpose, but so can a less extreme position which still permits a negotiated settlement.[53]

Conversely, a softer diplomatic line may follow in the wake of military successes. This is true not only because the need to delay the peace or to inspire the populace diminishes or disappears, but also because the two aspects of a nation's overall reputation under discussion here—bargaining fortitude and military capability—af-fect each other's importance. As with the reluctance to show weak-ness to the current opponent, the reluctance to acquire a general reputation for yielding under pressure is less apt to retard conces-

---

[52] Quoted in White, *The Diplomacy of the Russo-Japanese War*, p. 235.

[53] Italy toughened its negotiating position for this reason during the course of its war against Turkey in 1911–1912. Fairbanks, pp. 184–185.

sions when military circumstances are favorable; the side with the upper hand on the battlefield can afford to be less inhibited because it will not appear to be acting under duress. It was for this reason that France's military success in Algeria was an important ingredient in President De Gaulle's willingness to make concessions to the FLN, even after he came to realize that this success would not destroy the rebels' popular support. To him, the chief effects of the war went beyond the issues that separated his government and the FLN. Algeria had become a cruel sideshow that diverted attention from the great things that he and France had to do, and lessened the time he had to do them. *How* the settlement was reached, and its impact on France's international standing, were more important to him than the substance of the settlement itself. It was this concern which caused De Gaulle to stress military superiority. As he later explained in his memoirs, self-determination in Algeria was the only alternative, but it would be France alone, "from the height of her power," that would grant it. France must not be compelled to do so by military setbacks. "We would, therefore, put forth the effort required to make ourselves masters of the battlefield."[54] Had the French army been anything less than the military master of Algeria, he probably would have considered it too damaging to French prestige to make major concessions.[55]

Conclusion

We have now seen how the several different perspectives toward bargaining that were introduced in Chapter 3, and extended to the use of the military instrument in Chapter 4, also underlie diplomatic responses to military events. The discussion has gotten increasingly complicated as it has explored how each belligerent might interpret

[54] De Gaulle, *Memoirs of Hope,* pp. 45–46.

[55] Successful military action may lead to a softer diplomatic position, not just because concessions are less likely to damage one's prestige, but also because triumph on the battlefield can function as a sort of catharsis which fulfills desires to punish or humiliate the enemy. Triumph at the conference table then becomes less necessary. The sack of Washington in 1814 seemed to have this effect among many in Britain, where the urge had been strong to use the war to "give Jonathan a drubbing"—i.e., to punish the upstart republic for daring to go to war when Britain's hands were full in Europe. As one Minister observed, the burning of the capital helped to satisfy this urge; it "was felt as a reparation for the supposed insults our flag had suffered." Perkins, *Castlereagh and Adams,* p. 95.

or misinterpret both its own behavior and that of the enemy, but it has continued to analyze the belligerents as bargainers, not just as fighters. Their responses are distinguishable from those of fighters in at least two respects. First, to the extent that military activity affects the outcome of the conflict, it does so less through direct physical effects than through changes in the belligerents' expectations—expectations about their own bargaining strength, the enemy's strength, and future military events. Second, their diplomacy reflects not just the immediate battle but their overall bargaining relationship, which is also shaped by such factors as their reputations as negotiators and their involvement in outside conflicts.

Diplomatic responses to military activity are highly variable not only because of the complexity of the bargaining process itself but also because real bargainers often have widely divergent utility functions, particularly as they relate to the costs of combat. The principles of cost manipulation elucidated in Chapter 3 remain valid in spite of this divergence, as long as we remember that utility is not exactly equivalent to casualties, destruction, or other directly measurable physical effects.

The current chapter has also placed in sharper focus the limits to what military force can accomplish in a war, whatever a particular belligerent's military capabilities may be. We saw in Chapter 4 how the nature of the issues in some wars (i.e., those with a convex bargaining space, in which attractive compromise settlements are available) makes the probable diplomatic payoff of military effort relatively small. Now we see additional possible reasons that the military instrument is sometimes frustratingly ineffective in changing the enemy's diplomatic posture: the enemy may place little importance on his war costs or high value on his bargaining reputation, for example, or battlefield events may be sufficiently consistent with his prior expectations that he sees no reason to change his negotiating position. Successful military operations often do win political objectives, of course, but they are by no means the sole—and sometimes not even the most critical—influence on peace negotiations.

CHAPTER SIX

The Manipulation
of Multiple Issues

A peace negotiation generally involves several discrete issues. This fact was briefly noted in Chapter 3, in order to make an observation about the usual shape of the overall bargaining space and to introduce a discussion of how individual questions tend to be settled. But the existence of multiple issues also has some other implications, to which we now turn. The subject has been set aside until now because the manipulation of multiple issues becomes most important near the end of a peace negotiation, when the belligerents are searching for ways to bridge the remaining gaps that divide them and to assure enforcement of peace terms after the armistice. The problems and opportunities entailed in that search will be addressed in a moment, but first we consider why it is common for several issues to remain unsettled until near the end of the negotiation, rather than having been resolved separately earlier.

The Sequence of Consideration

Many collective decision processes, such as legislation by a parliament, use a formal agenda, specifying the issues to be resolved and the order in which they are to be considered. But in peace negotiations, an agenda is seldom used, and when one is, it often causes trouble and is later modified or abandoned. Korea was the only major case in which an agenda was ever adopted, and this only after two weeks of acrimony that got the truce talks off to an inauspicious start. The ordering of issues in the Korean agenda later broke down, with a given subject being taken up before the previous one was resolved, and item 5 being settled long before items 3 and 4. The preliminary talks between France and the FLN at Melun in June

1960 broke down partly because of differences over the agenda for the later substantive sessions. When the parties finally did start negotiating over substance at Evian the following spring, they did so without an agenda.[1] At Ghent and Geneva, the parties placed on the record their willingness to discuss particular issues, but no attempt was made to agree upon an agenda before substantive negotiations began. In the Vietnam peace talks, the matter was bypassed altogether.

One reason that prior adoption of an agenda is more of a hindrance than a help in a peace negotiation is that, far from being a mere convenience that makes the deliberations more orderly, an agenda inevitably embodies negotiating advantages and disadvantages for each side. Consequently, agreement on an agenda presupposes to some degree a prior narrowing of the substantive differences between the parties. There are two respects in which this is true.

First, it is sometimes difficult to state an issue without implying a certain resolution of it. This is most obvious when the question of whether a given topic is an issue is itself an issue, as was true of the fisheries privileges in the War of 1812. It is hard to see how the American commissioners could have accepted a formal agenda which listed it as a topic without appearing to abandon their position that the war had never called fisheries into question in the first place. Other topics may not be this intractable but nevertheless constitute stumbling blocks when exact phraseology must be agreed upon. In the Korean talks, the UNC accused the Communists of proposing a "loaded" agenda that included substantive demands, such as in their proposed item 1, which read in part: "Establishment of the 38th Parallel as the military demarcation line." But some of the topics on the UNC's own proposed agenda seemed equally "loaded," such as item 7: "Agreement on the principle of inspection within Korea by Military Observer Teams, functioning under the Military Armistice Commission."[2] This item implied a specific resolution of the issue of how the armistice would be policed, just as the Communists' item 1 implied a specific resolution of the issue of where the demarcation line would be located. The whole episode demonstrates not so much an attempt by one side to trick the other as the difficulty in disentangling answers from a statement of the questions.

[1] Tricot, *Les Sentiers de la Paix*, p. 234.
[2] Vatcher, *Panmunjom*, pp. 33–34.

Second—and of more direct concern to the subject of this chapter—if issues are to be considered sequentially, the sequence itself will be a bone of contention. One reason for this is that each party usually wants to turn first to those issues of greatest concern to it.[3] Neither wants to yield ground on other issues until it has secured what it views as its chief interests, lest it give up something that would have been more useful to withhold as a potential reward. We see evidence of this when, in the absence of an agenda, the parties attempt to steer the deliberations toward their favored subjects, even though they wind up negotiating several issues simultaneously. France at Geneva and the United States in the Paris peace talks both wished to give priority to military issues, while the Viet Minh/DRV preferred to talk first about political arrangements. Similarly, the French negotiators who conducted the final two rounds of bargaining with the FLN considered guarantees for the Europeans in Algeria to be their most important objective, and therefore planned to try to obtain such guarantees before they conceded on other issues, particularly arrangements for the transitional period, which they deemed less important.[4]

Another reason for different preferences regarding the sequence in which to consider issues is that the sequence helps to determine which issues would still be unresolved should the negotiation break down. That is important because it affects the strength of each side's case before the court of public opinion, both foreign and domestic. The proposals in supposedly secret negotiations are frequently leaked, and a belligerent usually considers an interruption or breakdown of talks as an excuse to reveal the exchanges more directly if it is in its interest to do so, as both sides in the Vietnam War did on more than one occasion when the secret talks hit snags. To the extent that a government's demands, once revealed, are widely viewed as reasonable, its bargaining position strengthens; the view that they are unreasonable weakens it. This means it is advantageous to leave until last those issues which would cause the most problems for the opponent's public relations, and the least for one's own.

Neither of these last two implications of the sequence of consideration is peculiar to peace negotiations, but an additional one is. Negotiation takes place against a military background that is subject

[3] Raymond Cohen and Stuart Cohen, *Peace Conferences: The Formal Aspects*, p. 15.

[4] Buron, *Carnets Politiques de la Guerre d'Algérie*, pp. 193–194.

to change, and may in fact be changing rapidly. Later bargaining is based upon different military facts than earlier bargaining. Accordingly, if the military situation is expected to improve, it is advantageous to delay consideration of those issues the settlement of which will be most dependent on the current state of play on the battlefield. A deteriorating situation implies the opposite. We saw in an earlier chapter that territorial issues tend to reflect the current military situation more than do other issues. Thus, for the side on the defensive, it is best to dispose of territorial issues first. The Communists in the Korean War tried to do so when they made the establishment of the demarcation line the first item on their proposed agenda. By agreeing to this proposal, the UNC forfeited some of the tactical advantage it had at the time.[5] Fixing the demarcation line meant that subsequent territorial gains would have to be given up at the armistice. And, because of this, it would be harder to maintain pressure on the Communists to induce them to concede on the other issues, since it would be difficult to justify an offensive domestically when everyone knew that any ground gained would not be kept. The UNC later tried to undo the damage by interpreting the agreement on the demarcation line as referring to the front line at the time the armistice was signed. But this looked like a retraction of a previous willingness to settle the location of the line first. The UNC wound up accepting the Communist interpretation if the armistice were concluded within thirty days. This gave the Communist armies a crucial respite (the so-called "Little Armistice" of November-December 1951), during which they improved their defenses and made later UNC offensive action that much more difficult.[6]

Package Proposals

Apart from the difficulty in reaching prior agreement on a list of topics that neither side believes will give an advantage to its opponent, the infrequency with which an agenda is used in peace negotiations also reflects a general disadvantage of sequential consideration of issues: it eliminates the flexibility afforded by being able to bargain over several issues simultaneously, and specifically to trade

---

[5] Cf. Leckie, *Conflict*, pp. 307–308, 315–316.

[6] Wilfred A. Bacchus, "The Relationship Between Combat and Peace Negotiations: Fighting While Talking in Korea, 1951–1953," p. 561; Vatcher, p. 86; and Leckie, p. 317.

concessions on one issue for counterconcessions on another. In line with this, experimentation has shown that when a negotiation is structured so as to permit logrolling, agreements are reached more quickly and with greater joint utility than when issues are considered sequentially.[7]

From the point of view of the individual bargainer, there are two advantages to using package proposals, in which a concession is offered on condition that the opponent makes some specified concession on another issue. The first is that reciprocation is built in, unlike simple concessions, where reciprocation is only to be hoped for and never assured. A package proposal moves the parties just as quickly—probably more quickly—toward an agreement than does a simple concession, while reducing the danger that the opponent will interpret the move as a sign of weakness and become less compliant as a result.[8]

The second advantage is that a package provides a way of coping with discontinuities in the bargaining space. Because many of the issues in a peace negotiation are matters of discrete choice and not of degree, the bargainer may face a situation in which he wants to make a concession but the only simple concessions available are too large. This could make him reluctant to move even if there is little danger that the opponent will misinterpret his action. This would be especially true of a Zeuthenian bargainer, who seeks to concede only enough to reverse the inequality of critical risks and no more. The farther a concession takes him beyond that point, the less desirable it would be in his eyes. Coupling his new offer with some sort of compensation from the opponent reduces this problem.[9]

It might seem that the ideal sort of issue to be used for compensation is one which is itself a matter of degree and not of discrete choice, like the payment of money. Indeed, demands for, or offers of, money have often been made in peace negotiations in various guises, such as a purchase of territory (e.g., in the Mexican-American War) or an indemnity for the war itself (e.g., in the Russo-Japanese War). But, in a peace settlement, even a divisible good may have indivisible symbolic value. This is certainly true of

[7] Rubin and Brown, *The Social Psychology of Bargaining and Negotiation,* pp. 146–147.

[8] See the comments of Admiral Joy, the UNC negotiator at Panmunjom, on this point. Joy, *How Communists Negotiate,* pp. 119, 170–171.

[9] On the general problem of bargaining with indivisible goods and the use of compensation, see Schelling, *The Strategy of Conflict,* pp. 31–33.

money. In the Mexican-American War, the U.S. offer of cash in return for the cession of New Mexico and California perhaps was more of a hindrance than a help, at least initially, in concluding a peace with Mexico. To give up part of the homeland in return for money seemed even more degrading to the Mexican government than to have it wrested away solely by force. (This feeling was heightened by the appropriation of $3 million by the U.S. Congress for "extraordinary expenses" in connection with the peace negotiation, on action which carried a whiff of bribery.)[10] At Portsmouth, the Russians rejected the payment of any indemnity as a symbol of defeat. They treated indemnity as a yes-or-no question, and their final answer was no.

It would thus be an exaggeration to say that package proposals make it possible to fine-tune one's diplomatic behavior, and to regulate the size of concessions as precisely as in an economist's model. But with a judicious juggling of the issues, they enable the bargainer to come closer to doing so than he could by considering each issue separately. Most mutually acceptable package proposals naturally involve a yielding by each side on matters of relatively less concern to it, in return for getting its way on items that it deems more important. Within this constraint, the bargainers have considerable flexibility regarding how many issues they try to dispose of in a single diplomatic move, and the extent to which they indicate their willingness to drop current demands. One manifestation of this flexibility is that a belligerent may have more than one proposal on the table at the same time. When the U.S. commissioners at Ghent sent a draft treaty to the British, they also included in their note a simpler offer to make peace on the basis of the *status quo ante bellum,* while reserving matters in dispute for future negotiation.[11] The draft treaty was the "real" U.S. position, embodying the demands to which the Americans intended to adhere as long as there was no movement by the British. The alternative offer was essentially a package proposal in which the United States showed its willingness to drop its position on the maritime issues on condition that the British give up their territorial demands. President Nixon did virtually the same thing in October 1970 when he made his stripped-down offer of a cease-fire in place in Vietnam while leaving his more comprehensive proposal

[10] Justin H. Smith, *The War with Mexico,* Vol. 2, pp. 121, 126.

[11] U.S. commissioners to British commissioners, 10 November 1814. *American State Papers,* pp. 733–740.

of the previous May on the table.[12] This kind of flexibility is especially valuable because of the inevitable uncertainty about the enemy's utilities. Offering alternative package proposals is part of the process of groping for a Pareto-optimal settlement when neither side knows in advance exactly how the opponent would value each possible resolution of each issue.

Package proposals have some pitfalls. One is that the anticipation they will be used encourages the raising of spurious demands for the sole purpose of trading them away for genuine concessions by the opponent. The Communists' approach to the bargaining on control and supervision arrangements in Korea, which was described in Chapter 3, is an outstanding example. The Communist negotiators made it clear through hints dropped at the conference table that they considered their sham positions, such as the refusal to allow any rotation of personnel, as trading material intended to wring concessions from the UNC on such matters as the construction of airfields.[13] As a result of this experience, the decision-makers on the UNC side apparently learned the lesson that against an opponent who behaves this way it is sometimes better to resort to consideration of issues seriatim. In the bargaining during the spring of 1953 on arrangements for handling prisoners (following the Communists' acceptance of the principle of voluntary repatriation), the UNC insisted on settling the identity of the neutral nation that would have custody of the prisoners, before discussing any of the other arrangements.[14] Washington no doubt painfully remembered the Communists' earlier designation of the Soviet Union as a "neutral nation" to serve on the supervisory commission, which was one of the sham positions which they had taken on control arrangements a year earlier, and which they dropped in return for the UNC's conceding on the airfield issue. They were denied the opportunity to use this tactic a second time, and the overall settlement on the handling of prisoners was more in line with the UNC's original position than were the arrangements for control and supervision of the armistice.

Another pitfall—one associated with actually making a package proposal rather than with the expectation that such deals will be used—is that the enemy might in effect accept the part of the pack-

---

[12] Broadcast address, 7 October 1970. Text in *Weekly Compilation of Presidential Documents*, 12 October 1970, pp. 1349–1352.

[13] Hermes, *Truce Tent and Fighting Front*, p. 153.

[14] *Ibid.*, pp. 424–425.

age that is in his favor and reject the rest.[15] This accounted for some of the negotiating ground which the UNC lost at Panmunjom on the control issue. At one point, for example, the UNC offered to abandon its demand for aerial reconnaissance if the Communists would accept the restriction on airfields. The Communist response was to gladly accept the concession on reconnaissance flights while standing pat on the airfield question.[16] The aerial reconnaissance issue did not come up again—the point was lost just as if no conditions had been attached to the concession in the first place—and the Communists eventually got their way on the airfield issue in return for giving up the designation of the Soviet Union as a neutral nation. The result may well have been different if the UNC had handled the proposal better than it did, making the conditional nature of the concession more explicit and reasserting its original demand on aerial reconnaissance when no counterconcession was forthcoming. But the episode also demonstrates that the distinction between one's "real" position at any point during the bargaining process and what one suggests as part of a package deal is so tenuous as to be at times virtually nonexistent. In a sense, *all* proposals are conditional; they are statements that "If you accept this, so do I."[17] The opponent is free to make what he wants of any new offer, however it is phrased, and to withhold what is in his power to withhold.

This does not mean that package proposals are not worth considering as a distinct diplomatic tactic, but only that their results are problematical. Two conditions help to prevent results as unfortunate as those in the example just cited from the Korean talks. The first is that the package be expressible in general terms which automatically link the concession offered with the one demanded.[18] This was true of the alternative proposal presented by the United States at Ghent. The proposal was to abandon *all* demands for departure from the *status quo ante bellum;* it was not necessary to identify the demands themselves. It was not true of the UNC proposal in Korea, which

[15] On this as a hazard of package proposals in any type of negotiation, see Zartman and Berman, *The Practical Negotiator,* p. 172.

[16] Hermes, p. 153.

[17] In this respect, armistice negotiations differ from negotiations in which the settlement can be implemented in stages as bargaining progresses, as with the disengagement agreements that followed the Yom Kippur War, considered together as part of the making of an overall territorial settlement in the Middle East. In the latter, the "real" positions are marked by physical placement of men and installations on the ground and are therefore clearly distinct from mere verbal offers.

[18] Cf. Zartman and Berman, p. 179.

entailed an arbitrary linkage of two issues that had nothing else in common. The second condition pertains to the distinction among phases of a negotiation discussed in Chapter 3. The reasons that simple concessions are more likely to be reciprocated at certain stages of a negotiation than at others apply as well to package proposals. It is during Phase Two, when diplomatic actions are interpreted chiefly as indicators of morale and of an overall concession rate, that the enemy is most likely to concentrate on what his opponent is giving up and to disregard the rest. Packages are more effective during the final phase of bargaining, when there are stronger incentives to accept an invitation to reciprocate. A package offered at this time helps to quickly identify which specific points a belligerent considers more important than others. It is in fact during Phase Three bargaining that packages are used most often. At Panmunjom they were employed during this phase in settling several matters of detail, when they were far more effective in hastening agreement than the UNC's earlier package proposals had been.

Leaving Outcomes to Chance

Even a careful and imaginative use of package proposals may not enable the negotiators to resolve definitively all of the questions that divide them. The peace agreements in all of the major cases left the eventual outcomes of several important issues uncertain. For example, the Treaty of Ghent referred most of the Anglo-American boundary disputes to commissions (which were seen as a form of arbitration, not negotiation). And in both of the wars in Indochina, the belligerents left the whole political future of Vietnam in the air as the Western power withdrew. The 1954 agreement created a supposedly temporary partition of the country, with reunification dependent upon a future election. The 1973 agreement left the Vietnamese parties poised at each other's throats and relying upon a yet-to-be established Council of Reconciliation as a forum in which to achieve a permanent settlement.[19]

One reason that uncertainty is often incorporated into a peace agreement is that uncertain peace terms also tend to be vague terms, and vague terms tend to be easiest to negotiate. They are the path of

[19] Oran Young has noted that agreements reached in crisis bargaining often rely in this way upon contingent devices, specifying procedure rather than substance. Young, *The Politics of Force*, pp. 284–285.

least resistance; if the lines in an image of the future are sufficiently blurred, they may appear to cover positions which are actually still some distance apart. Efforts to tidy up the lines only reveal the continuing differences underneath, and hinder rather than facilitate agreement. This happened when the Vietnam negotiations ran aground in December 1972, as the Nixon administration attempted to put greater precision into the draft agreement reached in October. In the end, much of the vagueness in the draft had to be retained, such as in a clause on the demilitarized zone which did not resolve the question of whether North Vietnamese troops were entitled to be in South Vietnam. Henry Kissinger later publicly justified this clause by stating that on such issues "ambiguity has its merits" and "it is best not to deal in a formal and legalistic manner."[20]

But uncertainty per se, not just vagueness, is a useful device in peace agreements, and for the same reason that package proposals are: it is a way of dealing with discontinuities in the bargaining space. A method of compromising between two discrete positions with no apparent middle ground is to establish a temporary situation or procedure capable of leading to either one of the preferred states. The utility of this situation or procedure to each side would be somewhere between the utilities of the two demands. To establish such a contingent device may require discussion of election rules, nomination of arbitrators, or similar questions that were not issues at the outset of the negotiation. In effect, new issues are created to dispose of an old one.

Alternatively, the contingent device may be, as in Vietnam, a whole set of political and military circumstances the future evolution of which is in doubt. Kissinger reportedly told the North Vietnamese in one of the secret negotiating sessions in Paris that the United States was willing to give the Viet Cong a "reasonable chance" to acquire political power in South Vietnam through nonviolent means.[21] He later described his goal as a negotiated settlement that would give the Saigon regime a "fair chance" to survive, and that would leave the future of South Vietnam to a "historical process."[22] Such comments recognized that when the issue was sovereignty over South Vietnam—which, as Kissinger acknowledged, was indi-

[20] Press conference of 24 January 1973. Transcript in *Background Information*, pp. 503–516 at p. 512.

[21] He is supposed to have made the remark in a September 1970 meeting with Xuan Thuy. Kalb and Kalb, *Kissinger*, p. 174.

[22] Henry Kissinger, *White House Years*, p. 1038.

visible[23]—the only possible compromise settlement was one that gave each side a possibility of becoming the sovereign. An either-or issue would be transformed into one of degree, with the remaining question being how much of a chance was "reasonable" or "fair."

Such contingent devices help bargainers to cope with the problems of a discontinuous or concave bargaining space, but they do not eliminate these problems altogether. Leaving the political future of South Vietnam uncertain was probably the only way that North Vietnam and the United States could have made a compromise agreement, but the difficulty in reaching that agreement attests to its meager utility and to the point made in Chapter 4 about the lack of *attractive* compromises in civil wars. The bargaining space in the Vietnam War was probably still concave; the case demonstrates that relatively *unattractive* compromises may be reached when attractive ones are unavailable, but usually not without long and difficult negotiations and a relatively large amount of violence.

Not Leaving Outcomes to the Enemy

It is one thing for an outcome to be uncertain because it depends on events not entirely under the control of either party; uncertainty regarding the future cooperation of the adversary is altogether different. Most provisions of a peace agreement other than the cease-fire itself cannot be implemented immediately. Given the usual level of distrust between two warring states, there may be considerable doubt as to whether they will be implemented at all. Therefore, governments negotiating a peace agreement usually try to assure that they will have sanctions to impose on the adversary if he does not keep his part of the bargain.

The greatest sanction is to start a new war. As mentioned in an earlier chapter, Britain relied on the implicit threat of a future war to try to assure France's compliance with the peace terms reached in 1801. When such is the case, governments will pay particular attention to provisions of the armistice agreement that affect their capacity for renewed combat, such as those concerning the stationing and resupply of forces. Initiating a fresh war, however, is apt to be too drastic a sanction for many purposes. Furthermore, it may be politically difficult to resume combat, even for a state that is militarily

[23] *Ibid.*, p. 1393.

strong. The British government discovered this to be true in the
immediate aftermath of the armistice that it concluded with Bonaparte, despite the Royal Navy's command of the seas. That peace
was the traditional two-stage kind, with a preliminary treaty that
incorporated the cease-fire and was accompanied by various verbal
assurances that were to form the basis of a final treaty. The armistice
unleashed a celebration among the British people that effectively
foreclosed for the time being the option of resuming hostilities.
When the French envoy arrived in London to deliver the ratification
of the preliminaries, he was greeted by a jubilant crowd that un-
hitched the horses and pulled his carriage to Downing Street.[24] London paid the price for this during the negotiation of the final treaty,
when Bonaparte and Talleyrand welshed on their earlier verbal commitments and added new demands. The British negotiators' hands
were tied, and the treaty turned out to be much less favorable than
what the government might have hoped for only a few months earlier. It was precisely to avoid this sort of problem during the Korean
War that General Clark and others within the Defense Department
persuaded President Truman to reject a State Department recommendation to defer the issue of nonrepatriated prisoners to a post-
armistice negotiation. They feared, with justification, that any armistice would incite a bring-the-boys-home sentiment in the United
States that would rapidly erode the UNC posture in Korea. Meanwhile, the Communists would strengthen their own position, and the
prisoner issue might never be settled satisfactorily.[25]

[24] Arthur Bryant, *The Years of Endurance, 1793–1802*, p. 345.

[25] This, incidentally, suggests a secondary reason for the transition away from the
post-armistice peace negotiation discussed in Chapter 1—viz., the spread of popular
sovereignty, in the sense not just of formal control of government by the masses but
also of the influence of mass opinion (democracy in Tocqueville's broadest sense).
With more governments constrained by a citizenry which thinks in simplistic terms of
wartime versus peacetime and which finds it hard to understand the need to support a
military machine not to "win" a war but merely to support a negotiation, there are
more governments with an incentive to resolve all issues before an armistice. It is no
accident that the only two wars in the first half of the nineteenth century which ended
with a pre-armistice negotiation both involved the nation in which popular sovereignty was most strongly rooted—the United States. In the first of these, the War of
1812, the federal government was so dependent on the states, and on fickle popular
feeling generally, for the meager land forces at its disposal that it could have made
few credible threats once fighting stopped and the militiamen went home. In the other
war, the one against Mexico, President Polk accepted a treaty negotiated by a diplomat who had defied orders for his recall because the President feared that to do
otherwise would result in Congress's cutting off funds for the army in Mexico. See
Robert A. Brent, "Nicholas P. Trist and the Treaty of Guadalupe Hidalgo," p. 469.

With a peace settlement negotiated entirely before the armistice, the uncertainty concerns the adversary's execution of terms already agreed upon rather than on future negotiating behavior, but the problem is basically the same. Apart from the threat of resuming hostilities, the principal method of coping with this problem is to withhold something that the enemy desires until he carries out his part of the bargain. One side's obligations, in other words, become hostage to the fulfillment of the other's. Sometimes literal hostages are involved; American prisoners of war held by North Vietnam served as such in the execution of the 1973 Paris agreement, with their release carefully timed to coincide with the withdrawal of the remaining American troops from South Vietnam. Although a schedule of this type makes explicit the idea of obligations as hostages, it is not essential. Any provision the execution of which is valued by the other side, and which can be delayed at little cost to oneself, may serve as a sanction. No schedule was specified in the Vietnam agreement for the U.S. clearing of mines from North Vietnamese waters, and the United States probably retarded the clearing operations in order to provide extra assurance that all American prisoners would be returned.[26] Similarly, Hanoi's withholding of information on missing American servicemen served as a convenient sanction against the United States.

With sufficient ingenuity, belligerents usually can arrange post-armistice obligations in such a way that neither side feels entirely dependent on the future good will of the other. Nevertheless, there are limits to what ingenuity can do. The nature of the issues may be such that obligations are asymmetrical, with one side finding it easier to renege on them after the armistice than the other. This is especially true if one side's obligations are open-ended while those of the other consist of finite acts which, once performed, are not easily retracted. France, in its relationship with the FLN, suffered from this disadvantage. The principal French obligations in the Evian accords were to grant independence and to withdraw French troops from Algeria. Once done, these acts could not be undone without starting a new war. Upon their completion, France lacked an easily usable sanction to assure that the FLN fulfilled its most important obligations, which were mostly open-ended ones such as the protection of minority rights. "That the agreements are hazardous in their application is certain," De Gaulle remarked privately.[27] That is, they were hazardous from the French point of view. For

[26] Porter, *A Peace Denied*, p. 235.
[27] Quoted in Hartley, *Gaullism*, p. 184.

their part, the FLN leaders fully realized and exploited the advantage they enjoyed. "The Evian accords," proclaimed Ahmed Ben Bella two weeks after they were signed, "are only a stage in the revolution."[28]

Conclusion

Several of the points made in earlier chapters have resurfaced in this discussion of multiple issues. One of these is that certain questions relating to the peace negotiation itself—its timing, structure, and procedure—often constitute a subsidiary bargaining problem, because how these questions are resolved may affect each side's bargaining strength and thus also affect the settlement of substantive issues. As discussed in Chapter 2, this is why belligerents can be expected to differ over when, and under what conditions, peace negotiations should open. It is also why they differ over the order in which multiple issues are to be considered, so much so that an agreed agenda is usually infeasible or unworkable. Another point made earlier is that different logics tend to prevail in different phases of the negotiation. In Chapter 3 we saw that a bargaining strategy that relies on the reciprocation of concessions is apt to be more successful in the final phase of a negotiation than in the middle phase, when a concession is more likely to be interpreted as a sign of weakness. By the same token, package proposals—which embody the concept of reciprocation—are most useful in the final phase as well.

What is most significant about the manner in which multiple issues tend to be manipulated, however, is what this suggests about how real bargainers conform to models of bargaining behavior. Several of the techniques described in this chapter are in effect ways of coping with problems in the models, and of narrowing certain gaps between theory and reality that often arise with single-issue bargaining. One such problem is discontinuity in the bargaining space: models may be constructed with smooth curves and an assumed infinity of possible outcomes, but real outcomes are often limited to a few discrete choices with markedly different utilities. Package proposals and uncertainty-producing contingent devices are both means of partially

[28] Quoted in Maurice Allais, *Les Accords d'Evian, le Référendum et la Resistance Algérienne*, p. 53.

filling the gaps in a discontinuous space. They create new alternatives with utilities somewhere between those of the original, simple demands. Indeed, the technique of leaving an outcome to chance is the real-life equivalent of the hypothetical lotteries that game theorists use to justify the assumption of a continuous bargaining space (although objective probabilities in peace agreements are not known with the same precision as those in the game theorist's lottery).

Another problem, noted in Chapter 3, is how to determine that one particular bargainer should concede before the other, given that both are engaged in an infinite regress of trying to outguess each other's intentions. Package proposals enable bargainers to avoid this puzzle, and the use of packages suggests that what is a problem in theory is perceived by bargainers to be a problem in practice as well. The idea underlying a package deal is that both bargainers concede simultaneously. The vexing question of who goes first is circumvented in order to get closer to a settlement that both parties would prefer to continued stalemate.

CHAPTER SEVEN

War Termination in
Theory and Practice

The Use of Theory in the Study of War

The theoretical framework with which this book began can now be briefly reconsidered. The primary assumption was that war termination is indeed susceptible to theorizing, and that it can largely be explained in terms of principles that apply to many wars, not just to the issues and circumstances involved in any one of them. This assumption has been borne out by numerous patterns of diplomatic and military behavior that have recurred in past conflicts. The regularity of the patterns is due in part to the fact that most wars have in common certain central features—a conflict of interest, substantial costs that end only when the war does, and the need for agreement between the belligerents to make it end—that impose a consistent logic on military and economic decisions. It also reflects the fact that those decisions are generally taken by leaders who have an interest in minimizing the costs to their own side of the war and maximizing the value to it of a peace agreement, and who usually pursue these goals rationally.

Much that appears irrational in warfare is really not. There is a tendency to believe that if war is waged rationally, the costs incurred should be commensurate with the issues at stake and the results achieved. We have seen earlier in this book, however, how the rational pursuit of war aims can entail costs out of proportion to the aims themselves. Incremental decision-making may follow the logic of the both-pay auction, in which each increment in cost is justifiable even though the increments add up to a total cost that, if it could have been foreseen, would have been unjustifiable. The belligerents *cannot* foresee either costs or the outcome of negotiation, and warfare—like other types of bargaining—is in large part an effort to get the adversary to revise his estimates of both. At least one side's estimates will turn out to be wrong, but this does not mean that the decisions based on them earlier were irrational.

Theory that does not treat the belligerents as unitary, rational actors can no doubt make additional contributions to the analysis of war termination, providing insights that complement those offered in this book. The subject is sufficiently multifaceted that no conceptual framework will ever have a monopoly of knowledge on it. This book has itself been intentionally eclectic in its methodology, and has in several places noted where internal politics, cognitive distortions, and other phenomena that are not part of economic bargaining models and other rational choice theory may affect a belligerent's behavior. The terminal stage of a war, however, is probably better suited to such theory than are most problems in international relations, because in it the issues, the interests at stake, and the players involved are all relatively clear. They are less clear in a new international crisis, for example, in which it may be just as important to understand how statesmen interpret information about the situation that suddenly faces them as it is to explain the logic and strategy behind the responses they will eventually have to make.[1]

None of the rational choice models introduced in this book were "applied" to warfare in the full-blown sense of cranking in values and obtaining *a priori* a specific outcome for a specific conflict. Such an application appears impossible. There are simply too many problems in measuring critical variables, and too many variables that can be critical. The models are useful, however, in elucidating several of the chief considerations that enter into the decisions of bargainer-belligerents, and thus in clarifying principles that may, in at least some circumstances, be important in bargaining decisions.[2]

The problems in any full application of formal bargaining models to warfare are not necessarily problems in this more modest use of them, and may indeed be the subject of additional insights. Consider, for example, the problem of incomplete information among the bargainers themselves. To take full account of this in applying a model to any individual war would mean immersion in a maze of

---

[1] A discussion of information interpretation in international crises is in Lockhart, *Bargaining in International Conflicts*, pp. 37–60.

[2] Cf. P. H. Gulliver in *Disputes and Negotiations*, pp. 36–48, where he strongly attacks the applicability of game theoretical and economic models of bargaining but also acknowledges his own debt to them in pointing to possibilities that might otherwise have been ignored.

possible perceptions and misperceptions that would soon become analytically intractable. But taking account of it in a more general way makes certain diplomatic and military behavior more explicable. We saw, for example, how uncertainty particularly shapes the bargaining during Phase One of a peace negotiation.

Another potential problem is the analyst's lack of knowledge of the bargainers' utilities. Again, this would prevent the use of a model to predict a specific settlement. Some of the most important and interesting topics of inquiry, however, do not concern which out of many possible settlements will be the final outcome. Instead, they are either-or questions with yes-or-no answers—e.g., will a concession likely be reciprocated, or, will escalation of the war strengthen one side's bargaining position? We saw how at least some of these questions can be analyzed, given only a crude idea of the overall shape of the bargaining space, such as whether it is convex or concave, and this is usually inferable from what is known about the issues at stake.

Yet another complication is discontinuity in the bargaining space, due to the discrete nature of both military and diplomatic options, in contrast to the simplifying assumption of continuity in most models. Again, this does not prevent the analysis of either-or questions concerning the relative advantages of different options. And, as with the problem of incomplete information, taking note of discontinuity makes certain patterns of bargaining even more understandable than they otherwise would be. We saw, for example, how the discontinuous nature of military options may impede the opening of peace negotiations, as it did in Korea, and how discontinuity in diplomatic options affects the handling of multiple issues.

The general advice to the model-builders that emerges from the foregoing is to pay less attention to the derivation of solutions and more to the relative likelihood or advantageousness of bargaining moves—in short, more to the process than to the outcome. Some of the assumptions underlying determinate solutions will always seem unreal in a world in which indeterminacy in bargaining seems inevitable. Besides, most of what is worth knowing about concessions, cost manipulation, and the like does not hinge on the often small differences between proposed solutions to the bargaining problem.[3]

[3] See W. Craig Riddell, "Bargaining Under Uncertainty," where it is demonstrated that responses to changes in uncertainty are not very sensitive to the differences between alternative solutions to the bargaining problem. Most of the propositions in the present book would be insensitive to them as well.

Peace Negotiations and the Statesman

The ingredients of a wartime bargaining problem place a heavy hand on the statesman and limit the amount that his policy can accomplish. How much better could, say, American decision-makers have performed in the Vietnam War? The mark of a better performance might have been more advantageous terms, a quicker agreement at lower cost, or some combination of the two; the precise definition would depend on one's particular values. But whatever the values, no U.S. statesman could have eliminated—or avoided the consequences of—the extraordinary motivation of the North Vietnamese leaders in pursuing their goals, some evidence of which was provided in earlier chapters. They saw themselves as having the "mandate of heaven"; to give up their struggle would have been deemed immoral. And for the successors of Ho Chi Minh, it would have been a betrayal of their revered leader, who in his will urged them to continue the war.[4] Given the logic of bargaining, such motivation in an enemy severely restricts what a statesman can accomplish. The nature of the issues and the capabilities of the belligerents also enter into this logic, and, like motivation, they have effects that are inescapable as long as the logic itself is inescapable, as it is for most wars.

Nevertheless, the statesman must make many difficult decisions that can shape events for better or for worse. The structure of the bargaining problem determines the general flow of events; the individual participants fashion the details. And, in warfare, the details, or the means or consequences of pursuing them, can be of immense importance. It is worth remembering that the last three, very violent, months of the Vietnam War were fought over details.

The analysis in this book, although oriented more toward explanation than prescription, contains five types of specific lessons that could guide the wartime leader toward sounder decisions. First, it has described problems and challenges that arise in most wars and that he should thus prepare for. Second, it has provided a guide to the rational use of armed force and diplomatic concessions in a wartime bargaining problem. Third, this guide has also described actions that it is rational for the enemy to take, and hence actions that the statesman should expect the enemy to take. Fourth, it has suggested techniques for coping with specific difficulties. And, fifth,

---

[4] Brian M. Jenkins, *Why the North Vietnamese Keep Fighting*, pp. 1–2, 9.

it has pointed out pitfalls to avoid. Most of the specific lessons for the statesman are recapitulated in Appendix A.

Two more general lessons for the wartime decision-maker can be offered in closing.

First, a peace settlement will be the outcome of a *process,* and a mastery of this process is as important in bringing a war to a successful conclusion as is any static judgment on the value of possible peace terms. In planning for peace, a government should go beyond deciding what it will presently accept or reject and think as well about what its subsequent moves will be. It should plan for various contingencies which may, depending on the enemy's moves, arise in the future, and should consider its own actions as parts of a sequence, not as isolated actions. The natural inclination, particularly for a harried statesman conducting a war, is not to plan ahead in this way.[5] Because of the effort involved, it is unlikely that any belligerent will construct a strategy in the game theorist's sense—i.e., a complete plan of moves for every contingency that may arise until bargaining concludes. A statesman can, however, at least strive to do what an able player does in chess. Chess, like war, is too complicated for anyone to construct a strategy in the game theoretical sense. But the good player plans further ahead than the poor player, and can better see how an apparently sound move may, given certain responses by the opponent, turn out to be unsound.

Second, this process involves two independent though interacting participants, and the only peace agreement that will be reached is one that reflects and takes into account the hopes, fears, calculations, and strategies of both. It is easy to think of the adversary's decision-making as somehow different—especially, simpler— than one's own. (The economic bargaining models reflect this, in that hypothetical bargainers use decision rules which are more complex than the ones that they assume the opponent is using.)[6] But doing so

---

[5] In most past wars, such plans have not been made. During the Johnson administration, for example, when much time and effort in Washington was spent on determining what might bring the North Vietnamese to the conference table, very little was devoted to considering exactly what would happen once they got there. See the *Pentagon Papers,* Vol. 3, pp. 225–228, 238–239.

[6] E.g., the Zeuthenian bargainer makes incremental concessions in order to manipulate the opponent's incentives, whereas he assumes the opponent will simply capitulate or break off the negotiation. Similarly, the Crossian bargainer bases his own demand on a fairly complicated weighing of marginal costs and benefits but expects his opponent to concede blindly at a fixed rate (but see also Cross, "Negotiation as a Learning Process"). On this general point, see Coddington, *Theories of the Bargaining Process,* p. 63.

is apt to lessen understanding of the enemy's behavior, of the entire bargaining process, and of what kinds of agreements are feasible. It is safer to assume that the adversary's decision calculus includes as many ingredients as one's own. And the statesman must accept the fact that in the process of negotiating peace the enemy is manipulating him as much as he is manipulating the enemy.

In short, the statesman who is waging war and negotiating peace should endeavor to expand his cognitive horizons in two respects: from the present into a variety of possible futures, and from his own calculations to those of his enemy. The shortsightedness involved in doing neither has been around for a long time. In the seventh year of the Peloponnesian War, in 425 B.C., the Spartans appealed to the Athenians—who at the moment had the upper hand in the war—to expand their thinking in these ways. If you do not accept the peace terms we offer you now, the Spartans argued, you risk future setbacks and having to deal with us when we will be vindictive and more demanding.[7] The Athenians, hopeful of further successes, refused and eventually met the fate about which they had been warned. Many others have made comparable mistakes since then, but perhaps at least some future statesmen will avoid similar errors by making an effort to better understand the processes in which, as leaders of nations at war, they take part.

[7] Thucydides, *The Peloponnesian War,* pp. 218–219.

APPENDICES

Lessons for
the Statesman at War

Recapitulated below are some of the specific lessons of this book for the wartime decision-maker.

Chapter 1: Patterns of War Termination

1. If the war is a civil war, expect it to end with the extermination or expulsion of one side. If the war is international but involves no major powers and has not lasted long, it may end through the action of an international organization. Otherwise, prepare to negotiate a settlement directly with the enemy.

2. If you anticipate negotiations, expect them to take place while combat continues.

Chapter 2: The Opening of Negotiations

3. The enemy will decline to negotiate if his objective does not require your continued cooperation, if he believes he is militarily capable of achieving it directly, and if his calculation of costs and benefits makes direct achievement appear more attractive than a negotiated settlement.

4. The enemy's willingness to negotiate will fluctuate with the fortunes of war. He will be least willing when he has suffered recent defeats but expects his fortunes to improve. He will be most willing when he has enjoyed recent successes but anticipates future defeats.

5. Beware of an enemy seeking negotiations only to benefit from their side-effects—in particular, to erode your side's support and morale.

6. As long as the military outcome is uncertain, the enemy's preferences regarding when to open negotiations are likely to be the

opposite of your own. Do not expect negotiations to commence until the course of a continued war has become fairly clear.

7. Although the enemy may use public statements to signal his intentions, he is probably more willing to reach a compromise settlement than such statements—which are tailored to maintain his side's domestic support and morale—would suggest.

8. Be cautious in making the first overt offer to negotiate, lest the enemy interpret this as a sign of weakness and harden his position. For the same reason, the enemy—especially if he is at a military disadvantage—will probably make no open, direct offer to talk. Watch for subtle and indirect signals of his willingness to do so.

9. You may use a conditional offer of negotiation to delay a firm offer and to shift blame for continued warfare onto the enemy. Before you do, however, consider the dangers of losing third party support because your conditions are perceived as unreasonable or of reducing your future flexibility.

10. Take advantage of third party initiatives to get negotiations started.

11. Consider the use of an unofficial agent with official connections to make initial contact with the enemy.

12. In order to overcome inflexibility caused by the prior imposition of conditions, begin negotiating with a supposedly limited agenda or with an ambiguous understanding about fulfillment of conditions. If both sides are willing to talk, negotiations on all issues will take place anyway.

Chapter 3: The Dynamics of Concession

13. The enemy may interpret your concession in any of several different ways.

14. If, and only if, the enemy is making obviously spurious demands in Phase One of the negotiation, make some spurious demands yourself to use as trading material.

15. In Phase Two, use a tough negotiating strategy. The enemy is likely to interpret your concessions as signs of weakening.

16. Revert to a softer overall strategy in Phase Three. The enemy will probably reciprocate by conceding on the issues that are less important to him.

17. Expect to compromise on individual quantitative issues in Phase Three. If the implications of a settlement of a given quantita-

tive issue are uncertain, start with a fairly extreme demand, because the settlement is likely to split the difference between the two initial positions.

18. Do not expect to compromise on nonquantitative issues in Phase Three. A partial concession on such an issue will probably do little to satisfy the enemy, who will wait for you to concede the issue entirely.

19. In general, the enemy will reciprocate your individual concessions but not the overall toughness or softness of your negotiating posture. Therefore, try to break your concessions into small pieces; concede often but concede little.

Chapter 4: The Military Instrument

20. Use only those military actions efficient enough to improve your bargaining position. Expect the enemy to observe a similar rule.

21. The more that your side cares—and the less the enemy cares—about the terms of settlement relative to its concern with disagreement costs, the less efficient a military action can be and still work to your advantage (and, conversely, the enemy's actions must be more efficient to work to his advantage).

22. If relative disagreement costs change to your advantage in a war in which attractive settlements are unavailable (e.g., a civil war), you may now use some military actions that previously were too inefficient. If such a change occurs in a war in which attractive compromises do exist, you will have to discontinue some military actions because they are now too inefficient. Expect the enemy to observe a similar rule.

23. If progress in the peace negotiations makes an agreement appear imminent, escalation in order to improve the terms may become worth while. In other circumstances, escalation may be advantageous because it hastens agreement even if it does not improve the terms.

24. The optimum level of violence is lower in a war having attractive compromise settlements than in an otherwise similar war lacking such compromises.

25. Remember that your next military decision will be followed by still another, and that the total cost of the war may exceed the value to you of any particular settlement terms.

26. Resist the tendency to think of past costs as an investment in a war in which the effects of violence on the enemy are not really cumulative.

27. Bargaining chips may be captured in order to impose disagreement costs on the enemy. This strategy works best when the bargaining chip clearly has some intrinsic value to you.

28. Denial of the enemy's war aims may be the best way to impose disagreement costs on the enemy, especially if you possess a disputed territory. Continue to observe the other rules governing manipulation of disagreement costs, however.

29. It is difficult to reach agreement on mutual de-escalation, but be alert to the possibilities anyway.

30. Consider military options that not only inflict violence but communicate the threat to inflict more.

31. You may need to employ more violence than is otherwise desirable in order to demonstrate your determination to the enemy, especially when other moves on your part could suggest weakness. Be careful not to appear desperate or impatient, however. Expect the enemy to escalate in similar circumstances; he may not be as determined as he is trying to make you believe.

32. Especially during critical stages of the negotiation, avoid military actions that could incorrectly signal an unwillingness to settle.

33. Try to improve, or at least to maintain, the war map if the disposition of territory is one of the issues to be decided. Emphasize targets the loss or capture of which would have clarity, drama, and shock effect.

Chapter 5: The Diplomatic Response to Military Activity

34. Concentrate your military efforts on engagements that will demonstrate the future capabilities of each side.

35. Leaving the enemy's capability for future combat intact may induce him to accept terms that he would otherwise reject.

36. Do not couple a threat with a deadline unless execution of the threat would involve a change of leadership on your side.

37. The enemy's assessment of war costs may differ from yours. Consider both the way that his nation values different targets and the extent to which he is responsive to the suffering of his citizens.

38. The enemy will probably have difficulty interpreting your armed actions. If you want to use military activity to send a message, make the message as unambiguous as possible.

39. Help the enemy to avoid the appearance of backing down under pressure. Describe your attacks in a restrained manner, without issuing public challenges.

40. When fighting a major power, you may need to let it redeem its military reputation with a victory or two before it will come to terms.

Chapter 6: The Manipulation of Multiple Issues

41. Do not waste time over the agenda. Any agenda will probably be disregarded later anyway.

42. Use package proposals to encourage reciprocation and to avoid overly large concessions. To minimize their exploitation by the enemy, however, restrict their use to Phase Three and to issues that are naturally linked.

43. In order to create compromises where none exist and to bridge the remaining gaps between the two sides, use terms the future value of which is uncertain.

44. Strive for an agreement in which you need not fulfill all of your obligations before the enemy fulfills his.

Some Conditions for Nonreciprocation of Concessions by Zeuthenian Bargainers

Let the possible Pareto-optimal outcomes of a bargaining problem involving A and B be described by the function $f(u_a) = u_b$, which is assumed to be continuous and differentiable and in which u_a and u_b are the utilities of A and B, respectively. Let (U_{aa}, U_{ba}) be an offer made by A, which may be anywhere on the curve described by $f(u_a)$ provided U_{aa} falls within the domain of u_a. (U_{aa}, U_{bb}) is an offer made by B, located anywhere on the same curve where $U_{ab} < U_{aa}$ and $U_{bb} > U_{ba}$. Define the additional function.

$$g(u_a) = u_a u_b = u_a f(u_a).$$

If $g'(u_a) < 0$ for the entire domain of u_a, then because $U_{aa} > U_{ba}$,

$$U_{aa} U_{ba} < U_{ab} U_{bb}.$$

Subtracting $U_{aa} U_{bb}$, a positive number, from each side of the inequality, dividing by the same amount, and simplifying yields

$$\frac{U_{aa} - U_{ab}}{U_{aa}} < \frac{U_{bb} - U_{ba}}{U_{bb}},$$

which means that A's critical risk is less than B's, implying according to Zeuthen that A will concede. Thus, $g'(u_a) < 0$ for the entire domain of u_a is a sufficient condition for A always to have the lower critical risk and for him to concede all the way to B's position. Similarly, $g'(u_a) > 0$ would reverse the inequalities and would be a sufficient condition for B always to have the lower critical risk.

To show the corresponding necessary conditions when the bargaining space that generates $f(u_a)$ is nonconcave, express $g(u_a)$ as $u_a f(u_a)$ and take the first and second derivatives:

$$g'(u_a) = u_a f'(u_a) + f(u_a)$$
$$g''(u_a) = u_a f''(u_a) + 2f'(u_a).$$

Within its domain u_a is always positive, and since $f(u_a)$ includes only the Pareto-optimal points in the bargaining space, it is a monotonically decreasing function and $f'(u_a)$ is always negative. If the bargaining space is nonconcave then $f''(u_a) \leq 0$, which implies that $g''(u_a) < 0$. Since $g'(u_a)$ is continually decreasing, if there is any value of u_a, other than the minimum value of the domain, for which $g'(u_a) \geq 0$, then $g'(u_a) > 0$ for all smaller values of u_a. For any two demands (U_{aa}, U_{ba}) and (U_{ab}, U_{bb}) within such a range in which $g'(u_a) > 0$, $U_{aa} U_{ba}$ would be greater than $U_{ab} U_{bb}$, which by the previous reasoning would mean that B would be the one to concede. Thus, for a situation to occur in which A always concedes to B, a necessary condition is that $g'(u_a) < 0$ for at least all values of u_a other than the minimum value. By similar reasoning, a necessary condition for B always to concede to A is that $g'(u_a) > 0$ for at least all values of u_a other than the maximum value.

Splitting-the-Difference as a Consequence of Zeuthenian Bargaining with Linear Utilities

Assume that A and B are bargaining over an issue the settlement of which is measurable along a single dimension for which the utility to each bargainer is linear. This means that the two utility scales are also linear with respect to each other, and that the possible settlements would take the form of a straight line, as in Figure 12. If both bargainers are strict Zeuthenians, one will make an arbitrary opening offer, but the other will then select his counteroffer so that his critical risk will be more than, but as close as possible to, that of his opponent (assuming that the line is not so short, or its slope so close to zero or minus infinity, or the opponent's offer so generous, that this is not possible). Thus the initial offers (U_{aa}, U_{ba}) and (U_{ab}, U_{bb}) will be such that

$$\frac{U_{aa} - U_{ba}}{U_{aa}} = \frac{U_{bb} - U_{ab}}{U_{bb}} + e, \qquad (C1)$$

where e is some small number that will be positive if B made the opening offer and A the counteroffer, and negative if the opposite sequence was followed.

Let M be the midpoint of the line between (U_{aa}, U_{ba}) and (U_{ab}, U_{bb}). Given the assumptions about linearity of utility, it is also halfway between the two offers on each bargainer's utility scale and on the objective dimension in terms of which the offers are expressed—i.e., it is the split-the-difference solution. If the utilities of a settlement at M to A and B are denoted by U_{am} and U_{bm}, respec-

FIGURE 12. **Splitting-the-difference with linear utilities.**

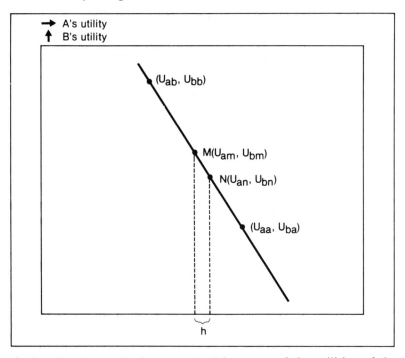

tively, then they may be expressed in terms of the utilities of the initial offers as follows:

$$U_{am} = U_{ab} + \frac{(U_{aa} - U_{ab})}{2} = \frac{(U_{aa} + U_{ab})}{2}$$

$$U_{bm} = U_{ba} + \frac{(U_{bb} - U_{ba})}{2} = \frac{(U_{bb} + U_{ba})}{2}.$$

Assume that at some time during the bargaining one of the parties, say B, has reached M and the other party, in this case A, is still some distance away at point N. Let h be the distance on A's utility scale from M to N. Then the utility to A of a settlement at N is

$$U_{an} = U_{am} + h = \frac{(U_{aa} + U_{ab})}{2} + h.$$

Since the slope of the line is

$$\frac{U_{ba} - U_{bb}}{U_{aa} - U_{ab}}$$

the utility to B of a settlement at N is

$$
\begin{aligned}
U_{bm} &= U_{bm} + h\left(\frac{U_{ba} - U_{bb}}{U_{aa} - U_{ab}}\right) \\
&= \frac{(U_{bb} + U_{ba})}{2} + h\left(\frac{U_{ba} - U_{bb}}{U_{aa} - U_{ab}}\right).
\end{aligned}
$$

Therefore the critical risk to bargainer B, at point M, is

$$
\begin{aligned}
C_b &= \frac{U_{bm} - U_{bn}}{U_{bm}} = \frac{U_{bm} - \left[U_{bm} + h\left(\dfrac{U_{ba} - U_{bb}}{U_{aa} - U_{ab}}\right)\right]}{U_{bm}} \\
&= \frac{-h\left(\dfrac{U_{ba} - U_{bb}}{U_{aa} - U_{ab}}\right)}{\dfrac{(U_{bb} + U_{ba})}{2}} = \frac{2h(U_{bb} - U_{ba})}{(U_{aa} - U_{ab})(U_{bb} + U_{ba})}, \quad \text{(C2)}
\end{aligned}
$$

and the critical risk to bargainer A, at point N, is

$$
\begin{aligned}
C_a &= \frac{U_{an} - U_{am}}{U_{an}} = \frac{(U_{am} + h) - U_{am}}{\dfrac{(U_{aa} + U_{ab})}{2} + h} \\
&= \frac{2h}{U_{aa} + U_{ab} + 2h}. \quad \text{(C3)}
\end{aligned}
$$

If M is the final solution, then B's critical risk should be greater than A's, meaning that A would concede. Assume that it is not—that $C_b \leq C_a$—so that

$$
\frac{2h(U_{bb} - U_{ba})}{(U_{aa} - U_{ab})(U_{bb} + U_{ba})} \leq \frac{2h}{U_{aa} + U_{ab} + 2h}. \quad \text{(C4)}
$$

Multiplying by the denominators, both being positive, and simplifying yields

$$
U_{ab}U_{bb} + h(U_{bb} - U_{ba}) \leq U_{aa}U_{ba}. \quad \text{(C5)}
$$

Multiplying Equation (C1) by $U_{aa}U_{bb}$ and simplifying yields

$$
eU_{aa}U_{bb} + U_{ab}U_{bb} = U_{aa}U_{ba}. \quad \text{(C6)}
$$

Subtracting (C6) from (C5) produces

$$
h(U_{bb} - U_{ba}) - eU_{aa}U_{bb} \leq 0. \quad \text{(C7)}
$$

Since both h and $(U_{bb} - U_{ba})$ are always positive, the inequality will not hold provided that e is sufficiently small relative to h. This means that if the graduation of the stakes into different possible outcomes is sufficiently fine (the finer the graduation, the smaller the absolute value of e will be), the inequality $C_b \leq C_a$ is false and A, at point N, will concede to B.

If A is the bargainer who first reaches the midpoint M, redefine N as a point above and to the left of M which B has reached and h as the distance of B's utility scale from M to N. Then C_a and C_b become

$$C_a = \frac{U_{am} - U_{an}}{U_{am}} = \frac{U_{am} - \left[U_{am} + h\left(\dfrac{U_{ab} - U_{aa}}{U_{bb} - U_{ba}}\right)\right]}{U_{am}}$$

$$= \frac{-h\left(\dfrac{U_{ab} - U_{aa}}{U_{bb} - U_{ba}}\right)}{\dfrac{(U_{aa} + U_{ab})}{2}} = \frac{2h(U_{aa} - U_{ab})}{(U_{bb} - U_{ba})(U_{aa} + U_{ab})}$$

and

$$C_b = \frac{U_{bn} - U_{bm}}{U_{bn}} = \frac{(U_{bm} + h) - U_{bm}}{(U_{bb} + U_{ba})}$$

$$= \frac{2h}{U_{bb} + U_{ba} + 2h},$$

which are the same as (C2) and (C3) but with the a and b subscripts reversed. If M is the final settlement, then A's critical risk should be greater than B's, with B conceding toward M. Making the contrary assumption that $C_a \leq C_b$ produces an inequality the same as (C4) but with subscripts reversed, which leads to

$$U_{ba}U_{bb} + h(U_{aa} - U_{ab}) \leq U_{bb}U_{ab}, \tag{C8}$$

the counterpart of (C5). Adding this to (C5) and simplifying yields

$$h(U_{aa} - U_{ab}) + eU_{aa}U_{bb} \leq 0, \tag{C9}$$

which is false if $|e|$ is sufficiently small relative to h, this again depending upon how fine the stakes are graduated. If it is false, then the assumption $C_a \leq C_b$ is also false and B must concede to A. The conclusion is that, to the extent that discontinuities in the outcome set permit, any bargainer making an offer not at the midpoint will concede to one offering the midpoint, which means that bargaining tends toward the midpoint as the final settlement. If there are no discontinuities, $|e|$ will be infinitesimally small, and (C8) and (C9) will be false for all h not also infinitesimally small, which is another way of saying that the settlement will be at a point infinitesimally close to the midpoint.

Since Zeuthenian bargainers will employ the same decision mechanism throughout the negotiation, (U_{aa}, U_{ba}) and (U_{ba}, U_{bb}) might be the pair of offers on the table at any moment. Hence, the bargainers will not only make their initial offers so that they are as nearly as possible at equal distances from what will be the final settlement; they will stay at equal distances from it as they concede.

Note that the results do not depend on the length of the line or its location with respect to the origin, provided only that an initial counteroffer is available which is more advantageous to the party making it than is the opening offer and which would make the critical risks as nearly equal as possible. In other words, they do not depend on the utility to each side of no agreement relative to the best, worst, or any other possible agreement. With the same proviso, they do not depend on the slope of the line, which means that no interpersonal comparison of utility is required.

BIBLIOGRAPHY

BIBLIOGRAPHY

This bibliography lists general and theoretical works as well as sources for individual wars. For the latter, bracketed numbers refer to the numbers in Table 1.

Abt, Clark C. *The Termination of General War.* Unpublished Ph.D. dissertation, MIT, 1965.

Acheson, Dean. *Present at the Creation.* New York: Norton, 1969. [112]

Adams, Henry. *History of the United States of America During the Administrations of Jefferson and Madison.* New York: Scribners, 1921. [7]

Adams, John Quincy. *Memoirs.* Ed. Charles Francis Adams. Volumes 2 and 3. Philadelphia: Lippincott, 1874. [7]

Albert, Stuart and Edward C. Luck (eds.). *On The Ending of Wars.* Port Washington, N.Y.: Kennikat Press, 1980.

Allais, Maurice. *Les Accords d'Evian, le Référendum et la Résistance Algérienne.* Paris: L'Esprit Nouveau, 1962. [117]

Allison, Graham T. *Essence of Decision.* Boston: Little, Brown, 1971.

American State Papers. Foreign Relations, Volume 3. Washington: Gales and Seaton, 1832. [7]

Anderson, R. C. *Naval Wars in the Levant.* Princeton: Princeton University Press, 1952. [21]

Andrews, William G. *French Politics and Algeria.* New York: Appleton-Century-Crofts, 1962. [117]

Askew, William C. *Europe and Italy's Acquisition of Libya, 1911–1912.* Durham, N.C.: Duke University Press, 1942. [83]

Bacchus, Wilfred A. "The Relationship Between Combat and Peace Negotiations: Fighting While Talking in Korea, 1951–1953," *Orbis,* 17 (Summer 1973), 545–574. [112]

Baldwin, Frank. "A 'Korean Solution' For Vietnam?" *New Republic,* 163 (18 July 1970), 19–21. [137]

Bar-Siman-Tov, Yaacov. *The Israeli-Egyptian War of Attrition, 1969–1970.* New York: Columbia University Press, 1980. [127]

Bartos, Otomar J. *Process and Outcome of Negotiation.* New York: Columbia University Press, 1974.

Bar-Yaacov, Nissim. *The Israeli-Syrian Armistice.* London: Oxford University Press, 1967. [110]

Behr, Edward. *The Algerian Problem.* London: Hodder & Stoughton, 1961. [117]

Bidault, Georges. *D'une Résistance a l'Autre.* Paris: Les Presses du Siecle, 1965. [113]

Bishop, Robert L. "A Zeuthen-Hicks Theory of Bargaining," *Econometrica,* 32 (July 1964), 410–417.

Bloomfield, Lincoln P., and Amelia C. Leiss. *Controlling Small Wars.* New York: Knopf, 1969.

Blunt, Wilfrid. *Desert Hawk.* London: Methuen, 1947. [25]

Boca, Angelo del. *The Ethiopian War, 1935–1941.* Trans. P. D. Cummins. Chicago: University of Chicago Press, 1969. [96]

Bodart, Gaston. *Losses of Life in Modern Wars.* Oxford: Clarendon Press, 1916. [2]

Boserup, Anders, and Andrew Mack. *War Without Weapons.* London: Frances Pinter, 1974.

Boulware, Lemuel R. *The Truth About Boulwarism.* Washington: Bureau of National Affairs, 1969.

Brant, Irving. *James Madison: Commander in Chief.* Indianapolis: Bobbs-Merrill, 1961. [7]

Brent, Robert A. "Nicholas P. Trist and the Treaty of Guadalupe Hidalgo," *Southwestern Historical Quarterly,* 57 (April 1954), 454–474. [26]

Brodie, Bernard. *Strategy in the Missile Age.* Princeton: Princeton University Press, 1959.

––––––. *War and Politics.* New York: Macmillan, 1973.

Bromberger, Merry. *Le Destin Secret de Georges Pompidou.* Paris: Fayard, 1965. [117]

Bruun, Geoffrey. *Europe and the French Imperium, 1799–1814.* New York: Harper, 1938. [1]

Bryant, Arthur. *The Years of Endurance, 1793–1802.* New York: Harper, 1942. [1]

Buron, Robert. *Carnets Politiques de la Guerre d'Algérie.* Paris: Paris: Plon, 1965. [117]

Buttinger, Joseph. *Vietnam: A Dragon Embattled.* New York: Praeger, 1967. [113]

Calahan, H. C. *What Makes a War End?* New York: Vanguard Press, 1944.

Callières, Francois de. *On the Manner of Negotiating with Princes.* Trans. A. F. Whyte. Notre Dame, Indiana: University of Notre Dame Press, 1963.

Calogeras, Joao P. *A History of Brazil.* Trans. and ed. Percy A. Martin. New York: Russell and Russell, 1963. [32, 52]

Cameron, Allen W. (ed.). *Vietnam Crisis, A Documentary History.* Ithica: Cornell University Press, 1971. [113]

Carr, Edward H. *The Bolshevik Revolution 1917–1923.* Vol. 1. London: Macmillan, 1950. [88]

Carroll, Berenice A. (ed.). *Journal of Peace Research,* 6 (1969, No. 4), entire issue.

Castlereagh, Viscount. *Correspondence, Despatches, and Other Papers of Viscount Castlereagh.* Volume 10. London: Shoberl, 1852. [7]

Catton, Bruce. *Never Call Retreat.* Garden City, N.Y.: Doubleday, 1965. [46]

Cheng, Tien-fong. *A History of Sino-Russian Relations.* Washington: Public Affairs Press, 1957. [93]

Chinh, Truong. *Primer for Revolt.* New York: Praeger, 1963 [113]

Clark, Mark W. *From the Danube to the Yalu.* New York: Harper, 1954. [112]

Clarke, H. Butler. *Modern Spain, 1815–1898.* Cambridge: Cambridge University Press, 1906. [39]

Clausewitz, Carl von. *On War.* Trans. J. J. Graham. London: Routledge and Kegan Paul, 1976.

Clifford, Clark M. "A Viet Nam Reappraisal: The Personal History of One Man's View and How It Evolved," *Foreign Affairs,* 47 (July 1969), 601–622. [137]

Coddington, Alan. *Theories of the Bargaining Process.* London: George Allen and Unwin, 1968.

_____. "A Theory of the Bargaining Process: Comment," *American Economic Review,* 56 (June 1966), 522–530.

Cohen, Raymond, and Stuart Cohen. *Peace Conferences: The Formal Aspects.* Jerusalem Papers on Peace Problems, No. 1. Jerusalem: Hebrew University, 1974.

Coles, Harry L. *The War of 1812.* Chicago: University of Chicago Press, 1965. [7]

Collins, J. Lawton. *War in Peacetime.* Boston: Houghton Mifflin, 1969. [112]

Contini, Bruno. "The Value of Time in Bargaining Negotiations: Some Experimental Evidence," *American Economic Review,* 58 (June 1968), 374–393.

Cooper, Chester L. *The Lost Crusade.* New York: Dodd, Mead, 1970 [137]

Coox, Alvin D. *The Anatomy of a Small War.* Westport, Conn.: Greenwood Press, 1977. [97]

Coser, Lewis A. "The Termination of Conflict," *Journal of Conflict Resolution,* 5 (December 1961), 347–353.

Courrière, Yves. *Les Feux du Désespoir.* Fayard, 1971. [117].

Crawford, Vincent P. "A Note on the Zeuthen-Harsanyi Theory of Bargaining," *Journal of Conflict Resolution,* 24 (September 1980), 525–535.

Cross, John G. *The Economics of Bargaining.* New York: Basic Books, 1969.

――――. "Negotiation as a Learning Process," *Journal of Conflict Resolution,* 21 (December 1977), 581–606.

Crozier, Brian. *De Gaulle.* New York: Scribners, 1973. [117]

Dallin, David J. *Soviet Russia and the Far East.* New Haven: Yale University Press, 1948. [99]

Davey, Harold W. *Contemporary Collective Bargaining.* Third edition. Englewood Cliffs, N.J.: Prentice-Hall, 1972.

Dawson, Thomas C. *The South American Republics.* Volume 1. New York: Putnam, 1903. [52]

De Gaulle, Charles. *Major Address, Statements and Press Conferences of General Charles De Gaulle, May 19, 1958–January 31, 1964.* New York: French Embassy Press and Information Division, 1964. [117]

――――. *Memoirs of Hope.* Trans. Terence Kilmartin. London: Weidenfeld and Nicolson, 1971. [117]

Dennett, Tyler. *Roosevelt and the Russo-Japanese War.* Garden City, N.Y.: Doubleday, Page, 1925. [79]

Department of State Bulletin. [137]

Deutsch, Morton, et al. "Strategies of Inducing Cooperation: An Experimental Study," *Journal of Conflict Resolution,* 11 (September 1967), 345–360.

Deutsch, Morton, and Robert M. Krauss. "Studies of Interpersonal Bargaining," *Journal of Conflict Resolution,* 6 (March 1962), 52–76.

Devillers, Philippe, and Jean Lacouture. *End of a War*. Trans. Alexander Lieven and Adam Roberts. New York: Praeger, 1969. [113]

Documents Relating to the Discussion of Korea and Indo-China at the Geneva Conference. Cmd. 9186. London: H. M. Stationery Office, 1954. [113]

Donovan, Robert J. *Eisenhower: The Inside Story*. New York: Harper, 1956. [112]

Douglas, Ann. *Industrial Peacemaking*. New York; Columbia University Press, 1962.

Douhet, Giulio. *The Command of the Air*. Trans. Dino Ferrari. New York: Coward-McCann, 1942.

Druckman, Daniel. *Human Factors in International Negotiations: Social-Psychological Aspects of International Conflict*. Beverly Hills: Sage, 1973.

————, Kathleen Zechmeister, and Daniel Solomon. "Determinants of Bargaining Behavior in a Bilateral Monopoly Situation: Opponent's Concession Rate and Relative Defensibility," *Behavioral Science*, 17 (November 1972), 514–531.

Duncanson, Dennis J. *Government and Revolution in Vietnam*. New York: Oxford University Press, 1968. [137]

Earle, Edward Mean (ed.). *Makers of Modern Strategy*. Princeton: Princeton University Press, 1944.

Eden, Anthony. *Memoirs: Full Circle*. Boston: Houghton Mifflin, 1960. [113]

Eisenhower, Dwight D. *The White House Years: Mandate for Change, 1953–1956*. Garden City, N.Y.: Doubleday, 1963. [112]

Ely, Paul. *Mémoires: L:Indochine dans la Tourmente*. Paris: Plon, 1964. [113]

————. *Mémoires: Suez . . . le 13 Mai*. Paris: Plon, 1969. [117]

Engelman, Fred L. *The Peace of Christmas Eve*. New York: Harcourt, Brace & World, 1962. [7]

Fall, Bernard B. *Street Without Joy*. Harrisburg, Pa.: Stackpole, 1961. [113]

————. *The Two Viet-Nams*. Revised edition. New York: Praeger, 1964. [113]

Fasai, Hasan ibn Hasan. *History of Persia under Qajar Rule*. Trans. Heribert Busse. New York: Columbia University Press, 1972. [14]

Fehrenbach, T. R. *Fire and Blood*. New York: Macmillan, 1973. [50]

Festinger, Leon. *A Theory of Cognitive Dissonance*. Stanford: Stanford University Press, 1957.

Foldes, Lucien. "A Determinate Model of Bilateral Monopoly," *Economica,* 31 (May 1964), 117–131.

Foreman, John. *The Philippine Islands*. Second edition. New York: Scribners, 1899. [73]

Fortescue, John W. *History of the British Army*. 13 Volumes. London: Macmillan, 1899–1930. [3, 10, 13, 24]

Fox, William T. R. (ed.). *Annals of the American Academy of Political and Social Science,* 392 (November 1970), entire issue.

France, Ministère des Affaires Etrangères. *Conférence de Genève sur l'Indochine*. Paris: Imprimerie Nationale, 1955. [113]

Friedjung, Heinrich. *The Struggle for Supremacy in Germany 1859–1866*. Trans. A. J. P. Taylor and W. L. McIvee. London: Macmillan, 1935. [49]

Garner, William R. *The Chaco Dispute*. Washington: Public Affairs Press, 1966. [95]

Gelb, Leslie H. "The Essential Domino: American Politics and Vietnam," *Foreign Affairs,* 50 (April 1972), 459–475. [137]

————. "Vietnam: The System Worked," *Foreign Policy,* No. 3 (Summer 1971), 140–167. [137]

George, Alexander L., and Richard Smoke. *Deterrence in American Foreign Policy*. New York: Columbia University Press, 1974.

George, Alexander L., David K. Hall, and William E. Simons. *The Limits of Coercive Diplomacy*. Boston: Little, Brown, 1971.

Giap, Vo Nguyen. *People's War, People's Army*. Hanoi: Foreign Languages Publishing House, 1961. [113]

Gillespie, Joan. *Algeria: Rebellion and Revolution*. New York: Praeger, 1960. [117]

Goodman, Allan E. *The Lost Peace*. Stanford: Hoover Institution Press, 1978. [137]

Goodrich, Leland M. *Korea: A Study of U.S. Policy in the United Nations*. New York: Council on Foreign Relations, 1956. [112]

Gordon, David C. *The Passing of French Algeria*. London: Oxford University Press, 1966. [117]

Gulliver, P. H. *Disputes and Negotiations: A Cross-Cultural Perspective*. New York: Academic Press, 1979.

Gurtov, Melvin. *The First Vietnam Crisis*. New York: Columbia University Press, 1967. [113]

Haas, Ernst B., Robert L. Butterworth, and Joseph S. Nye. *Conflict Management by International Organization*. Morristown, N.J.: General Learning Press, 1972.

Halperin, Morton H. *Limited War in the Nuclear Age*. New York: Wiley, 1963.

Hammer, Ellen J. *The Struggle for Indochina*. Stanford: Stanford University Press, 1954. [113]

———. *The Struggle for Indochina Continues*. Stanford: Stanford University Press, 1955. [113]

Hancock, Anson U. *A History of Chile*. Chicago: Sergel, 1893. [48]

Harnett, Donald L., Larry L. Cummings, and W. Clay Hamner. "Personality, Bargaining Style and Payoff in Bilateral Monopoly Bargaining Among European Managers," *Sociometry*, 36 (September 1973), 325–345.

Harsanyi, John C. "Approaches to the Bargaining Problem Before and After the Theory of Games: A Critical Discussion of Zeuthen's, Hicks's and Nash's Theories," *Econometrica*, 24 (April 1956), 144–157.

Hartley, Anthony. *Gaullism*. New York: Outerbridge & Dienstfrey, 1971. [117]

Heggoy, Alf A. *Insurgency and Counterinsurgency in Algeria*. Bloomington: Indiana University Press, 1972. [117]

Henao, Jesus M., and Gerardo Arrubla. *History of Colombia*. Trans. and ed. J. Fred Rippy. Chapel Hill: University of North Carolina Press, 1938. [42]

Henissart, Paul. *Wolves in the City*. New York: Simon and Schuster, 1970. [117]

Hermes, Walter G. *Truce Tent and Fighting Front*. Washington: Office of the Chief of Military History, United States Army, 1966. [112]

Hicks, J. R. *The Theory of Wages*. London: Macmillan, 1932.

Hinton, Bernard L., W. Clay Hamner, and Michael F. Pohlen. "The Influence of Reward Magnitude, Opening Bid and Concession Rate on Profit Earned in a Managerial Negotiation Game," *Behavioral Science*, 19 (May 1974), 197–203.

Hoffman, Stanley. "Vietnam: An Algerian Solution?" *Foreign Policy*, No. 2 (Spring 1971), 3–37. [137]

Holmes, John G., Warren F. Throop, and Lloyd H. Strickland. "The Effects of Prenegotiation Expectations on the Distributive Bargaining Process," *Journal of Experimental Social Psychology*, 7 (November 1971), 582–599.

Holsti, Ole R. *Crisis Escalation War*. Montreal: McGill-Queens University Press, 1972.

Hoopes, Townsend. *The Limits of Intervention*. New York: McKay, 1969. [137]

Horne, Alistair. *A Savage War of Peace*. New York: Viking Press, 1977. [117]

Horsman, Reginald. *The War of 1812*. New York: Knopf, 1969. [7]

Hourani, Albert H. *Syria and Lebanon*. London: Oxford University Press, 1946. [92]

Houssaye, Henry. *Napoleon and the Campaign of 1814*. Trans. R. S. McClintock. London: Rees, 1914. [8]

Howard, Harry N. *The Partition of Turkey*. Norman: University of Oklahoma Press, 1931. [90]

Howard, Michael. *The Franco-Prussian War*. New York: Macmillan, 1961. [53]

Hytier, Adrienne D. *Two Years of French Foreign Policy*. Geneva: Droz, 1958. [100]

Iklé, Fred C. *Every War Must End*. New York: Columbia University Press, 1971.

————. *How Nations Negotiate*. New York: Praeger, 1967.

Irving, R. E. M. *The First Indochina War*. London: Croom Helm, 1975. [113]

Isard, Walter (ed.). *Vietnam: Some Basic Issues and Alternatives*. Cambridge, Mass.: Schenkman, 1969. [137]

Jacob, Samuel, et al. *History of the Ottoman Empire*. Second edition. London: Griffin, 1854. [16]

Jakobson, Max. *The Diplomacy of the Winter War*. Cambridge, Mass.: Harvard University Press, 1961. [102]

James, Alan. *The Politics of Peacekeeping*. New York: Praeger, 1967.

Jenkins, Brian M. *Why the North Vietnamese Keep Fighting*. Rand P-4395-1. Santa Monica: Rand Corporation, 1972. [137]

Jervis, Robert. *The Logic of Images in International Relations*. Princeton: Princeton University Press, 1970.

Johnson, Lyndon B. *The Vantage Point*. New York: Holt, Rinehart and Winston, 1971. [137]

Johnson, Willis F. *The History of Cuba*. New York: Buck, 1920. [56]

Joseph, Myron L., and Richard H. Willis. "An Experimental Analog to Two-Party Bargaining," *Behavioral Science,* 8 (April 1963), 117–127.

Joy, C. Turner. *How Communists Negotiate*. New York: Macmillan, 1955. [112]

———. *Negotiating While Fighting: The Diary of Admiral C. Turner Joy at the Korean Armistice Conference*. Ed. Allan E. Goodman. Stanford: Hoover Institution Press, 1978. [112]

Kaas, Albert, and Fedor de Lazarovics. *Bolshevism in Hungary*. London: Grant Richards, 1931. [87]

Kahin, George McT., and John W. Lewis. *The United States in Vietnam*. Revised edition. New York: Dell, 1969. [137]

Kalb, Marvin, and Elie Abel. *Roots of Involvement*. New York: Norton, 1971. [137]

Kalb, Marvin, and Bernard Kalb. *Kissinger*. Boston: Little, Brown, 1974. [137]

Kaplan, Morton A., et al. *Vietnam Settlement: Why 1973, Not 1969?* Washington: American Enterprise Institute for Public Policy Research, 1973. [137]

Kecskemeti, Paul. *Strategic Surrender*. Stanford: Stanford University Press, 1958.

Keesing's Contemporary Archives. [109, 123, 125, 126, 130, 132, 133, 134]

Kelman, Herbert C. (ed.). *International Behavior*. New York: Holt, Rinehart and Winston, 1965.

Kennan, George F. *Memoirs*. Volume 2: 1950–1963. Boston: Little, Brown, 1972. [112]

King, Bolton. *A History of Italian Unity*. 2 volumes. London: Nisbet, 1899. [27, 31, 38, 41]

Kissinger, Henry A. "Domestic Structure and Foreign Policy," *Daedalus,* 95 (Spring 1966), 503–529.

———. "The Viet Nam Negotiations," *Foreign Affairs,* 47 (January 1969), 211–234. [137]

———. *White House Years*. Boston: Little, Brown, 1979. [137]

Klerck, Edward S. de. *History of the Netherlands East Indies*. Volume 2. Rotterdam: Brusse, 1938. [57]

Klingberg, Frank L. "Predicting the Termination of War: Battle Casualties and Population Losses," *Journal of Conflict Resolution,* 10 (June 1966), 129–171.

Knapp, Wilfrid. *A History of War and Peace 1939–1965*. London: Oxford University Press, 1967.

Knorr, Klaus. *Military Power and Potential*. Lexington: Heath, 1970.

_____. *The Power of Nations*. New York: Basic Books, 1975.

_____ (ed.). *Historical Dimensions of National Security Problems*. Lawrence: Kansas University Press, 1976.

Kofos, Evangelos. *Nationalism and Communism in Macedonia*. Thesaloniki: Institute for Balkan Studies, 1964. [78]

Kraft, Joseph. *The Struggle for Algeria*. Garden City, N.Y.: Doubleday, 1961. [117]

Kraslow, David, and Stuart H. Loory. *The Secret Search for Peace in Vietnam*. New York: Random House, 1968. [137]

Landau, David. *Kissinger: The Uses of Power*. Boston: Houghton Mifflin, 1972. [137]

Lebow, Richard Ned. *Between War and Peace*. Baltimore: The Johns Hopkins University Press, 1981.

Leckie, Robert, *Conflict: The History of the Korean War, 1950–53*. New York: Putnam, 1962. [112]

Lefebvre, Georges. *Napoleon: From Tilsit to Waterloo, 1807–1815*. Trans. J. E. Anderson. New York: Columbia University Press, 1969. [8]

Leslie, R. F. *Reform and Insurrection in Russian Poland*. London: London University Press, 1963. [8, 44]

Liddell Hart, B. H. *Strategy*. 2nd revised edition. New York: Praeger, 1967.

_____. *Thoughts on War*. London: Faber and Faber, 1943.

Lockhart, Charles. *Bargaining in International Conflicts*. New York: Columbia University Press, 1979.

_____. *The Efficacy of Threats in International Interaction Strategies*. Beverly Hills: Sage, 1973.

MacArthur, Douglas. *Reminiscences*. New York: McGraw-Hill, 1964. [112]

MacDermott, Marcia. *A History of Bulgaria*. London: Allen and Unwin, 1962. [67]

Mackenzie, David. *The Serbs and Russian Pan-Slavism, 1875–1878*. Ithaca: Cornell University Press, 1967. [55]

Madelin, Louis. *The Consulate and the Empire*. Volume 2: 1809–1815. London: Heinemann, 1936. [8]

Mahajan, Vidya Dhar. *Fifty-Five Years of Modern India*. New Delhi: Chand, 1975. [105]

Mahon, John K. *The War of 1812*. Gainesville: University of Florida Press, 1972. [7]

Markham, Clements R. *Peru*. London: Low, Marston, Searle & Rivington, 1880. [22]

Martinengo-Cesaresco, Evelyn. *The Liberation of Italy, 1815–1870.* London: Seeley, 1902. [40]

Matthews, Tanya. *War in Algeria.* New York: Fordham University Press, 1961. [117]

May, Arthur. *The Hapsburg Monarchy, 1867–1914.* Cambridge, Mass.: Harvard University Press, 1951. [59]

McAlister, John T., Jr. *Viet Nam: The Origins of Revolution.* New York: Knopf, 1969. [113]

McGarvey, Patrick J. *Visions of Victory.* Stanford: Hoover Institution, 1969. [137]

Mendès-France, Pierre. *Choisir.* Paris: Stock, 1974. [113]

Michener, H. Andrew, and Eugene D. Cohen. "Effects of Punishment Magnitude in the Bilateral Threat Situation: Evidence for the Deterence Hypothesis," *Journal of Personality and Social Psychology,* 26 (June 1973), 427–438.

Michener, H. Andrew, et al. "Factors Affecting Concession Rate and Threat Usage in Bilateral Conflict," *Sociometry,* 38 (March 1975), 62–80.

Miller, John, Jr., Owen J. Carroll, and Margaret E. Tackley. *Korea 1951–1953.* Washington: Office of the Chief of Military History, Department of the Army, 1956. [112]

Miller, William. *The Balkans.* New York: Putnam, 1903. [33, 37]

————. *The Ottoman Empire 1801–1913.* Cambridge: Cambridge University Press, 1913. [72]

Milstein, Jeffrey S. *Dynamics of the Vietnam War.* Columbus: Ohio State University Press, 1974. [137]

Mitchell, Ted, and Roger Heeler. "Toward a Theory of Acceptable Outcomes," *Behavioral Science,* 26 (April 1981), 163–176.

Monroe, James. *Writings.* Volume 5. New York: Putnam, 1901. [7]

Morse, Hosea B., and Harley F. McNair. *Far Eastern International Relations.* New York: Russell & Russell, 1931. [43, 63, 65, 68]

Morfill, William R. *A History of Russia.* London: Methuen, 1905. [4]

Mowat, R. B. *The Diplomacy of Napoleon.* London: Edward Arnold, 1924. [8]

Nash, John F., Jr. "The Bargaining Problem," *Econometrica,* 18 (April 1950), 155–162.

————. "Two-Person Cooperative Games," *Econometrica,* 21 (January 1953), 128–140.

Navarre, Henri. *Agonie de l'Indochine.* Paris: Plon, 1956. [113]

Nechkina, Militsa V. *Russia in the Nineteenth Century.* Trans.

Bernard Pares and Oliver J. Frederiksen. Ann Arbor: Edwards, 1953. [6, 16]

New York Times. [66, 81, 94, 104, 109, 111, 119, 120, 121, 122, 126, 130, 135, 137]

Nicolson, Harold. *Diplomacy.* Third edition. New York: Oxford University Press, 1964.

Nixon, Richard M. *RN: The Memoirs of Richard Nixon.* New York: Grosset & Dunlap, 1978. [137]

Nye, J. S. *Peace in Parts.* Boston: Little, Brown, 1971.

Oakley, Stewart. *The Story of Denmark.* London: Faber, 1972. [28].

O'Ballance, Edgar. *The Algerian Insurrection, 1954–62.* London: Faber and Faber, 1967. [117]

————. *The Indo-China War, 1945–1954.* London: Faber and Faber, 1964. [113]

Oberdorfer, Don. *Tet!* Garden City, N.Y.: Doubleday, 1971. [137]

Okamoto, Shumpei. *The Japanese Oligarchy and the Russo-Japanese War.* New York: Columbia University Press, 1970. [79]

O'Neill, Robert J. *General Giap: Politician and Strategist.* New York: Praeger, 1969. [113]

Osgood, Robert E. *Limited War.* Chicago: University of Chicago Press, 1957.

———— and Robert W. Tucker. *Force, Order, and Justice.* Baltimore: Johns Hopkins Press, 1967.

Palmer, Alan W. *Metternich.* London: Weidenfeld & Nicolson, 1972. [9]

Paret, Peter. *French Revolutionary Warfare from Indochina to Algeria.* New York: Praeger, 1964. [117]

Pen, J. "A General Theory of Bargaining," *American Economic Review,* 42 (March 1952), 24–42.

The Pentagon Papers. Senator Gravel edition. Boston: Beacon Press, 1971. [137]

Perkins, Bradford. *Castlereagh and Adams.* Berkeley: University of California Press, 1964. [7]

Peters, Edward. *Strategy and Tactics in Labor Negotiations.* New London, Conn.: National Foreman's Institute, 1955.

Phillips, G. D. R. *Russia, Japan and Mongolia.* London: Muller, 1942. [99]

Phillipson, Coleman. *Termination of War and Treaties of Peace.* New York: Dutton, 1916.

Pickles, Dorothy. *Algeria and France.* New York: Praeger, 1963. [117]

Pike, Douglas. *War, Peace, and the Viet Cong*. Cambridge, Mass.: MIT Press, 1969. [137]

Porter, Gareth. *A Peace Denied*. Bloomington: Indiana University Press, 1975. [137]

Pruitt, Dean G. *Negotiation Behavior*. New York: Academic Press, 1981.

Puryear, Vernon J. *England, Russia, and the Straits Question, 1844–1856*. Berkeley: University of California Press, 1931. [34]

Quester, George. "Bargaining and Bombing during World War II in Europe," *World Politics,* 15 (April 1963), 417–437. [103]

Rambaud, Alfred N. *History of Russia*. Trans. L. B. Long. Volume 2. Boston: Estes and Lauriat, 1880. [5, 14]

Randle, Robert F. *Geneva 1954*. Princeton: Princeton University Press, 1969. [113]

———. *The Origins of Peace*. New York: Free Press, 1973.

———. "Peace in Vietnam and Laos: 1954, 1962, 1973," *Orbis,* 18 (Fall 1974), 868–887. [131]

Rees, David. *Korea: The Limited War*. London: Macmillan, 1964. [112]

Richardson, Lewis F. "War Moods: I," *Psychometrika,* 13 (September 1948), 147–174.

Riddell, W. Craig. "Bargaining under Uncertainty," *American Economic Review,* 71 (September 1981), 579–590.

Ridgway, Mathew B. *The Korean War*. Garden City, N.Y.: Doubleday, 1967. [112]

———. *Soldier: The Memoirs of Matthew B. Ridgway*. New York: Harper, 1956. [112]

Ripley, R. S. *The War with Mexico*. Volume 2. New York: Harper & Brothers, 1849. [26]

Rives, George R. *The United States and Mexico, 1821–1848*. New York: Scribner, 1913. [26]

Rodger, Alexander B. *The War of the Second Coalition, 1798 to 1801*. Oxford: Clarendon Press, 1964. [1]

Roos, Hans. *A History of Modern Poland*. London: Eyre & Spottiswoode, 1966. [88]

Rosenau, James N. (ed.). *International Aspects of Civil Strife*. Princeton: Princeton University Press, 1964.

Roth, Alvin E., and Michael W. K. Malouf. "Game-Theoretic Models and the Role of Information in Bargaining," *Psychological Review,* 86 (November 1979), 574–594.

Rouanet, Pierre. *Mendès-France au Pouvoir*. Paris: Laffont, 1965. [113]

Roy, Jules. *The Battle of Dienbienphu*. Trans. Robert Baldick. New York: Harper and Row, 1965. [113]

Rubin, Jeffrey Z., and Bert R. Brown. *The Social Psychology of Bargaining and Negotiation*. New York: Academic Press, 1975.

Rudin, Harry R. *Armistice 1918*. New Haven: Yale University Press, 1944. [86]

Sabry, M. *L'Empire Egyptien sous Mohamed-Ali et La Question d'Orient*. Paris: Geuthner, 1930. [19]

Schelling, Thomas C. *Arms and Influence*. New Haven: Yale University Press.

———. *The Strategy of Conflict*. New York: Oxford University Press, 1963.

Schlenker, Barry R., et al. "Compliance to Threats as a Function of the Wording of the Threat and the Exploitativeness of the Threatener," *Sociometry*, 33 (December 1970), 394–408.

Schlenker, Barry R., and Thomas V. Bonoma. "Fun and Games: The Validity of Games for the Study of Conflict," *Journal of Conflict Resolution*, 22 (March 1978), 7–38.

Seton-Watson, R. W. *The Southern Slav Question and the Habsburg Monarchy*. London: Constable, 1911. [59]

Shaplen, Robert. *The Road from War: Vietnam 1965–1971*. Revised edition. New York: Harper, 1971. [137]

Siegel, Sidney, and Lawrence E. Fouraker. *Bargaining and Group Decision Making*. New York: McGraw-Hill, 1960.

Sights, A. P., Jr. "Graduated Pressure in Theory and Practice," *U.S. Naval Institute Proceedings*, 96 (July 1970), 41–45.

Simmons, Robert R. *The Strained Alliance*. New York: Free Press, 1975. [112]

Singer, J. David. "Inter-nation Influence: A Formal Model," *American Political Science Review*, 57 (June 1963), 420–430.

——— and Melvin Small. *The Wages of War 1816–1965*. New York: Wiley, 1972.

Singletary, Otis. *The Mexican War*. Chicago: University of Chicago Press, 1960. [26]

Small, Melvin, and J. David Singer. *Resort to Arms*. Beverly Hills: Sage, 1982.

Smith, Justin H. *The War with Mexico*. New York: Macmillan, 1919. [26]

Smoke, Richard. *War: Controlling Escalation*. Cambridge, Mass.: Harvard University Press, 1977.

Snyder, Glenn H., and Paul Diesing. *Conflict Among Nations.* Princeton: Princeton University Press, 1977.

Stein, Janice G. "War Termination and Conflict Resolution or, How Wars Should End," *Jerusalem Journal of International Relations,* 1 (Fall 1975), 1–27.

Stoessinger, John G. *Henry Kissinger: The Anguish of Power.* New York: Norton, 1976. [137]

Swingle, Paul (ed.). *The Structure of Conflict.* New York: Academic Press, 1970.

Sykes, Percy M. *A History of Afghanistan.* 2 volumes. London: Macmillan, 1940. [23, 61]

Szulc, Tad. "How Kissinger Did It: Behind the Vietnam Cease-fire Agreement," *Foreign Policy,* No. 15 (Summer 1974), 21–69. [137]

———. *The Illusion of Peace.* New York: Viking Press, 1978. [137]

Tan, Chester C. *The Boxer Catastrophe.* New York: Octagon, 1975. [75]

Tanham, George K. *Communist Revolutionary Warfare.* New York: Praeger, 1967. [113]

Terrenoire, Louis. *De Gaulle et l'Algérie.* Paris: Fayard, 1964. [117]

Thies, Wallace J. "Searching for Peace: Vietnam & the Question of How Wars End," *Polity,* 7 (Spring 1975), 304–333. [137]

———. *When Governments Collide.* Berkeley: University of California Press, 1980. [137]

Thomas, Hugh. *The Spanish Civil War.* London: Eyre & Spottiswoode, 1961. [98]

———. *Suez.* New York: Harper & Row, 1967. [115]

Thompson, Robert. *Peace Is Not at Hand.* New York: McKay, 1974. [137]

Thompson, Virginia, and B. Richard Adloff. *The Malagasy Republic.* Stanford: Stanford University Press, 1965. [69, 106]

Thucydides. *The Peloponnesian War.* Crawley translation. New York: Modern Library, 1951.

Tricot, Bernard. *Les Sentiers de la Paix.* Paris: Plon, 1972. [117]

Tripier, Phillippe. *Autopsie de la Guerre d'Algérie.* Paris: Editions France-Empire, 1972. [117]

Tropper, Richard. "The Consequences of Investment in the Process of Conflict," *Journal of Conflict Resolution,* 16 (March 1972), 97–98.

Truman, Harry S. *Memoirs,* Volume 2: *Years of Trial and Hope.* Garden City, N.Y.: Doubleday, 1956. [112]

United States Congress, Senate, Committee on Armed Services, Preparedness Investigating Subcommittee. *Air War Against North Vietnam*. Hearings. Washington: GPO, 1967. [137]

United States Congress, Senate, Committees on Armed Services and Foreign Relations. *Military Situation in the Far East*. Hearings. Washington: GPO, 1951. [112]

United States Congress, Senate, Committee on Foreign Relations. *Background Information Relating to Southeast Asia and Vietnam*. Seventh revised edition. Washington: GPO, 1975. [137]

United States Congress, Senate, Committee on Foreign Relations. *Briefing on Vietnam*. Hearings, Washington: GPO, 1969. [137].

United States Department of Defense, Office of the Assistant Secretary of Defense (Comptroller). Table 1006, Statistics on Southeast Asia (final update). Washington: 1975. [137]

United States Department of Defense, Vietnam Task Force. *United States-Vietnam Relations, 1945–1967*. Volumes VI.C.1-4. Washington, 1968. [137]

Updyke, Frank A. *The Diplomacy of the War of 1812*. Baltimore: John Hopkins Press, 1915. [7]

Vagts, Alfred. *Defense and Diplomacy*. New York: King's Crown Press, 1956.

Vatcher, William H., Jr. *Panmunjom*. New York: Praeger, 1958. [112]

Vlekke, Bernard. *Nusantara*. Chicago: Quadrangle, 1960. [17]

Wagner, R. Harrison. "On The Unification of Two-Person Bargaining Theory," *Journal of Conflict Resolution*, 23 (March 1979), 71–101.

Walder, David. *The Short Victorious War*. London: Hutchinson, 1973. [79]

Warner, Denis, and Peggy Warner. *The Tide at Sunrise*. New York: Charterhouse, 1974. [79]

Weekly Compilation of Presidential Documents. [137]

Wehl, David. *The Birth of Indonesia*. London: Allen & Unwin, 1948. [108]

Wei, Henry. *China and Soviet Russia*. Princeton: Van Nostrand, 1956. [93]

Welles, Sumner. *Naboth's Vineyard*. Volume 1. New York: Payson & Clarke, 1928. [47]

Wellington's Supplementary Despatches. Volume 9. London: Murray, 1862. [7]

White, John A. *The Diplomacy of the Russo-Japanese War*. Princeton: Princeton University Press, 1964. [79]

Whiting, Allen S. *China Crosses the Yalu*. Stanford: Stanford University Press, 1968. [112]

Whitney, Courtney. *MacArthur: His Rendezvous with History*. New York: Knopf, 1956. [112]

Winham, Gilbert R. "Practitioners' Views of International Negotiation," *World Politics*, 32 (October 1979), 111–135.

Witte, Serge Y. *The Memoirs of Count Witte*. Trans. Abraham Yarmolinsky. Garden City, N.Y.: Doubleday, Page, 1921. [79]

Wittman, Donald. "How a War Ends: A Rational Model Approach," *Journal of Conflict Resolution*, 23 (December 1979), 743–763.

Work, Ernest. *Ethiopia, a Pawn in European Diplomacy*. New Concord, Ohio: author, 1935. [71]

Wright, Quincy. *A Study of War*. Second edition. Chicago: University of Chicago Press, 1965.

Young, Oran R. *Bargaining: Formal Theories of Negotiation*. Urbana: University of Illinois Press, 1975.

_____. *The Politics of Force*. Princeton: Princeton University Press, 1968.

Yukl, Gary A. "Effects of Situational Variables and Opponent Concessions on a Bargainer's Perception, Aspirations, and Concessions," *Journal of Personality and Social Psychology*, 29 (February 1974), 227–236.

_____. "Effects of the Opponent's Initial Offer, Concession Magnitude, and Concession Frequency on Bargaining Behavior," *Journal of Personality and Social Psychology*, 30 (September 1974), 323–335.

Zartman, I. William. *The 50% Solution*. Garden City, N.Y.: Doubleday, 1976.

_____. "Negotiations: Theory and Reality," *Journal of International Affairs*, 29 (Spring 1975), 69–77.

_____ and Maureen Berman. *The Practical Negotiator*. New Haven: Yale University Press, 1982.

Zeuthen, F. *Problems of Monopoly and Economic Warfare*. London: Routledge, 1930.

Zinnes, Dina A. and John V. Gillespie (ed.). *Mathematical Models in Internatonal Relations*. New York: Praeger, 1976.

Zook, David H., Jr. *The Conduct of the Chaco War*. New York: Bookman, 1960. [95]

INDEX